P9-DEN-757

THE LONGING FOR A FORM

The Longing
for a Form

ESSAYS ON THE FICTION
OF C. S. LEWIS

edited by Peter J. Schakel

THE KENT STATE UNIVERSITY PRESS

Copyright © 1977 by The Kent State University Press
All rights reserved
Library of Congress Catalog Card Number: 77-2586
ISBN: 0-87338-204-8
Printed in the United States of America

Library of Congress Cataloging in Publication Data
Main entry under title:

The Longing for a form.

Includes index.
1.   Lewis, Clive Staples, 1898-1963—Criticism and interpretation
—Addresses, essays, lectures.   I.   Schakel, Peter J.
PR6023.E926Z79   823'.9'12   77-2586
ISBN 0-87338-204-8

Contents

IV. TILL WE HAVE FACES

Editions of Frequently Used Texts

For the convenience of contributors and readers, the following American editions, usually paperback, have been employed uniformly throughout this book and will be cited by page number in brackets in the text.

FICTION

The Pilgrim's Regress: An Allegorical Apology for Christianity, Reason and Romanticism (1933; rpt. Grand Rapids, Michigan: William B. Eerdmans Publishing Company, 1958)

Out of the Silent Planet (1938; rpt. New York: The Macmillan Company, 1965)

Perelandra: A Novel (1943; rpt. New York: Macmillan, 1965)

That Hideous Strength: A Modern Fairy-Tale for Grown-Ups (1945; rpt. New York: Macmillan, 1965)

The Great Divorce (New York: Macmillan, 1946)

The Lion, the Witch and the Wardrobe (1950; rpt. New York: Collier Books, 1970)

Prince Caspian: The Return to Narnia (1951; rpt. New York: Collier, 1970)

The Voyage of the "Dawn Treader" (1952; rpt. New York: Collier, 1970)

The Silver Chair (1953; rpt. New York: Collier, 1970)

The Horse and His Boy (1954; rpt. New York: Collier, 1970)

The Magician's Nephew (1955; rpt. New York: Collier, 1970)

The Last Battle (1956; New York: Collier, 1970)

Till We Have Faces: A Myth Retold (1956; rpt. Grand Rapids: Eerdmans, 1966)

NONFICTION

The Problem of Pain (1940; rpt. New York: Macmillan, 1962)

Miracles: A Preliminary Study (New York: Macmillan, 1947)

Mere Christianity (New York: Macmillan, 1952)

Surprised by Joy: The Shape of My Early Life (New York: Harcourt, Brace and World, 1955)

Letters to Malcolm: Chiefly on Prayer (New York: Harcourt, Brace and World, 1964)

Letters of C. S. Lewis, ed. W. H. Lewis (New York: Harcourt, Brace and World, 1966)

Preface

THIS book grew out of the need for a critical study of Lewis's works in fiction. Our aim was to make it sound literary scholarship, but in a style and manner suitable to general readers of Lewis. Three of the essays have been previously published and have been well received by students of Lewis. Several others have been presented at professional literary meetings: the essays by Professors Zogby, Hannay, Huttar, Cox, and Van Der Weele were used for various groups at conventions of the Modern Language Association of America in 1974, 1975, and 1976. The essay by Professor Christopher was given before a meeting of the Southwest Regional Conference on Christianity and Literature. Each of the other authors has written a book or scholarly thesis on Lewis.

We are grateful to *The Hudson Review*, *Children's Literature*, and *Orcrist* for permission to reprint the essays by Professor Shumaker, Father Hooper, and Professor Kilby. We are grateful also to the Trustees of the Estate of C. S. Lewis for permission to quote from unpublished letters of Lewis, to the Marion E. Wade Collection at Wheaton College, Wheaton, Illinois, and the Bodleian Library, Oxford—each of which has a collection of Lewis manuscripts and copies of the originals held by the other—for approval to publish the quotations, and to the Executors of the Estate of W. H. Lewis and the Marion E. Wade Collection for permission and approval to quote from the Diary of W. H. Lewis.

I wish to thank Professor Kilby personally for encouragement and suggestions in the early stages of this project. I am grateful to Father Hooper for reading the typescript and indicating several needed corrections and possible improvements and to Maryam Komejan for typing, and often retyping, parts of the book and a great deal of correspondence. I am grateful also to my wife, Karen, for reading several essays, checking the proofs, listening to problems, and proposing solutions. Finally, thanks to my colleague, Charles Huttar, who offered suggestions and read several manuscripts as the essays were being collected, and suffered throughout the project as involuntary consultant on large and small editorial matters: the editorial task would have been longer, and the result less satisfactory, without his willing help.

P.J.S.

Peter J. Schakel

Introduction

> Every poem has two parents—its mother being the mass of experience, thought, and the like, inside the poet, and its father the pre-existing Form (epic, tragedy, the novel, or what not) which he meets in the public world. By studying only the mother, criticism becomes one-sided. It is easy to forget that the man who writes a good love sonnet needs not only to be enamoured of a woman, but also to be enamoured of the Sonnet.[1]

IT is one of the minor ironies of fate that the criticism of Lewis's own artistic works should have become one-sided in just such a way. Many valuable studies of Lewis have appeared in recent years,[2] but the emphasis, even in books and articles on his fiction, has been on the ideas; comparatively little attention has been given to Lewis as creative artist. This volume is intended as a step toward rectifying that imbalance. It seeks to lay a foundation for further analyses of Lewis's craftsmanship by focusing attention on "Form," in the two senses in which Lewis uses the word in his own criticism.

The first implication Form carries for Lewis is literary "kind," almost "genre," as in the opening quotation above. For Lewis, both as artist and critic, Form in this sense is of vital importance. As a critic he devotes over a third of his book on Milton to the epic, because "the biography of the literary kind will help our reading of *Paradise Lost* at least as much as the biography of the poet" [*A Preface to Paradise Lost*, p. 8]. And he uses the opening chapters of *The Allegory of Love* to trace "the rise both of the sentiment called 'Courtly Love' and of the allegorical method" because "the allegorical love poetry of the Middle Ages is apt to repel the modern reader both by its form and by its matter."[3] As an artist he carefully specifies on the title pages that *Perelandra* is "A Novel" and *That Hideous Strength* is "A Modern Fairy-Tale for Grown-Ups," with the assumption, apparently, that these distinctions will be meaningful and important to the reader. And, in the note he prepared for the dust jacket of the first edition of *Till We Have Faces*, he comments on the significance of Form in the creative process itself: "This reinterpretation of an old story has lived in the author's mind . . . since he was an undergraduate. . . . Recently, what seemed to be the right form presented itself and themes suddenly interlocked."

One must not be misled by Lewis's metaphors, however, into thinking of Form as some sort of Coleridgean "organic form," shaping itself from within, disclosing itself by intuition and the emotional fervor of composition. Lewis always refers to Form in the classical sense of traditional "types":

> In the Author's mind there bubbles up every now and then the material for a story. For me it invariably begins with mental pictures. This ferment leads to nothing unless it is accompanied with the longing for a Form: verse or prose, short story, novel, play or what not. When these two things click you have the Author's impulse complete. It is now a thing inside him pawing to get out. He longs to see that bubbling stuff pouring into that Form as the housewife longs to see the new jam pouring into the clean jam jar.[4]

The matter longs not for an innate Form but for a pre-existing Form, one which exists independently with characteristics already defined, as the simile of the jam jar brings out clearly. Despite Lewis's romantic leanings in other areas of life, his theory of creativity is based on the thoroughly classical premise that freedom is most fully achieved through restraint:

> It would, in my opinion, be the greatest error to suppose that this fertilization of the poet's internal matter by the pre-existing Form impairs his originality. . . . *Materia appetit formam ut virum femina.* The matter inside the poet *wants* the Form: in submitting to the Form it becomes really original, really the origin of great work. The attempt to be oneself often brings out only the more conscious and superficial parts of a man's mind; working to produce a given kind of poem which will present a given theme as justly, delightfully, and lucidly as possible, he is more likely to bring out all that was really in him, and much of which he himself had no suspicion. [*A Preface to Paradise Lost*, p. 3]

The metaphor here is organic: the union of Form and matter parallels the union of male and female. But note that *Form* is not "organic," growing and perfecting itself; rather the *work* as a whole can develop and deepen, can grow to fullest potential, from the union of matter with a pre-existing Form.

Similarly Lewis's thoughts on how an artist comes to use a certain Form always involve choice, thoughtful and calculated selection. Thus it was for Lewis himself as he worked with the mental pictures which became *The Lion, the Witch and the Wardrobe*:

> Then came the Form. As these images sorted themselves into events (i.e., became a story) they seemed to demand no love interest and no close psychology. But the Form which excludes these things is the fairy tale. And the moment I thought of that I fell in love with the Form itself: its brevity, its severe restraints on description, its flexible traditionalism, its inflexible hostility to all analysis, digression, reflections and "gas." . . . I wrote fairy tales because the Fairy Tale seemed the ideal Form for the stuff I had to say. [*Of Other Worlds*, pp. 36-37]

Perhaps, of course, this is hindsight, supplying a rationale after the fact. If so, however, the moment of inspiration would be, in Lewis's eyes, the product of the hours of reflection and the years of preparation that preceded it. The key process involves the mind, not emotions or inspiration. Thus it was for Milton also. Lewis spends five pages in *A Preface to Paradise Lost* [pp. 3-7] following the steps through which Milton eliminated alternative Forms and fixed upon the epic. Again the metaphor, in Lewis's summary statement, implies emotion, but the process being described is almost totally rational:

> By observing how Milton subdivides the Epic into its sub-species, we are again brought face to face with the problem of Forms—with the virginal *materia* inside the poet hesitating, as it were, between different suitors. When he wrote the *Reason of Church Government* the different types of poem were all present to Milton's mind, all different, all attractive, each offering its own unique opportunities, but each also demanding peculiar sacrifices. His sentence about epic is really a short history of epic poetry. To know what he was talking about, to feel as he felt, and so, in the end, to know what he was really choosing when he finally chose and what kind of thing he was making when he acted on that final choice, we also must attend to epic. [*A Preface to Paradise Lost*, p. 8]

To Lewis, then, Form, in the sense of "literary kind," is a vital part of the artistic process. It is one of the two parents of a literary work, and by no means the less important of the two. Form, in the artist, is not spontaneous and self-determining, but is at least partially subject to control. Because Lewis's comments on his own manner of composition frequently imply a large measure of spontaneity and inspiration, a closer analysis of his use of Form is necessary. To have written as voluminously as he did, much must have "come to him" when or before he sat down to write. But we must never forget that his writing was preceded by more reading, probably, than done by any other person of his time, that he had an enormously large stock of literary knowledge and literary Forms to draw upon. If Lewis was "inventing" material, it was in the eighteenth-century sense of making "a new combination of those images which have been previously gathered and deposited in the memory." A detailed formal analysis of his fiction, then, is needed and should be rewarded by new and fuller insights into his works and into Lewis himself as artist and thinker.

A sizeable portion of this book is devoted to Lewis's use of Form, in the sense discussed above. The essay by Scott Oury, by illustrating Lewis's attraction to "the object itself," to things (and thus Forms) which have objective, independent existence outside the perceiver or user, supplies a theoretical framework for the emphasis on Form as "literary types." The essays by Wayne Shumaker and Chad Walsh consider the "genre" of the Ransom trilogy, Lewis's adaptation of science fiction to his own purposes. Three essays discuss Form in the Chronicles of Narnia. Walter Hooper shows that the Chronicles are not "allegories," with characters and situations which "stand for" something else, but "extremely well-written adventure stories" whose success derives from their intrinsic "meaning." Charles Huttar views the Chronicles as "scripture," containing the same "grand design" as God incorporated in history and in the Bible. And Eliane Tixier explains how use of the Fairy Tale enabled Lewis to capture in the Chronicles his own experience with Holiness and to convey it in a nondogmatic way.

The second implication the term Form carries for Lewis is "shape," the internal arrangement and handling of material, including the degree to which that handling produces a unity of effect. Thus he says of tragedy and comedy that "both [Forms] were deliberate patterns or arrangements of possible . . . events chosen for their harmonious unity in variety, deliberately modified, contrasted, balanced in a fashion which real life never permits."[5] Much of Lewis's work as a critic redirected attention to this aspect of literature, as well as to its generic part. This, indeed, was the theme of the interchange between Lewis and E. M. W. Tillyard, which became *The Personal Heresy: A Controversy*. The crucial point for Lewis may be summed up in these lines:

Poetry is an art or skill—a trained habit of using certain instruments to certain ends. This platitude is no longer unnecessary; it has been becoming obscured ever since the great romantic critics diverted our attention from the fruitful question, "What kind of composition is a poem?" to the barren question, "What kind of a man is a poet?"[6]

Again and again Lewis's criticism focuses on the shaping and unity of a work: "A work of literary art . . . both *means* and *is*. It is both *Logos* (something said) and *Poiema* (something made). As Logos it tells a story, or expresses an emotion, or exhorts or pleads or describes or rebukes or excites laughter. As Poiema, by its aural beauties and also by the balance and contrast and the unified multiplicity of its successive parts, it is an *objet d'art*, a thing shaped so as to give great satisfaction."[7] Lewis's interest in the techniques which produce those shapes can be illustrated by the titles of five of the essays collected in *Studies in Medieval and Renaissance Literature*: "What Chaucer really did to 'Il Filostrato,' " "The Fifteenth-Century Heroic Line," "Variation in Shakespeare and Others," "Dante's Similes," and "Imagery in the Last Eleven Cantos of Dante's 'Comedy.' "[8] The critical approaches range widely, from source studies to metrical analysis, but everywhere the method is close examination of the text, of the specific skills employed by the writer in achieving "something like a balance, but never a too perfect symmetry, so that the shape of the whole work will be felt as inevitable and satisfying" [*An Experiment in Criticism*, p. 83].

Nowhere is his attention to the details which compose the Form in this second sense more impressive than in a series of unpublished letters to Ruth Pittar. In some letters he writes about her poems; his comments are so detailed, sensitive, and perceptive as to make her declare, in her remarks on his letters, "Here is someone who really read the poems." In other letters he discusses the poems of others:

Have you read Andrew Young's *Into Hades*, and what do you think of it. I found the content absorbing and the images, like all his, simply enchanting (There's a bit about reflected water-drops from a raised oar rushing to meet the real water drops—lovely!) but my *ear* was a bit unsatisfied. I believe "Blank Verse," unrhymed five footers, is not a metre to be written loosely. I think the unrhymed Alexandrine, written without a break at the 6th syllable wd. be far better: e.g.

> I know far less of spiders than that poetess
> Who (like the lady in *Comus* in the perilous wood)
> Can study nature's infamies with secure heart . . .

The third line is here the best: one wants plenty of trisyllables to leap across the threatened medial pause. Try a few.[9]

And in still others he asks for her responses to his own poems. But he has already considered his poems himself, with concern for the same qualities he looks for in others' works: "Get clear what the question is. I know (or think) that some of these contain important thought and v. great metrical ingenuity. That isn't what I'm worrying about. But are they real poems or do the content and the form remain separable—fitted together only by force?" [24 July 1946]. Much evidence suggests that Lewis was a careful, thoughtful craftsman in fiction as well as verse. And the kind of detailed analysis Lewis did of his own poems should be equally justified and valuable for his fiction. The remainder of this book, therefore, deals with this implication of Form, as various essays examine the techniques by which Lewis shaped and unified his novels as "objects of art," and how he achieved the beauty and significance apparent so often in them.

Edward Zogby, S.J., establishes the theoretical background for this endeavor by demonstrating that a pattern of triadic relationships, of opposites existing in tension with each other until they are resolved into a "third thing," appears throughout Lewis's life, thought, and art. Janice Neuleib extends this by showing how, for Lewis, the artist and the work of art become a model of Providence: the reader, by seeing and coming to understand the artist's relationship to the work he or she has created, can come to grasp more readily God's relationship to the work He has created. Chad Walsh, Richard Purtill, and Clyde Kilby show how a similar attention to pattern is valuable within individual novels: in the growth/education theme of *Out of the Silent Planet*, the contrasting pairings throughout *That Hideous Strength*, and the purposeful series of "witnessings" to Orual in *Till We Have Faces*. Several essays illuminate novels by analyzing how Lewis handled the sources from which he drew ideas or structures. Wayne Shumaker shows how Lewis gave renewed meaning to a prepared world view by incorporating that view into space fiction. Margaret Hannay illustrates how Lewis's criticism of Milton influenced the novel he was writing at the same time: "Those things which disappointed Lewis in *Paradise Lost* have been altered in . . . *Perelandra*; those elements which he most approved in Milton he has sought to emulate." John Cox examines a wide range of influences on and analogues to *The Silver Chair* and demonstrates the depths of this, the most philosophical of the Narnia books. Steve Van Der Weele supplies a detailed discussion of both small and sweeping changes Lewis made in the Apuleian myth he is retelling in *Till We Have Faces*. And J. R. Christopher shows how Lewis used a variety of literary allusions and analogues to establish the universal human patterns which give so much depth and power to *Till We Have Faces*.

The book will achieve its highest aim if it sends readers back to the novels, better enabled to "receive" the novels as Lewis wrote them:

> A work of (whatever) art can be either "received" or "used." When we "receive" it we exert our senses and imagination and various other powers according to a pattern invented by the artist. When we "use" it we treat it as assistance for our own activities. . . . "Using" is inferior to "reception" because art, if used rather than received, merely facilitates, brightens, relieves or palliates our life, and does not add to it. [*An Experiment in Criticism*, p. 88]

For that reason the one-sided type of criticism mentioned in the opening quotation must be avoided. Too great an emphasis on Lewis's ideas, unbalanced by attention to what the works really *are* and how they really work upon an objective reader, can lead to sheer "use" of them, usually to reinforce a pre-existing world or life view. The focus upon Form in this book—on the kinds of novels these are, and on their shapes, their patterns, their total effects— should help readers to attain the chief end of imaginative writing, according to Lewis, that of "entering fully into the opinions, and therefore also the attitudes, feelings and total experience, of other men" [*An Experiment in Criticism*, p. 85].

I: GENERAL STUDIES

Scott Oury

"The Thing Itself": C. S. Lewis and the Value of Something Other

ANYONE who has read C. S. Lewis with the least bit of attention finds himself confronted with a set of difficult—even annoying—paradoxes. He stressed objectivity, but everywhere a strong personal bent seems to obtrude. He converted to Christianity and defended its doctrines, yet he evidenced an insatiable thirst for new worlds of experience and ideas:

> Reality, even seen through the eyes of many, is not enough. I will see what others have invented. Even the eyes of all humanity are not enough. I regret that the brutes cannot write books.[1]

For one who professed such openness, he dismissed entire philosophies with something just short of contempt. Atheism and pantheism were for him "boys' philosophies" [*Mere Christianity*, p. 33]. Yet he maintained an almost intolerable confidence in the main outlines of his own philosophy. His reputation as a great scholar seems to clash with his distrust of abstractions in almost any form: A "mere dexterous playing with counters" [*Letters*, p. 147]. And as a literary critic who by his own admission (not to mention the opinion of some of his critics) belonged to another age, he stirred some of the most heated literary controversies of his day. John Wain called him "England's chief literary controversialist" after Orwell's death.[2]

The paradoxes suggest that Lewis is difficult to understand from any single perspective, literary, theological, or personal. Read him for his theories of literature and you run sooner or later into theology. Read him for either his theology or his critical theories and the man himself seems to be facing you, that warm but un-

1

compromising tutor, friendly enemy, or partner in an intellectual game of chess.

Pull any strand and all the rest come along. And the smaller patterns of his life integrate with the whole tapestry. Those who knew him best agree. Owen Barfield suggests that Lewis was thoroughly committed in *practice* to his intellectual beliefs.[3] Chad Walsh, who wrote the first full-length book on him and to whom *The Four Loves* was dedicated, was frustrated in every attempt to find the *real* Lewis behind the literary personage; they seemed identical.[4] And Dabney Hart, who wrote a definitive study of Lewis's theory of mythopoeia, concludes that Lewis's theological and critical stances were thoroughly integrated.[5]

Out of these paradoxes and this unity the question arises: Where is the key? Where is the main strand, the strand that makes a pattern of the paradoxes and contributes most basically to the whole? Perhaps his Christianity. Orthodox, historical Christianity did become central and indispensable to every facet of his life and literature. But Lewis was thirty-one at the time of his conversion. Certainly he did not suddenly, or subsequently, become all that he was from that point on. Nor can the literary man be understood entirely from the perspective of his beliefs.

There is a strand more basic—though not more important in the final analysis—to an understanding of C. S. Lewis. It was, in fact, the thread that drew him to Christianity and became the dominant quality of his life work. This thread was his attention and commitment to the value of something other than himself, to "the object itself." None of the studies of C. S. Lewis that I am aware of treats this preoccupation with "the object itself." The purpose of this paper, therefore, will be to trace the occurrence of this preoccupation first in his life, then briefly in his nonfictional works and in his theories of literature, and finally in his major effort in adult fiction, the science-fiction trilogy.

At start a hesitation must be expressed. This is an attempt to shed some light, not to obscure. Yet one feels like a man with a candle attempting to illuminate a beacon. If he was anything, C. S. Lewis was the essence of clarity. Every attempt will be made to let him frequently speak for himself.

C. S. Lewis's conversion, first to theism and then to Christianity, was due in good part to his attention to "the object itself." The result was to confirm this habit of attention and establish it as a basis for his subsequent life and work.

Since the term "the object itself" (or "the object") is basic to this entire discussion, an attempt will be made to define Lewis's use of it. An immediate qualification, however, is necessary. The very attempt to define "the object itself" abstracts it from its perceived completeness and from its proper setting. One inevitably endows "the object" with qualities out of one's own personal makeup. And one perceives "the object itself" in its wholeness as having these added qualities. Strictly speaking, "the object itself" can only be encountered and experienced, in the sense that one *undergoes* an experience. This is its proper setting.

To C. S. Lewis, the very idea of "the thing itself" assumed as its starting point something real *out there* with qualities that belong to it or inhere. "Certain things, if not seen as lovely or detestable, are not being correctly seen at all."[6] "The object itself" includes physical objects, persons and beings, their movements, and their communications. It excludes only those qualities that one encountering "the object" *adds* to it—in short, the projection of one's own makeup upon "the object." Lewis also viewed "the object" on a larger scale:

> It is Nature, it is the Way, the Road . . . the Way in which the universe goes on, the Way in which things everlastingly emerge, stilly and tranquilly, into space and time . . . the Way which every man should tread in imitation of that cosmic and supercosmic progression.[7]

And it is God, the "sheerly objective, . . . the naked Other" [*Surprised by Joy*, p. 221], "the most concrete of all Facts."[8]

As far as I am aware, Lewis never embarked upon an extended philosophical discussion of "the object itself"; it was defined for him concretely in the process of attending to it, or, as he puts it in the subtitle of his autobiography, in "The Shape of My Early Life." In the preface to *Surprised by Joy*, Lewis explains that his purpose is not general autobiography, but telling the story of his conversion, especially as it concerns the experience of "Joy." Recalling his late childhood, Lewis relates three experiences, all characterized by an element of intense desire, "an unsatisfied desire . . . itself more desirable than any other satisfaction," which he called "Joy."[9] This continuing experience of Joy became the most important experience of his life, though he did not become aware of its origin until much later. The essence of his involvement with Joy is summed up in the preface to *The Pilgrim's Regress*:

> It appeared to me . . . that if a man diligently followed this desire, pursuing the false objects until their falsity appeared and then resolutely abandoning them, he must come out at last into the clear knowledge that the human soul was made to enjoy some object that is never fully given . . . in our present mode of . . . experience. [p. 10]

The desire, however, did not reappear until early adolescence (he had never been able to command it). But when it did appear, he immediately embraced what seemed to produce it: Norse mythology, or "Northernness." His attention to "the object itself" began to sharpen. In his involvement with Norse mythology there was a "quite disinterested self-abandonment to an object which securely claimed this by simply being the object it was" [p. 77]. The "Northernness" eventually began to fade; instead of drawing the conclusion that Joy was "further away, more external, less subjective," he concluded for a time that it was a mood or state within himself, and he attempted to produce it again, by sex [p. 68] and by magic [p. 176], only to be disappointed once more.

Then he picked up George MacDonald's *Phantastes* and all was changed: "It was as though the voice which had called to me from the world's end were now speaking at my side" [p. 180]. An important step occurred here in Lewis's search for the source of Joy. He had previously confused Joy with the objects that invited it and, as a result, the objects had quickly faded. With *Phantastes* the Joy was nearly inseparable from the story itself, yet it was a distinct element, *light*, that transformed not only the objects of the story but even the common things of his own life:

> For I now perceived that while the air of the new region made all my erotic and magical perversions of Joy look like sordid trumpery, it had no such disenchanting power over the bread upon the table or the coals in the grate. [p. 181]

Evidently Joy was not to be found in any particular kind of experience, object, or imaginative construct. It was to be found, paradoxically, in something inseparably bound to the qualities of things, yet distinctly itself.

MacDonald's *Phantastes* was an early taste of what Lewis was to realize fully later. First came increased attention to "the qualities of things" through a friend at Oxford. He learned from Hamilton Jenkin to "attempt a total surrender to whatever atmosphere was offering itself at the moment, . . . to rub one's nose in the very quiddity of each thing, to rejoice in its being . . . what it was" [p. 199]. At the same time, however, he adopted a "New Look," which served to explain away all his previous experiences of Joy as merely aesthetic experience. Then, with the reading of Langland, Donne, Browne, and especially George Herbert, the New Look was shaken; Joy began to approach once more. Herbert conveyed to him "the very quality of life as we actually live it from moment to moment" [p. 214], an echo of his experience with *Phantastes*.

But it took rereading the *Hippolytus* of Euripides to bring him once again into the world of desire. "In one chorus all that world's end imagery which I had rejected when I assumed my New Look rose before me" [p. 217].

The next step provided an intellectual explanation for this experience, and for the quality of all his past experiences of Joy. It also established the pattern of attention to "the object itself" which had been developing, though perhaps erratically, and put a definitive stamp on his character. The occasion was his reading of Alexander's *Space, Time, and Deity*. The sharp distinction between attention to an object and attention to one's *feelings about* an object suddenly became apparent:

> It seemed to me self-evident that one essential property of love, hate, fear, hope, or desire was attention to their object. To cease thinking about or attending to the woman is, so far, to cease loving; to cease thinking about or attending to the dreaded thing is, so far, to cease being afraid. But to attend to your own love or fear is to cease attending to the loved or dreaded object. In other words the enjoyment and the contemplation of our inner activities are incompatible. You cannot hope and also think about hoping at the same moment; for in hope we look to hope's object and we interrupt this by (so to speak) turning around to look at the hope itself. [p. 218]

Once he accepted the distinction—"an indispensable tool of thought" —its consequences bore in and put his entire life in a new light:

> I saw that all my waitings and watchings for Joy, all my vain hopes to find some mental content on which I could, so to speak, lay my finger and say, "This is it," had been a futile attempt to contemplate the enjoyed. [p. 219]

All the objects, the images, and sensations mistaken for Joy had merely been its "mental track"—"not the wave but the wave's imprint on the sand" [p. 219]. This, he admits, he had already learned through attention to the objects that had been associated with his experiences of Joy.

What of Joy itself then? Lewis became aware that Joy, being a desire, "turned not to itself but to its object" and "owes all its character to its object" [p. 220]. In answering his next question, "What is it?", Lewis found himself in the "region of awe":

> For I thus understood that in the deepest solitude there is a road right out of the self, a commerce with something which, by refusing to identify itself with any object of the senses, or anything whereof we

have biological or social need, or anything imagined, or any state of
our own minds, proclaims itself sheerly objective. Far more objective
than bodies . . . the naked Other, imageless (though our imagination
salutes it with a hundred images), unknown, undefined, desired. [p.
221]

It was not—yet—the God of Christianity, or any God at all, not even
the Absolute. His realization did not proceed from a system of
theology or philosophy to the awareness of the "sheerly objective";
it was a progression from *experience* to realization. The "naked
Other" was discovered primarily in attention to the concrete experiences of life, both those of Joy and those substituting for Joy,
not in attention to mental constructions.

The succeeding events of Lewis's conversion, for the purposes of
this paper, are all but epilogue—though hardly so for Lewis. This
"Other" became identified with the Absolute. Then the Absolute, to
his horror, began to stir, "became a living presence," and demanded
to be recognized [p. 227]. To Lewis this was no cheerful "search
for God." One "might as well have talked about the mouse's
search for the cat" [p. 227]. Finally his "adversary" won on His
own terms. "I gave in, and admitted that God was God, . . . perhaps, that night, the most dejected and reluctant convert in all
England" [pp. 228-29]. This was only a conversion to theism, with
no belief in an afterlife. His conversion to Christianity came later,
with nearly as much resistance as he had mustered against his conversion to theism. But it was a step in character with the rest:
"Toward the more concrete" [p. 237].

This emphasis on "otherness," objectivity, attention to "the object itself," appears throughout Lewis's theological, apologetical,
and critical works. A few examples must suffice here. One occurs
in the sermon "The Weight of Glory":

> The books or the music in which we thought the beauty was located
> will betray us if we trust to them; it was not *in* them, it only came
> *through* them, and what came through them was longing. These things
> —the beauty, the memory of our own past—are good images of what
> we really desire; but if they are mistaken for the thing itself they turn
> into dumb idols, breaking the hearts of their worshippers. For they are
> not the thing itself; they are only the scent of a flower we have not
> found, the echo of a tune we have not heard, news from a country we
> have never yet visited.[10]

And the aim of the entire sermon is to lead its hearers beyond
their "present experiences" [p. 8] to a more adequate perception

of "reality" [p. 11]. Quite a different example appears in *The Four Loves*. In discussing pleasure, Lewis comments on man's general tendency toward subjectiveness:

> The human mind is generally far more eager to praise and dispraise than to describe and define. It wants to make every distinction a distinction of value; hence those fatal critics who can never point out the differing quality of two poets without putting them in an order of preference as if they were candidates for a prize.[11]

One must, in other words, see clearly "the thing itself" before attempting any evaluation. Lewis took his own advice in the actual writing of *The Four Loves*. Far from being content to write "fairly easy panegyrics" out of his own preconceptions, he met the reality—the "puzzles and contradictions"—on its own terms. His method was to "describe and define" rather than to evaluate. In *Reflections on the Psalms* he again approaches his subject with preconceptions behind him, as an "amateur" (to use his own understatement) "talking about difficulties I have met, or lights I have gained, when reading the Psalms" themselves.[12]

The quasi-apological book *A Grief Observed* gives perhaps the strongest evidence of Lewis's unqualified attention to things for what they are in themselves. The book is a series of notebook entries following the death of his wife by cancer. In spite of his Christian orientation, Lewis does not compromise with the reality of death or the character of his own initial reactions to it:

> It is hard to have patience with people who say "There is no death" or "Death doesn't matter." There is death. And whatever is matters. . . . I look up at the night sky. Is anything more certain than that in all those vast times and spaces, if I were allowed to search them, I should nowhere find her face, her voice, her touch? She died. She is dead. Is the word so difficult to learn?[13]

> Meanwhile, where is God? This is one of the most disquieting symptoms. When you are happy, so happy that you have no sense of needing Him, . . . you will be . . . welcomed with open arms. But go to Him when your need is desperate, when all other help is vain, and what do you find? A door slammed in your face, and a sound of bolting and double bolting on the inside. After that, silence. [p. 9]

And he will not compensate with his memory of her:

> What pitiable cant to say "She will live forever in my memory!" *Live?* That is exactly what she won't do. . . . What's left? A corpse, a memory, and . . . a ghost. All mockeries or horrors. Three more ways of

spelling the word *dead*. It was H. I loved. As if I wanted to fall in love
with my memory of her, an image in my own mind! It would be a sort
of incest. [p. 19]

By a process similar to that described in *Surprised by Joy*, only when
he can lay aside his own passionate grief, the "mental track" [see
p. 7] of her death upon him, can "the real shape" [p. 19] be re-
membered:

> As I have discovered, passionate grief does not link us with the dead
> but cuts us off from them. This become[s] clearer and clearer. It is just
> at those moments when I feel least sorrow . . . that H. rushes upon my
> mind in her full reality, her otherness. Not, as in my worst moments,
> all foreshortened and patheticized and solemnized by my miseries, but
> as she is in her own right. [pp. 44-45; also see p. 42]

Dealing with God in "his own right" is more difficult, but a similar
process obtains. Lewis sees his first fierce reactions—imagining
God bolting the door against his desperate need, God torturing him
—as the very element that separated him from the reality:

> You can't, in most things, get what you want if you want it too desper-
> ately. . . . So, perhaps, with God. I have gradually been coming to
> feel that the door is no longer shut and bolted. Was it my own frantic
> need that slammed it in my face? . . . Perhaps your own reiterated
> cries deafen you to the voice you hoped to hear. [pp. 37-38]

In coming to terms with both God and his wife's death, he was
unable to attend to "the object itself" until he got something of
himself, his needs, his emotions, out of the way:

> All reality is iconoclastic. The earthly beloved, even in this life,
> incessantly triumphs over your mere idea of her. And you want her to;
> you want her . . . in her foursquare and independent reality. And this,
> not any image or memory, is what we are to love still, after she is dead.
> But "this" is not now imaginable. In that respect H. and all the dead
> are like God. In that respect loving her has become, in its measure,
> like loving Him. In both cases I must stretch out the arms and hands of
> love—its eyes cannot here be used—to the reality, through—across—all
> the changeful phantasmagoria of my thoughts, passions, and imagin-
> ings. I musn't sit down content with the phantasmagoria itself and
> worship that for Him, or love that for her. [pp. 52-53]

And upon that note "the object itself" emerges as the theme of the
entire book:

Not my idea of God, but God. Not my idea of H., but H. Yes, and also not my idea of my neighbour, but my neighbour. For don't we often make this mistake as regards people who are still alive—who are with us in the same room? Talking and acting not to the man himself but to the picture—almost the *précis*—we've made of Him in our own minds? And he has to depart from it pretty widely before we even notice the fact. [p. 53]

As the emphasis on "the object" expands from Lewis's life to his theology and ethics, its full importance as the unifying strand begins to become clear.

Lewis's critical theory also was based on attention to the work itself. In *An Experiment in Criticism*, he accepts and builds on a critical principle from Matthew Arnold, that "the important thing is 'to see the object as in itself it really is' " [p. 119]. He applies this principle first to the visual arts:

We must not let loose our own subjectivity upon the pictures and make them its vehicles. We must begin by laying aside as completely as we can all our own preconceptions, interests, and associations. . . . After the negative effort, the positive. We must use our eyes. We must look, and go on looking till we have certainly seen exactly what is there. We sit down before the picture in order to have something done to us, not that we may do things with it. The first demand any work of art makes upon us is surrender. Look. Listen. Receive. Get yourself out of the way. [pp. 18-19]

He applies this principle also to the verbal arts:

The same is true of a novel or narrative poem. They are complex and carefully made objects. Attention to the very objects they are is our first step. To value them chiefly for reflections which they may suggest to us or morals we may draw from them, is a flagrant instance of "using" instead of "receiving." [pp. 82-83]

Thus the good reader yields himself to the work of art, immerses himself in it: "When we 'receive' it we exert our senses and imagination and various other powers according to a pattern invented by the artist. When we 'use' it we treat it as assistance for our own activities" [p. 88].

Critical attention to literary works as "the very objects they are" must begin, for Lewis, with consideration of what kinds of works they are:

The first qualification for judging any piece of workmanship from a corkscrew to a cathedral is to know *what* it is—what it was intended to

do and how it is meant to be used. After that has been discovered the
temperance reformer may decide that the corkscrew was made for a
bad purpose, and the communist may think the same about the
cathedral. But such questions come later. The first thing is to understand the object before you: as long as you think the corkscrew was
meant for opening tins or the cathedral for entertaining tourists you
can say nothing to the purpose about them. [*A Preface to Paradise
Lost*, p. 1]

Thus nearly a third of *A Preface to Paradise Lost* is devoted to
the epic form. Similarly, Lewis emphasizes that "the Psalms must be
read as poems. . . . Otherwise we shall miss what is in them and
think we see what is not" [*Reflections on the Psalms*, p. 3]. Much
of Lewis's critical work is devoted to clarifying for modern readers
literary forms which have become unfamiliar: in *The Allegory of
Love* he illuminates the form of the medieval love allegory, and in
Spenser's Images of Life, the iconography central to Spenser's
style. For C. S. Lewis, then, the critic's job is "to show others the
work they claim to admire or despise as it really is; to describe,
almost to define, its character, and then leave them to their own
(now better informed) reactions" [*An Experiment in Criticism*, p.
120]. All is aimed at enhancing the reader's encounter with the
work of art, with "the object itself."

Literary works, as Lewis sees them, are "objects" in the sense of
being real things *out there* with inherent qualities. But literature,
perhaps in contrast to the other arts, has also the potential to approach and convey "the object" in its *ultimate* sense, as *reality*.
"Approach" is used advisedly here. Lewis makes a careful distinction at this point between life and literature. One may only *experience* or *encounter* "the object"—reality—in its ultimate sense
in the course of living day to day. This we have seen in Lewis's
account of his own experience. In literature (the realm of language)
one may only hope to *approach* "the object itself." One cannot even
hope to demonstrate the nature of "the object"—reality—with
literature. This was the subject of lengthy correspondence between
C. S. Lewis and Owen Barfield (which they called "The Great
War"), Barfield maintaining that the poet could demonstrate the
nature of reality with true poetic images, Lewis maintaining that
the poet makes his metaphors unconscious of their connection with
reality, i.e., of the truth of the metaphor. It gives him " 'the right
feeling' and there's an end on't."

But Lewis did feel that literature of a certain type or quality could
approach and somehow *convey* "the object"—reality—in its ultimate
sense. And not surprisingly this literature, as Lewis describes it,

comes closest in character to the character of "the object" in life. He labels this literature (somewhat reluctantly in view of its ambiguities) *myth*, and lists these characteristics: 1) it has "a value in itself"—apart from any particular account of it; 2) it introduces us "to a permanent object of contemplation—more like a thing than a narration—which works upon us by its peculiar flavour or quality, rather as a smell or a chord does"; 3) it has a "simple narrative shape," a "pattern of . . . movements [with] a profound relevance to our own life"; and 4) it is " 'fantastic,' " "grave," and "awe-inspiring" [*An Experiment in Criticism*, pp. 41-44].

In short, one finds myth to be literature—itself the shape and character of reality—"that creates an image which impresses and haunts the mind of the reader as an incarnation of reality."[14] Thus literature that pretends to be nothing more than itself, professes no actuality, and claims no truth, paradoxically gives us the fullest image of "the object itself," of reality.

> The highest reach of the whole poetic art turns out to be a kind of abdication, and is attained when the whole image of the world the poet sees has entered so deeply into his mind that henceforth he has only to get himself out of the way.[15]

"What flows into you from the myth," Lewis sums it up elsewhere, "is . . . reality."[16]

Lewis was concerned, as a critic, with literature as object on both levels. As a novelist, he wrote literature which contains both levels. Elsewhere in this volume, Chad Walsh considers the form of the trilogy, indicating the importance of seeing the trilogy initially as science fiction. Walsh, Margaret Hannay, and Richard Purtill consider the three parts of the trilogy, respectively, as objects in the first sense, offering readers a clearer understanding of the shape and themes of each of the novels. And Wayne Shumaker shows that the trilogy also includes the wider dimension of "object" as myth. The remainder of this paper will examine the importance of "the thing itself" within the novels, showing a concern for attention to objects at least equal to that we have already seen in his life, his religious writings, and his critical theories.

Lewis's concern with "the object" in the trilogy shows itself in his close attention to: 1) setting, especially in its atmosphere; 2) persons, especially the encounter with persons in respect to their uniqueness; and 3) the shapes of persons' lives. With this last, of course, we take a quantitative jump to the "larger scale" of "the object." The progressively wider scope of these three areas is parelleled by an increase in the message component of Lewis's attention to "the object," and thereby perhaps ultimately a problem or two with Lewis's fiction and "the object itself."

The starting point of *Perelandra* (and most, if not all, his fiction), Lewis tells us, was images that occurred to him, images of floating islands.[17] Through attention to these images he built a world in which floating islands could exist, and finally a story, the story of an averted fall. But the images were first. And it is Lewis's close attention to details of setting and atmosphere consonant with those images that bring them alive. The result is two very believable and unique worlds, Malacandra and Perelandra, which compel our attention. Who could imagine space as cold and dead after reading of the voyage to Malacandra?

> The very name "Space" seemed a blasphemous libel for this empyrean ocean of radiance in which they swam. He could not call it "dead"; he felt life pouring into him from it every moment. [*Out of the Silent Planet*, p. 32]

Malacandra becomes enchanted as well. Its description is attended to with such detail and completeness that the mention of earth (the silent planet) later in the book comes almost as a shock. One has been on another world, thoroughly engrossed with the "experience." Perelandra, if anything, is more engrossing, again almost an experience:

> His eyes were stabbed by an unendurable light. A grading, blue-to-violet illumination made the golden sky seem dark by comparison and in a moment of time revealed more of the new planet than he had yet seen. He saw the waste of waves spread illimitably before him, and far away, at the very end of the world, against the sky, a single smooth column of ghastly green standing up, the one thing fixed and vertical in this universe of shifting slopes. [*Perelandra*, p. 37]

And after the sea, the nearly indescribable pleasures of the floating islands:

> He put out his hand to touch [the globe]. Immediately his head, face, and shoulders were drenched with what seemed . . . an ice-cold shower bath, and his nostrils filled with a sharp, shrill, exquisite scent that somehow brought to his mind the verse in Pope, "die of a rose in aromatic pain." [p. 47]

And the "world" of *That Hideous Strength* is no less engrossing, even its smaller features. How can one regard those woods at the edge of his own town as anything less than enchanted after reading Lewis's description of Bragdon Wood?

As might be expected, the characters to which Lewis commits himself are those who attend to the qualities of things, for instance the atmosphere of a landscape. It is through Ransom's eyes that we see Perelandra and Malacandra. The Dennistons love "Weather" [*That Hideous Strength*, p. 113]. And it is the fellowship at St. Anne's who "enjoy things for their own sake" [p. 248]. On the other hand, the opposition ignores *all that*, sometimes studiously. Devine thinks of Ransom's walking tour as "sheer masochism" [*Out of the Silent Planet*, p. 16]. Weston evidences not the slightest interest in the features of either Malacandra or Perelandra. He has a job to do. And the crew at N.I.C.E. not only coop themselves up in one large building, but would scour the planet clean of organic life [*That Hideous Strength*, p. 173]. Quaint villages such as Cure Hardy [p. 87] are mere fodder for their sociological theories. The Deputy Director of N.I.C.E., Wither, embodies the extreme of studious avoidance of setting and atmosphere, the outer world:

> Colours, tastes, smells, and tactual sensations no doubt bombarded his physical senses in the normal manner: they did not now reach his ego. [p. 250]

The description of Wither's state is particularly effective as placed; it falls in the middle of the search for Merlin through a very "Wet and Windy Night" full of sensations: "The wind had risen and was roaring about them. . . . The branches of the hedge beside which they were tramping swayed and dipped and rose again so that they looked as if they were lashing the bright stars" [p. 253].

The encounter with persons (and beings) in their uniqueness, often a fearful encounter, is the second feature of "the object itself" to which Lewis gives a great deal of attention. The point is *encounter*, undergoing the experience of that *otherness*. Where necessary, understanding and comprehension—even fear—of the otherness must be courageously sacrificed for the encounter itself, the experience. Ransom's *initial* idea of meeting with the *sorns* of Malacandra is full of fears: "He could face death, but not the *sorns*. He must escape" [*Out of the Silent Planet*, p. 35]. But he learns; his first extraterrestrial encounter is with a Malacandrian *hross*:

> Neither dared let the other approach, yet each repeatedly felt the impulse to do so himself, and yielded to it. It was foolish, frightening, ecstatic and unbearable all in one moment. It was more than curiosity. It was like a courtship—like the meeting of the first man and the first

woman in the world; it was like something beyond that; so natural is
the contact of sexes, so limited the strangeness, so shallow the reticence,
so mild the repugnance to be overcome, compared with the first tingling intercourse of two different, but rational, species. [p. 56]

Subsequently the *hrossa* overturn his primitive estimates of their
species; Ransom increasingly sees them as unique, rational, and
intelligent creatures.

Although Ransom loses most of his fear of extraterrestrial encounters, he loses none of his attentiveness to the uniqueness and
mystery of other beings. He meets the Oyarsa, the ruler of Malacandra:

> Like a silence spreading over a room full of people, like an infinites-
> imal coolness on a sultry day, like a passing memory of some long-
> forgotten sound or scent, like all that is stillest and smallest and most
> hard to seize in nature, Oyarsa passed between his subjects and drew
> near and came to rest. . . . Ransom felt a tingling of his blood and a
> pricking on his fingers as if lightning were near him; and his heart
> and body seemed to him to be made of water. [p. 119]

Ransom's meeting with the Green Lady of Perelandra similarly
proves "overwhelming," just because he has paid enough attention to her godlike person to feel ridiculous by comparison [p. 59].
But, as with the *hrossa*, his freight of preconceptions must be, and is,
unlearned as he comes to know her in her own right. His encounter
with the Oyarsa of Perelandra, accompanied by the Oyarsa of Malacandra, is full of revelation as he takes in what he can of their
character, so unlike his own or that of any other being he has experienced.

With *That Hideous Strength*, encounter is the order of the day.
The general structure of the book concerns the encounter of the
young married couple, Mark and Jane, with the other's real self.
With Jane this is accomplished by the unmaking of her tight and
tidy world through the meeting with Ransom, and through Ransom,
God. This process is described as an experience of "joy" [p. 151],
parallel to Lewis's own encounter with God. Jane's encounter with
God is the essence and archetype of Lewis's idea of personal encounter: all one's personal baggage sacrificed for the Otherness.

> There was nothing, and never had been anything, like this. And now
> there was nothing except this. Yet also, everything had been like this;
> only by being like this had anything existed. In this height and depth
> and breadth the little idea of herself which she had hitherto called *me*
> dropped down and vanished. [p. 318]

And it is this encounter that opens the way for a full appreciation of Mark. Mark's own road to Jane is full of personal baggage which must be cleared away before he can meet her unique self:

> Inch by inch, all the lout and clown and clod-hopper in him was revealed to his own reluctant inspection; the coarse, male boor with horny hands and hobnailed shoes . . . blundering, sauntering, stumping in where great lovers, knights and poets, would have feared to tread. An image of Jane's skin, so smooth, so white . . . floated before him. How had he dared? [pp. 380-81]

Ransom's encounter with Merlin proceeds along similar lines, each respecting the sharp differences found in the other.

By contrast, the assemblage at N.I.C.E. avoid encounter wherever possible. The chapter "Real Life Is Meeting" shows the comic aspect of this avoidance. Wither and company, in search of Merlin, have captured a bum. Mark's meeting with the bum as bum becomes a part of his journey to Jane. But the N.I.C.E. folks treat the bum with utmost deference, never discovering who their scraggly captive is, so blind are they to personal encounter. The entire atmosphere at N.I.C.E. is one of fear, avoidance, and projection of one's *own* feelings and wishes upon others. Wither, again, is the extreme. Projection is his mode of operation; others' feelings and thoughts must quite simply be his own: " 'Ah! The post at last!' said Wither. 'Perhaps, Mr. Studdock, er—you will have letters of your own to attend to' " [p. 105].

The antagonists of *Out of the Silent Planet* and *Perelandra* are similarly blind to personal encounter. Both Devine and Weston mistake a senile *hross* for the Oyarsa of Malacandra, and talk to him as if he were a savage. Lewis makes comic with the encounter. Devine and Weston have just been addressed by the Oyarsa.

> "God!" exclaimed Devine in English. "Don't tell me they've got a loud-speaker."
> "Ventriloquism," replied Weston. . . . "Quite common among savages. The witch-doctor or medicine-man pretends to go into a trance and he does it. The thing to do is to identify the medicine-man and address your remarks to *him* wherever the voice seems to come from; it shatters his nerve. . . . Do you see any of the brutes in a trance? By jove—I've spotted him." [*Out of the Silent Planet*, p. 126]

Not only do the antagonists of the trilogy avoid real encounter, they abuse and finally murder other persons in response to the notion of somehow prolonging human existence indefinitely. Individual human relationships are readily sacrificed to an abstract concept.

With "the object itself" as the shape of persons' lives, our third category, we begin to enter the heart of Lewis's concern with "the object" and paradoxically seem to leave sensible objects altogether. Of course, with human relationships we have already gone beyond the purely sensible. But for Lewis, as we have seen above, the shape of life, that is, life directed a certain way, has a solidity analogous to sensible objects. As he describes it in *The Abolition of Man*, it is quite simply "the Way, the Road" [p. 28], the imitation in human life of the shape of Nature and the Universe.[18]

Particular attention is given to the Way, the shape of life, in *Perelandra*—understandably, since the ideal pattern of life is essential to its subject. The central metaphors (for Lewis the primary images) are the fixed and floating islands. The Way, quite literally, is an unrolling sequence of delights on the floating islands, each delight beyond the one previous [p. 83] and none quite repeated, all by Maleldil's command and from his hand. The *fixed* island is forbidden to the Green Lady for more than a day's length; she must never spend the night there [p. 74]. She turns, not to expected and repeated delights, but to an acceptance of that good which she will be given next, the next wave Maleldil is rolling toward her [p. 68].

Ransom has already sensed the shape of life on Perelandra in a feeling of reluctance to repeat his first pleasurable taste of Perelandrian fruit [pp. 42-43]. With his experience of an entirely new pleasure, the rich refreshment of the bubble trees, Ransom's intuitions are strengthened:

> This itch to have things over again, as if life were a film that could be unrolled twice or even made to work backwards . . . was it possibly the root of all evil? [p. 48—ellipsis in the original]

Apparently (at least for Perelandra) it was. The antagonist Weston's entire effort is simply to bring the Green Lady to the fixed land for an extended stay [p. 103], to substitute her own little drama for the one Maleldil was unfolding to her. And it is Ransom's arduous task to prevent that evil.

At its core, the Way is a conviction that *this* must be done and *that* avoided, that only thus does life take the shape of the Way. And the confirmation is found in an increasing awareness of that shape, an increasing understanding of one's own life and destiny, and, of course, an increasing joy. (We have met this before.) Ransom's career is a prime example. The Way begins for him in carrying out the simple duty of returning a son to his worried mother. The result is the voyage to Malacandra and a key part in the cosmic drama. It proceeds in the conviction that he must engage and defeat Weston at all costs. The confirmation is his fulfillment of his name and destiny.

In *That Hideous Strength*, it is primarily Mark and Jane who learn the Way. Jane experiences it primarily as a demand out of her encounter with the Director and then God:

> This demand which now pressed upon her was not, even by analogy, like any other demand. It was the origin of all right demands and contained them. [p. 318]

And within that demand her life takes shape, "a shape it had never dreamed of. And the making went on amidst a kind of splendour or sorrow or both" [p. 319].

Mark experiences the Way during his initiation at N.I.C.E. Its beginning is his desperate cry for help against his own lust for N.I.C.E.'s specific version of the anti-human. As the initiation continues, a sense of something Mark vaguely calls the "Normal" grows:

> He had never thought about it before. But there it was—solid, massive, with a shape of its own, almost like something you could touch, or eat, or fall in love with. It was all mixed up with Jane and fried eggs and soap and sunlight and the rooks cawing at Cure Hardy. [p. 299]

His realization grows: this thing is not simply an idea in his own head, but "something which obviously existed quite independently of himself and had hard rock surfaces which would not give, surfaces he could cling to" [p. 310].

But for the antagonists of the trilogy, the shape of human life is valueless; *continued existence* is all that matters. That is Weston and Devine's reason for traveling to Malacandra. And it is Weston's "fixed idea" upon Perelandra [p. 89]. In *That Hideous Strength* the idea reveals itself in its full intention, the creation of an artificial and deathless man (perhaps "Un-man," Weston's title, is better) free from nature. The careers of all those who serve the Head, and of the Head itself, reveal the shapelessness and horror of the result.

> Mark felt an insane doubt whether he [Wither] was there at all. . . . What looked out of those pale watery eyes was, in a sense, infinity —the shapeless and the interminable. [p. 188]

N.I.C.E. at bottom is a single, shapeless personality [p. 120] that absorbs and assimilates fresh individuals such as Mark [p. 243]. Far from understanding, fulfillment, and joy, the Hideous Strength bewilders, enslaves, and kills. As Ransom says, "their Masters hate them" [p. 317]. With Belbury in riot and ruins the Head demands, and receives, human sacrifice—if Filostrato and Straik can still be considered human—and is then itself destroyed [pp. 355, 358].

In its further reaches "the object itself" is the shape and character of the universe, a universe of infinite richness and depth, full of life and full of God. The heavens serve as the primary metaphor for "the Way" in its fullest dimensions:

> To dissolve into the ocean of eternal noon, seemed . . . a consummation even more desirable than their return to Earth. And if he had felt some such lift of the heart when first he passed through heaven on their outward journey, he felt it now tenfold, for now he was convinced that the abyss was full of life in the most literal sense. [*Out of the Silent Planet*, p. 146]

At the opposite reach from absorption in "the Way" is absorption in the self and a shrinking universe. It is the temptation of the Green Lady, Jane, and Mark, and the condition of all the antagonists in some degree. The result is best described in Weston's tormented words, as the inside of the rind or the exchanged self: "Darkness, worms, heat, pressure, salt, suffocation, stink" [*Perelandra*, p. 169].

The shapes of the books of the trilogy are analogous to the contrasting shapes of the lives they describe. In *Out of the Silent Planet* as Ransom's life takes shape, Weston's and Devine's are brought to comic absurdity. Ransom fulfills his highest destiny, the fulfillment of his name, in *Perelandra*, while Weston loses his personality entirely and is reduced physically to a shapeless mass. (Meanwhile Ransom, physically, is a new man.) In *That Hideous Strength* the contrasts between the shape and shapelessness of lives are pursued within chapters and from chapter to chapter, culminating in the individual and collective disasters of lives at Belbury, and the individual and collective fulfillment of lives at St. Anne's.

Before we finish, the "message" component of the trilogy must be taken into account. It is here that a reservation must be expressed concerning Lewis's attention to "the object itself," and the application of his own theory of good literature. First a reminder of an aspect of his theory. Good literature, for Lewis, must invite attention, interest, and pleasure for itself alone and not for such secondary considerations as its truth or philosophy. It is here that Lewis's fiction suffers. In the trilogy Lewis is not content to present a mythical story involving the conflict of good and evil (as Tolkien has done, for example, in *The Lord of the Rings*); nor does he settle for a story with obvious affinities to the Christian story. He teaches; he instructs. And in this instruction, truth and philosophy *are* primary considerations. His instruction is worth its weight in gold, as W. H. Auden has commented,[19] but it calls attention away from "the object itself" and therefore reduces the mythopoeic and imaginative value of the work.

The instruction is accomplished mainly through conversations, in some cases long conversations, or the protagonists' philosophical speculations and conclusions. And some of the ideas are driven home repeatedly. Ransom speculates that myth in one world may well be fact in another [*Perelandra*, p. 102]. This arbitrary distinction between myth and fact is discussed at least twice more in *Perelandra*, and is picked up again for several discussions in *That Hideous Strength*. Though the shape of Mark and Jane's lives suggest a certain viewpoint on marriage, the Director lectures Jane at length on the topic [pp. 146-50]. And though N.I.C.E. manifests at least the potential shape of the modern world, it must also be discussed between Merlin and Ransom [p. 293] and, in a long passage, between Frost and Mark [pp. 254-60].

Perhaps the least necessary of these "messages" are those that link specifically fictional elements of the trilogy with those of the actual world. Thus we are told Maleldil might really be God [*That Hideous Strength*, pp. 233-34]. No attentive reader could have missed the implication. Nor is the explicit statement that *Space* should be replaced by the idea of *Heaven* in the minds of readers any more necessary [*Out of the Silent Planet*, pp. 154]. Lewis's descriptions of the voyages through deep heaven are quite sufficient. The straightforward message might well have the opposite effect. In general the imaginative shape, the "mythic core," of Lewis's fiction invites a far more attentive reading for the thing that it is in itself than do his messages. With many of his messages, secondary considerations of validity and, at this point, datedness, are bound to obtrude.

The weight of message in Lewis's fiction may well limit the length of its stay. One cannot help but feel that the nearly messageless (in any obvious sense) *Lord of the Rings* will be read when the trilogy has been forgotten. As W. H. Auden has said, it would have been a pity for C. S. Lewis to have written fewer books ["Red Lizards," p. 23]. But they might have been more lasting if he had.

Edward G. Zogby, S. J.

Triadic Patterns in Lewis's Life and Thought

IT seems a fair statement of the state of Lewis criticism to date
to say that most of the criticism being published falls into the
category of appreciation and applause. There is little written which
attempts to see Lewis as more than a moralist and Christian apolo-
gist. No one but Owen Barfield has written about the man behind
the works, and no one has written about the man *in* the works
themselves. The endeavor of this paper is to be comprehensive,
to look at all of Lewis's writings, excluding for the most part his
Allegory of Love, A Preface to Paradise Lost, and *English Literature in the Sixteenth Century Excluding Drama.* This view follows
Owen Barfield's discovery of "the two Lewises," Lewis the dialectician and the "mythopoeic Lewis." A comprehensive view of the
two Lewises reveals that there was in Lewis, as he himself admitted
in his reply (undated) to the Milton Society of America, a central
man trying to "get out," trying to assert himself over Lewis the
dialectician. Lewis said: "The imaginative man in me is older,
more continuously operative, and in that sense more basic than
either the religious writer or the critic. It was he who made me
first attempt (with little success) to be a poet" [*Letters,* p. 260].

How successful was Lewis in uniting the two halves? Certainly,
if we read the 1943 preface to *The Pilgrim's Regress,* we can see
that at the heart of his "dialectic of desire" there is a *quest* for unity
within himself. But Lewis was too astute a dialectician to let himself believe that his savior would be any other person, whether
Freud or Jung. His quest was leading him, as it led Arthur, to
Mother Kirk, who alone could lead him to Christ: "This Desire
was, in the soul, as the Siege Perilous in Arthur's castle—the chair
in which only one could sit. And if nature makes nothing in vain,

the One who can sit in this chair must exist" [p. 10]. Since Lewis himself demonstrates this on his own behalf, this study will avoid any Freudian or Jungian interpretations to explain how the two Lewises finally were united. They were finally united in the *person* of Jesus, not in an idea of Him. Yet it took Lewis until 1955-56 to indicate to his readers how he, the central man, finally broke through the *idea* of Jesus the ransomer of man to the *person* of Jesus who ransomed not only all men but also *each* man, including C. S. Lewis.

It is instructively curious to see how Owen Barfield repeats, after so many years, and after having said the same thing many times before, his view of the two Lewises seeking unity of self. In a recent article on *The Great Divorce*, Barfield writes:

> Lewis was not only a moralist and Christian apologist. He was also a distinguished literary critic, a writer of imaginative fiction and a poet. And in all three of these capacities he evinced a strong and warm feeling for myth; one might better say a firm intuition of the substantial reality of myth. There were, in fact, two Lewises. . . . There was the "bonny" fighter of the Socratic Club (see Austin Farrar's essay in *Light on* [C. S.] *Lewis*); but there was also mythopoeic Lewis, the author of *Till We Have Faces*, the planetary novels, of the Narnia series and of many of the poems. *The Great Divorce*, as I have said, is itself a kind of myth and in that book, as perhaps not quite in any other, this ever diverse pair—atomically rational Lewis and mythopoeic Lewis—I will not say unite, but they do at least join hands.[1]

My own contention is that Barfield has his finger on the pulse, but I do see a further evolution towards union which can be found when we see *Surprised by Joy* and *Till We Have Faces* in polar relationship. As genres they are as much coinciding opposites as the two halves of Lewis, but when seen as *in relation* to one another, the linear ghost-Lewis of *The Great Divorce* is ripped away and the triadic Lewis emerges. This, however, must be seen on an anagogic level, as this paper will soon demonstrate. And since the anagogic is to be found in a literary mode, a world all in itself, Lewis's metaphoric use of masculine and feminine as *gender-in-polarity* (the primordial relationship from which our sex differences of male and female take their metaphorical origin for Lewis), we shall employ the terms masculine and feminine as the literary metaphors which Lewis uses to express the deepest relation of creature to Creator.

How much this was in Lewis's own thinking in the fiction can be seen in *The Pilgrim's Regress*, in which both John and Vertue must gain the opposite quality by fighting victoriously over the male and female dragons of the North and South; also, in the masculine Malacandra and the feminine Perelandra, in the struggle between the harsh N.I.C.E. of no compromise with life and St. Anne's lush fertility, in the struggle between Mark and Jane Studdock, as well as the struggle within Jane to discover her true self. In *The Great Divorce* it is the hard-questioning dialectician Lewis submitting himself to the master of imaginative fiction, George MacDonald. In Narnia the tame and the wild are found to coincide in Aslan, who embodies both the masculine and the feminine. Lewis extends the bafflement even further in *Till We Have Faces*, in which the tension between the masculine and feminine takes place not only between Psyche and the god, but also between the two sisters, and then within each one of them. Lewis gives what I consider his theological intention in the fiction when he has Ransom say in *That Hideous Strength*: "The masculine none of us can escape. What is above and beyond all things is so masculine that we are all feminine in relation to it" [p. 316].

What further definition can we give to these terms? In *Letters to Malcolm* there is much discussion of the relation between Creator and creation. The qualities of life-giving, or life-dealing, belong to the Father and to those to whom He wishes to delegate that power. This is never equated by Lewis with reproduction but rather with the presence of God in the soul. *Agape*, he says in *The Four Loves*, is the love of God for His creatures as well as "the Christian's love for the brethren." The traditional understanding of the effectiveness of the Sacrament of Baptism is certainly being given the priority here. The Feminine follows the path of obedience, for only a creature which can receive this life and contain it can also deal it out; this Lewis extends in his discussion of imagination in *An Experiment in Criticism*. There the imagination has both feminine and masculine qualities and the differences are unmistakable.

While the use of a genetic model can and does arouse the feeling that Lewis is being anti-feminist (in today's legitimate concern for women's rights), we can also see that Lewis was trying to give expression to the reality which theologians over many centuries in the West have labored hard to define: how does *grace* operate in man? how does God give Himself to a creature free to reject Him? Gender, not sexual difference, is the metaphor which Lewis chooses; the fact that his genetic model involves the Thomistic distinction between act and potency shows that Lewis is consciously working within a long and solid Christian theological tradition. It also furthers Lewis's insistence against the modern trend to make words simply be and not mean. He continues to parry and thrust even after his death. Although, as he admits in *The Discarded Image*, each age needs, and develops according to its need, a Model which provides a controlling principle of order, we, while we wait for the emergence of the Model which will serve our own age, must continue to use what we have. He said in his Cambridge Inaugural address in 1955 that he was one of the last of the dinosaurs, one of the last who could speak the mother tongue; everyone else would speak the mother tongue with foreign accents. But the practised dialectician forces us, unwilling perhaps, to fight the perilous siege on the field which he himself designates.

Since Lewis and Barfield were concerned with saving the appearances, it would help at this point to show part of the background which was prompting Lewis's selection of these precise metaphors. Barfield expresses in his article on *The Great Divorce* the same sentiment which he (and Lewis said he shared this) gave us in his second preface to *Poetic Diction*:

> There are two things above all that characterise the world we have lived in since what is called the scientific revolution, by contrast with the world before it. One is the overriding importance of solidity in our estimate of what constitutes reality and the other is our tendency to conceive of space as an infinite number of points and of time as an infinite succession of moments. The two together—the notion of "extended substance," used by Descartes to designate everything in the universe that is not mind or spirit, and the habit of thought induced by the calculus—led inevitably to "atomism" in physical theory. Atoms were the only ultimate reality, and atomism the only reality principle. (I am not refering to modern atomic theory, but to the "billiard ball" atoms, as they are sometimes called, of classical, nineteenth century physics.)
>
> What was disastrous was the failure to distinguish between atomism as *method* and physical atomism as the sole reality principle. For the result was that people gradually became incapable of thinking precisely, or indeed without hopeless confusion, about anything at all that was *not* reducible to physical units. It remained for the twentieth century, in the person of C. S. Lewis, to detect and expose the disastrous confusion, to discover that thinking atomically is not the same thing as thinking about atoms, and especially to show that it is possible to think in that way even about ethics without simply turning it into an offshoot of psychology or physiology.[2]

In Lewis we find the dialectician urging the man of imagination to rediscover the central man. Lewis wrote in terms of the dangerous alteration of traditional moral values and led a direct attack on it in *The Abolition of Man* and *That Hideous Strength*. Hell became his symbol of the world in which everything flows, where men are

ghosts who shun the decision which saves their souls, as Lewis
learned from MacDonald. Heaven is the opposite; it is represented
by "solid" images. Barfield explains:

> Both during Lewis's life and since his death, there has been a steadily
> growing interest, a growing awareness of the fact that there was once a
> time when that kind of consciousness [the "solid," which Lewis equates
> with salvation, and the choice of the good as opposed to the evil which
> one must undo when it is discovered] was collective; a time when it
> was, for mankind, the normal way of apprehending the world around
> him; when it was his "common sense"; when it was the ground beneath
> knowledge itself. And there has been a growing tendency to ask whether
> it may not have been a way of knowing things, including things about
> the spirit, which we no longer know—except in what we call "the uncon-
> scious." In this mythic, or symbolic type of consciousness, which was not
> finally extinguished until the time of the scientific revolution, Lewis, as
> he showed in *The Discarded Image* and elsewhere, was very much at
> home.[3]

It is the "ground beneath knowledge itself" which Lewis emphasizes and pursues. This leads him to present his thesis concerning
the Tao in *The Abolition of Man*. Lewis saw the Tao at the heart
of the "dialectic of desire"; it is the Tao, as the reality beyond all
predicates, which directs one's natural desire for God. He saw that
the universal pattern of the Tao was in line with the primary story
told through the downward ascent[4] of the Incarnation and Resurrection of Christ, the *Evangelium*. The *Evangelium* story of the
tragic Creator and Redeemer is the main subject of Lewis's fiction;
Lewis's representative anecdote is that of ransoming man's capacity
for the Tao-Christ; his key metaphor for the divine-human activity
is the downward ascent. Lewis symbolized creation in his fiction
by the archetype of gender; gender is where he focuses on the
masculine and the feminine in polar tension. The union resulting
from participation in the polar tension is holiness, which corrects
the distortions of human loves in relation to divine love. The cosmic
result is that Man becomes the Feminine, receptive and expectant
of the Divine gift, which is the Presence of the Masculine God
through the free, unilateral, and continuing gift of Himself to His
creation.

Through the dialectic of desire Lewis discovered a naturally polar
relation between reason (mind) and imagination (spiritual sensation), the tension of the coinciding opposites producing the third
thing. The triadic pattern in Lewis's life and autobiographies is
delight: pain: fruit; in his social criticism—*tradition* (Tao): *anti-tradi-
tion* (being outside of the Tao): *the Tao realized* in the individual

person; in his theology—*begetting* (*zoe*): *making* (*bios*): *participation in the life of the Trinity*; in his fiction—*masculine: feminine: union* (*marriage*); in his literary theory—*Logos: poiema: Evangelium* in the imagination of the reader.

By way of summary for this introduction we can say that in biblical theology the act of creation is described in both masculine and feminine terms. Barfield has shown us that this principle has been lost: C. S. Lewis tried to restore it because its loss has brought about spiritual illiteracy. His complaints were, first, that Christians have more in common with Pagans than with modern scientistic man, who has lost his belief in any Creator God; and, second, that the modern scientistic mind, through its various "mythologies" (such as eugenics and evolutionism) has replaced the life-giving role traditionally attributed to the Masculine God and has given that role to its own inventions. Pursuit of the Masculine-Feminine tension in Lewis's view of life and creativity runs into so many degrees of application and multiple suggestion that we shall have to limit detailed exploration of it here to the space trilogy and to *Till We Have Faces*, considered together with *Surprised by Joy*.

In novels subsequent to *The Pilgrim's Regress* Lewis focuses less on social criticism and more on a type of spiritual autobiography. As he moves from allegory to myth, Lewis is able to unpack the universal elements in his personal belief as Christian converted from paganism. Having discovered the archetype of *gender* in the tension between human love and divine love, Lewis began seriously to explore the archetype. In the polar opposition between the Masculine and the Feminine, Lewis found the natural reasonableness for belief in Christ and in the Trinity. The space trilogy *as a trilogy*, which includes *Out of the Silent Planet*, *Perelandra*, and *That Hideous Strength*, is an exploration on a grand scale of this archetype of gender.

Out of the Silent Planet is a story of Malacandra, or Mars. It is a dying planet whose death has been willed by God or Maleldil. It is a planet governed by the archon Malacandra, who represents the Masculine per se but is not to be confused with God, the absolute Masculine. None of the inhabitants of the planet have human form, but they are creatures who are bound by affection, which comes from being "in the will of Maleldil."

Perelandra is a story of Perelandra, or Venus, a planet on the brink of new life. It is under the guardianship of the archon Perelandra, who is the Feminine per se. Couched in the creation mythology of Genesis, the novel ends with the Morning Day of the planet's

birth in innocence. Evil had been averted by the intervention of
Dr. Elwin Ransom, who had defeated the Devil's attempt to corrupt
the Green Lady, the Queen of Perelandra, through the devil-
possessed body of Dr. Edward Rolles Weston, a famous Oxford
physicist-evolutionist. By refusing evil, by remaining obedient to
Maleldil, the Queen feminized the planet. Morning Day, in our
reckoning 1943 A.D., is an annunciation scene in which all the creatures of Perelandra were gathered by the new King and Queen of
Perelandra. Together on top of a mountain in a vast crater lush
with vegetation, they were overshadowed by the power of Maleldil
and given life which will know no effects of evil. The Masculine
was able to enter freely into a virginal planet willing to be Feminine.
It is significant that the King and Queen had totally human bodies
and emerald green skin: the human form is the elected species
because of what Maleldil achieved on Thulcandra, or Earth, through
His victory over death. What the devil tried to achieve through evil,
Weston's dream of a human utopia, a eugenically perfect world,
Maleldil achieved through Ransom's victory.

That Hideous Strength begins with the word "matrimony" and
ends with the consummation of real marriage in the flesh. While
the novel satirizes the spiritual death which the popularizers of
evolution have brought to Thulcandra, it is more fundamentally
a movement from archetype to anagoge, from speculation on the
universal truth to that same truth brought into contemporary personal experience. In other words, it is the universal seen in concrete terms of human love accepting divine love freely. Lewis is
here dealing with what Christians call the *eschaton* or the end-time,
when Christ will come to establish definitively His victory over
evil. Feminized creation can receive the Masculine directly.

Lewis sets this story up in a highly complex use of ancient and
modern mythology, the Arthurian legend, and the modern evolutionary myth.[5] Both myths are "popular" myths. The Arthurian
myth, which promised that a descendent of Arthur would come to
ransom Britain from final defeat, was a popular myth, as popular
as the story of Aeneas coming to found Rome was to Romans. The
evolutionary myth presents man as no longer either pagan or Christian. He is so masculinized as to attempt to replace God with his
own artifacts. Ransoming can happen only by the defeat of the
creaturely masculine, which is the property of evil.

That which moves this story and the trilogy from archetype to
anagoge is the story within the story, the failing marriage of Jane
and Mark Studdock. Jane is an archfeminist who is unwilling to
surrender herself to being a proper wife to Mark. Mark, in turn,
has greedily sold himself, seeking fame and prestige by joining

forces with N.I.C.E., the National Institute of Co-ordinated Experiments, a politico-behavioral organization seeking a Nazi-like
domination of the world. Dr. Ransom, having returned from Perelandra in a transfigured or glorified state (i.e., already beyond
death), is now the Pendragon sent to ransom Britain in its final
conflict with evil. He functions as the Director of St. Anne's, a
haven of order, life, and fertility. St. Anne's represents creation,
the human Feminine in preparation for the coming of the Masculine. Redemption is to issue from this place. The key figure,
however, is Merlin, who is awakening after centuries of sleep.
N.I.C.E. wants Merlin for his magical powers. St. Anne's hopes
that he will be swayed to their side (the side of good) because
of a residual "eldilic power" latent in the Great Tongue tradition
in which Merlin was educated. Lewis facilitates the winning over of
Merlin not only by making Ransom the Pendragon but also by showing that in the Old Order Merlin was more a Christian than a "black"
magician. After Ransom informs him of his mission to rid Britian
of N.I.C.E., the gods descend to empower Merlin for the battle
facing him. Lewis makes much of the healing of Jane's distorted
self-actualization and of her broken marriage. The descent of the
gods, especially the descent of Perelandra, restores Jane and Mark
to the Feminine. We are told that Jane and Mark were to have been
the parents of the descendent of Arthur but, because they had prevented conception in their marriage, they had foiled the divine plan.
In the end they are reconciled in their marriage bed, once they have
learned the true nature of the relation of the Feminine to the
Masculine.

The anagogic level of the story is thus located in the reordering
of the archetype within the self of both Jane and Mark so that the
Presence which gives the archetype power to reconcile coinciding
opposites without destroying their particular individuality can deal
life to them. Creation is Feminine, receptive and life-nurturing.
The life it deals out is borrowed life; the Feminine is delegated to
hand on the capacity for the Masculine. This is what St. Anne's and
the reconciled marriage of Jane and Mark represent.

In this trilogy we have a complete triad which celebrates the
central man. Modern man has become spiritually illiterate and
thus falls victim to evil: his evil consists in pretending to be the
Masculine. Lewis claims that this illiteracy prevents modern man
from being a pagan, who recognizes the Tao, that law of obedience
planted in the heart drawing man to goodness, and from being a
Christian (this term includes the Jew, for Lewis), who knows that
the Masculine has historically entered into the Feminine. Through
Incarnation the coinciding opposites are in perpetual tension but

unified by personality; the Masculine and the Feminine co-inhere
without one taking over the other.[6] As Lewis states in *Miracles*,
and further suggests in his fiction, man was made for God and
made by Him in His image. Similarly, God could not be related to
man as Creator without entering into that creation. Lewis is suggesting that in the act of creation God willed to participate in His
creation and that He willed also to have that creation participate
in His own being.

At this point in the chronological development, Lewis has made
two assertions which leave us on the bridge between archetype
and anagoge-in-depth. First, he has accepted the Christian dogma of
the Incarnation, God the Word become flesh in the person of Jesus.
But because of what Christ has done on Earth by His death and
victory over death, Lewis considers the *human form* itself to be
the definitively elected species over all other specific forms. That
is why pre-Christ Malacandra is a dying planet, and why the King
and Queen of Perelandra are human in every respect except that
their obedience is unspoiled by evil choices. For this reason, too,
the ransoming of Perelandra and Thulcandra from the power of
the Bent One is done through men who, because of their Christian
baptism, are also Maleldil. The victory over evil, although definitive in Christ, is wrought in post-Resurrection time through human
mediation and the power of the Holy Spirit. Lewis has used the
Myth of Deep Heaven of the space trilogy to portray this cosmic
drama. The move from cosmic drama as known speculatively to
the cosmic drama as experienced within the individual self has been
established. The third step will be to see this same thing happening
to Lewis himself in 1955-56 in *Surprised by Joy* and *Till We Have
Faces*. Support for this argument can be found in the fact that Lewis
had been writing *Till We Have Faces* since 1922. Its completion
waited upon his maturity, when he was able to get past the
idea of God to the experience of the real presence of God. It is not
a book which an atheist could have written.

The second assertion is that the archetypes of Masculine and
Feminine as understood by pagans had to undergo their own
Christian conversion. In a key passage in *Perelandra*, Dr. Ransom
saw both living archetypes materialize before his eyes and from this
vision he learned that life itself presents itself in terms of two forces
co-inhering in one power.[7] His vision of creation is in terms of the
Masculine and the Feminine. But by the will of Maleldil, both
Malacandra and Perelandra live on as servants of the *human*. On
Perelandra they both function as parts of creation; they are not as
great as Maleldil, for He created them, as He did the rest of creation. But the power of creation is a *delegated* power, as Lewis says

in *Letters to Malcolm*. By holding this hierarchical notion of creation, Lewis is able to avoid both pantheism and polytheism. The
archons are, in a word, subcreators; so is the Christian literary
artist for Lewis. They are powers carrying out the will of Maleldil
to create and to give freedom and unity so that His creatures would
delight to live in His will. They pass their power to humans, both
on Thulcandra and Perelandra, but they can do so effectively only
when the matter of the "new creation," that is, men willing to live
freely in the will of Maleldil, is properly feminized. And that can
take place only when the tendency of humans to be gods without
living in the will of Maleldil is corrected.

Lewis, as a chronicler in his own novel, says of Ransom's vision,
"Malacandra was like rhythm and Perelandra like melody. He
[Ransom] has said that Malacandra affected him like a quantitative, Perelandra like an accentual, metre." In his vision Ransom
realized that

> Gender is a reality, and a more fundamental reality than sex. Sex is,
> in fact, merely the adaptation to organic life of a fundamental polarity
> which divides all created beings. Female sex is simply one of the things
> that have feminine gender; there are many others, and Masculine and
> Feminine meet us on planes of reality where male and female would be
> simply meaningless. Masculine is not attenuated male, nor feminine
> attenuated female. On the contrary, the male and female of organic
> creatures are rather faint and blurred reflections of masculine and
> feminine. Their reproductive functions, their differences in strength and
> size, partly exhibit, but partly also confuse and misrepresent, the real
> polarity. All this Ransom saw, as it were, with his own eyes. The two
> white creatures were sexless. But he of Malacandra was masculine
> (not male); she of Perelandra was feminine (not female). Malacandra
> seemed to him to have the look of one standing armed, at the ramparts
> of his own remote archaic world, in ceaseless vigilance, his eyes ever
> roaming the earth-ward horizon whence his danger came long ago.
> . . . But the eyes of Perelandra opened, as it were, inward, as if they
> were the curtained gateway to a world of waves and murmurings and
> wandering airs, of life that rocked in winds and splashed on mossy
> stones and descended as the dew and arose sunward in thin-spun delicacy
> of mist. On Mars the very forests are of stone; in Venus the lands
> swim. For now he thought of them no more as Malacandra and Pere-
> landra. He called them by their Tellurian names. [*Perelandra*, pp. 200-01]

In this second assertion, Lewis is seeking to establish the polarity
which co-inheres in central man.[8] It is this which explains why opposites such as reason and imagination, *bios* (the strictly biological
nature of man) and *zoe* (the spiritual nature of man), are in dialecti-
cal relation in man. The archetypal realities are not the less real

for being archetypes, but their relation as Masculine and Feminine produce the third thing: the human, Man.

The most crucial of all of Lewis's writings, the companion works *Surprised by Joy* and *Till We Have Faces*, examine the same relationship within the individual self of Lewis. It does not seem accidental that Lewis, who began his writing of fiction with an allegorized autobiography, *The Pilgrim's Regress*, should publish these two books at the height of his maturity as an artist. They parallel by their genres and style the two main literary influences on Lewis's Christian life, Chesterton and MacDonald. They also parallel the two halves of Lewis, reason and imagination, the Masculine and the Feminine. *Surprised by Joy* is not fiction. Rather it is the story of the feminization of Lewis as he had to submit finally to the masculine God. Lewis found that God had been tracking him down through all of his experiences of Joy. Indeed, this is the way Lewis himself presents God's action.

When the two books are taken as companion works depicting the two halves of Lewis, and when one examines the relationship of the two sisters, Psyche and Orual, in *Till We Have Faces*, it is difficult not to see these as comprising together an anagoge in depth. Northrop Frye says that "the anagogic view . . . leads to the conception of literature as existing in its own universe, no longer a commentary on life or reality, but containing life and reality in a system of verbal relationships."[9] Stanley Romaine Hopper, the author of the phrase "anagoge in depth," says that reality is *presential*. Hopper claims a "between" ground "where Being is unconcealed in the concealment of beings." For Hopper, to see is not to see the differences but "in the case of the poem, [to] stand *within* the magnetic field of the elements in tension, and see as the poem sees." Hopper continues,

> In the old rhetoric *logic* presides via syllogistic exactness; in the new grammar Logos presides as utterance in the realm of the "difference" between Being and beings: it *presences* there as *Mythos* or as radical metaphor containing the opposites—an unconcealing that at the same time necessarily conceals. . . . I only add that contemporary literature is effecting a *translatio* of this awareness into ontology itself, which means that at its depth one may take the part for the whole. . . , that everything *is* in its depth identical with everything else anagogically, that "it [God, or the universe] is an infinite sphere of which the center is everywhere and the circumference is nowhere."[10]

Frye adds, "when poet and critic pass from the archetypal to the anagogic phase, they enter a phase of which only religion, or something as infinite in its range as religion, can possibly form an external goal."[11] In the same sense, Lewis says, "we are, not metaphorically but in very truth, a Divine work of art, something that God is making, and therefore something with which He will not be satisfied until it has a certain character" [*The Problem of Pain*, p. 42].

The Christian literary artist, once aware that he has been created and that he is "something that God is making," is able to "take the part for the whole"; he is transformed inwardly by the new relations which he sees. He works from within that universe wherein "Logos" presides anagogically. His works of literary imagination will be charged with this "presencing God" of Hopper. It is this God who indwells the metaphors, images, symbols, and stories of the Christian literary artist and who, through these literary means, steals into the imagination of the reader. In this way the reader is "feminized," and enabled to receive and nurture the good seed of *Evangelium* which he had ingested through the image, symbol, and metaphor. Once this presencing God had penetrated the hard atheistic core of Lewis the dialectician, Lewis saw the real relation between myth and fact. Christ was the Myth become Fact without ceasing to be Myth; history had been established as the meeting point of this coincidence for Lewis. He wrote to Malcolm:

But in order to find God it is perhaps not always necessary to leave the creatures behind. We may ignore, but we can nowhere evade, the presence of God. The world is crowded with Him. He walks everywhere *incognito*. And the *incognito* is not always hard to penetrate. The real labour is to remember, to attend. In fact, to come awake. Still more, to remain awake. [*Letters to Malcolm*, p. 75]

Lewis wrote in the same vein in *The Problem of Pain*:

If any message from the core of reality ever were to reach us, we should expect to find in it just that unexpectedness, that wilful, dramatic anfractuosity which we find in the Christian faith. It has the master touch—the rough, male taste of reality, not made by us, or, indeed, for us, but hitting us in the face. [p. 25]

It is a fact that Lewis did not confuse Christ with man-made myth. But, for Lewis, Christ is the reality which all myths are suggesting, provided they are sincere in following the dialectic of desire through suffering, grief, and the problem of death. His most important statement on the subject of myth is in *Miracles*:

On the factual side, a long preparation [of all previous Myths] culminates in God's becoming incarnate as Man, so, on the documentary
side [story], the truth first appears in *Mythical* form and then by a
long process of condensing or focussing finally becomes incarnate as
History. This involves the belief that Myth in general is not merely
misunderstood history . . . nor diabolical illusion . . . nor priestly
lying . . . but, at its best, *a real though unfocussed gleam of divine
truth falling on human imagination* [so that we might realize, through
reason, the Tao in each of us]. . . . Just as God is none the less God
by being Man, so the Myth remains Myth even when it becomes Fact.
[p. 139n—latter italics added][12]

By pairing Lewis's last autobiography and last novel, we are
able to see that not only is Lewis the subject of what is written
but so too is the Trinity. The Trinity is for him, as for Coleridge,
the "antecedent factual unity" of all polar existence. Here, at last,
in Lewis's writings, we get a clear picture of Lewis's own struggle
for self-realization. Owen Barfield, known to be one of Lewis's
closest friends, provides a commentary on Coleridge which applies
equally well to Lewis. Barfield says that polarity applies both to
the nature of human reason and to the nature of God, both of which
are the polar elements in tension in the two books now under
consideration.

Another name for the principle of polarity is triunity: the two poles,
with their originating unity as the relation between them. The operations
of the understanding are always, whether knowingly or unknowingly,
based on a bare principle of identity. . . . Psychologically and theologically . . . [the] apprehension of the bare principle of identity can
give us no more than the bare *fact* of personal identity. The *content*
of self-consciousness on the other hand is always tri-une, or three "in"
one and one "in" three, and it is only in realising tri-unity that we
can be said to realise our actual selves.[13]

Barfield explains that while this truth certainly transcends human
reason, it is also something which reason can grasp, because reason, and with it the principle of tri-unity, is itself the source and
existential condition of the understanding. It cannot itself therefore
be "understood," but only *experienced* by the understanding as
self-evident. Furthermore, "the Holy Spirit is that polarity and
'the spirit' its realisation in human life."[14]

The polarity of gender represents for Lewis a paradoxical transposition, the "downward ascent" movement of the transforming
love of God. It is, indeed, for Lewis, the unique way in which rational creatures can share in the superpersonal presence of the God
of love. As he said in *That Hideous Strength*, "what is above and

beyond all things is so masculine that we are all feminine in relation to it" [p. 316]. Lewis, the Christian literary artist himself,
becomes for us the transposed and transformed personification, to
use Barfield's term, of the polar tension existing between human
love and divine love. Indeed, five moments of this transposition
are discernible in his fiction, life, and theology. They map out the
journey one takes from noetic to ontic faith, from faith known
intellectually to an experienced knowledge of that faith as reality
itself.

The first is *interposition*, which causes a crucial moment of
paradox or enigma arresting the imagination of the artist and preparing it for loss or humility. The second is *iconoclasm*, which
shatters the artist's ideas or conceptions of systems and then wres-
tles with the artist through the pain of the dialectic of loss and gain,
desolation and consolation, dejection and joy, to raise him up out
of the death of idolatry to the presence of God Himself: to the
why of existence at all. Third is *eucatastrophe*, a term borrowed
from Tolkien. This brings about a sense of joy at the healing possibility which a shattering can bring. There is joy in being delivered
from a universal and final defeat, which the iconoclasm figures.
Christ's birth and death were eucatastrophic events; they are the
assurance of the final victory over death; they show the way to
the exit from the fear of permanent death.[15] The fourth moment is
the *ascent to the universal*. The Christian literary artist shows that
mystical union with God involves a death to self which is true
liberation. He is not speaking philosophically, but theologically;
not about self-transcendence alone, but a self-transcendence which
comes about as a result of one's search for God. The fifth is the
personal descent to the particular. This empowers or inspires the
believing artist to possess a unifying belief and to give biblical
overtones to his myths, symbols, and metaphors.

These five moments can be seen clearly in *Surprised by Joy*,
particularly since Lewis uses the chess game metaphor to describe
his conversion. The final four moves are God's strategy against
the hard-boiled dialectician. These four moves directly parallel the
four tasks which Psyche has to perform before both she and Orual
can return to divine favor. The parallel between the two books is
so remarkable that I have elsewhere devoted a separate study to it.
The moves are feminizing for Lewis as well as for Psyche and
Orual.

In *Till We Have Faces*, a retelling of Apuleius's myth of Cupid
and Psyche, Orual is Queen of Glome and the sister of Psyche,
who was marked with divine favor from her birth. Orual is a
masculine-assertive woman, possessive to the point of destructive-

ness in her love of Psyche; Psyche is almost too feminine for one
born from flesh and blood. Both must undergo transformation—
one must be softened and the other hardened, just as Vertue and
John were softened and hardened respectively by their combat
with the hot female dragon and the cold male dragon in *The Pilgrim's Regress*. All of Lewis's polarities are recapitulated in one
form or another in this novel. But the anagogic value of this novel
lies in seeing the two women as the two halves of the soul, really
the two halves of Lewis, reason and imagination in tension. Only
the God of love, who is also transformed in this case, can bring each
of them to their proper state, but it is not done without all three of
them suffering. Lysias, the Greek slave who taught Orual and
Psyche from the time they were children, was an enlightened
sceptic-atheist. His name in Greek, ironically, means ransomer. He
fails to ransom them but instead must suffer with them in their own
suffering before he too arrives at a realized faith. He fails because
without Christ there can be no ransoming, not even for the pagan
when he refuses to accept the Tao. The ransoming occurs only
when they realize that the God of Mountain, the Shadowbrute (or
God as the pagans saw him), is the God of love.

The irony of *Till We Have Faces* is that one cannot face God
until one has been fully feminized—until then even the god Eros
has no face for humans to behold. Orual and Psyche do not become
real characters until they are one at the end of the tale. Orual
must become Psyche. They represent possibilities of what is to
come. They are more like the material out of which myth is built.
They are in constant growth, casting off old life forms and ideas
in preparation for the central act of reconciliation. All is focused
on this realization of the myth: it is the center of the circle in
which all lines intersect. This story portrays the last chapter of pagan
myth before the Incarnation, which is also the story of Lewis, who
was truly a pagan until his conversion. He said of himself, "I have
been a converted Pagan living among apostate Puritans" [*Surprised by Joy*, p. 69].

Just as Perelandra, a planet at the pitch of ripeness awaiting the
new creation, begins with the dreary business of the temptation
and the defeat of evil, so Glome, at the pitch of pagan ripeness for
Christ, begins with the gloom of Glome and the House of Ungit
which precedes the union of ancient religious feeling with a personal, living God. Everything is ready for the universal to be par-
ticularized, one freely suffering for the other.

Here there is a sense of change, preparation, anticipation, and
dissatisfaction with feelings as they exist. Orual must undergo

many deaths before she can be softened and feminized, and Psyche must undergo real suffering for Orual before she can become *humanly* real. No one can be outside *the law of the Cross*. When Orual and Psyche each wanted to commit suicide, they were being religiously premature. " 'Do not do it,' said the god. 'You cannot escape Ungit by going to the deadlands, for she is there also. Die before you die. There is no chance after' " [*Till We Have Faces*, p. 279].

The difference between *Till We Have Faces* and *The Pilgrim's Regress* is that in the former there is the evolution of a fully conscious person, while in the latter we have not evolution but rather an accomplished and staged fact. In *Till We Have Faces*, just as the characters do not yet have faces with which to meet the god, so too the god does not yet have the face with which to meet the Feminine *humanly*. The Myth is on the way to becoming Fact through the Virgin Birth. The Feminine before the Masculine must be virginal—nothing else will do. Both men and god are moving towards visible personality, just as Lewis is moving toward holiness.

All, in a sense, are parts of that last vibration after a series of vibrations which has been the Great Dance of the world since the beginning. It takes shape as the Myth itself takes on deeper and more discernible features in the years following the historical birth of Christ. The story of Christ as tragic Creator and Redeemer, as Lewis says in *Letters to Malcolm*, could not be told until the long preparation through the line of David led to Mary, who also had to suffer. The story of the whole person in Lewis's retelling of the ancient myth, which he began in verse form in 1922, could not be told until Psyche was hardened by suffering and grief. Only after both women had suffered for one another were they able to convert the extreme rationality of Lysias and alter the decadent religion of Ungit. A new religion grew around Psyche. She became the symbol of the new relationship of human love to divine love, but Psyche was to become two people; she and Orual became one through mutual suffering. The once ugly Orual, who had kept her face hidden behind a veil for years, was transformed into Psyche's own beauty, which had captured the eye of God. Psyche's marriage to Eros (a prefigurement of Christ) provided what was lacking and what was needed to complete the whole person. Lewis is saying that the cerebral and visceral, the rational and the imaginative, are united by the Incarnate Christ, who alone was able to unite the human and the divine within Himself. Lewis's own struggle was to let the dialectician in him die so that the central man in him, the man of imagination [*Letters*, p. 260], could live. The Orual-reason in him had to die to her own absoluteness and realize the Logos that moves within Psyche-imagination.

Polarities yield trinities; this is what the imagination knows. This the Feminine knows as it stands before the Masculine. When polarities remain simply two poles without a relationship of coinciding opposition, no marriage or union is possible. Without the imagination impressed by God's grandeur, one is condemned to a sterile, barren marriage bed; such was the problem facing Jane and Mark Studdock in *That Hideous Strength*. Lewis concludes in *The Four Loves* that human love and natural loves can be truly "human" only when they are impregnated by divine love and not made ends in themselves. This key principle guides everything he writes, whether it be social criticism, poetic theory, theology, autobiography, poetry, or fiction.

Lewis, in his opposition to the "modern" distortion of the Tao, achieved two things: he opposed the "flatlander" anti-metaphysical result of strict linear analysis, but in doing so he underwent a spiritual development and discovered that human experience participated in a mode of triadic revelation. In opposition to Shaw and Wells, Lewis discovered affection at the heart of the universe of space, time, and the self. Affection is the life-blood of the Tao, and the Tao is the continuing revelation of *agape* or divine love, welling up from within man. Lewis felt that the modern man had put himself outside of the Tao, alien now to both Pagans and Christians alike.

By discovering *storge*, or affection, at the core of the universe, as Lewis does by beginning in his own experiences with the dialectic of desire, it seems rather inevitable that he would find *agape*, or the Creator's love for creation, as the love which empowers all the other loves (*storge*, *eros*, and *philia*) to be loves at all. For Lewis, the Tao is what moves the loves towards *agape*, but, at the same time, it is *agape* which draws the Tao to itself through the loves, just as a third log draws flame upwards from two smoldering logs lying side by side.

When we see in *The Pilgrim's Regress* and in *Surprised by Joy* how Joy led Lewis to Christ *through* the dialectic of desire, so that Joy itself became a pointer to Christ rather than the desired end itself, we begin to get a glimpse into Lewis's *way* of discovering Christ. We know from the early poems *Spirits in Bondage* and *Dymer* that Lewis believed in life and goodness, but the presence of evil in the world had led him to question how, despite evil, man could predicate goodness, mercy, and love to a Creator God. Lewis had resented God for making such a bad job of creation. Only gradually was Joy able to effect that change in him which allowed him to see that the answer to the problem of pain lay in *relation*. Linear thought, he argues in *The Problem of Pain*, was always jolted by unexpected epiphanic leaps; this is the way from numinous religions down to the historical event of Christ. He came to see that the tension in man between *bios* (matter) and *zoe* (spirit) resulted in the unexpected third thing, the unification of the two halves of the self by divine love. This he expresses in his treatise on the Trinity in *Mere Christianity*.

Lewis discovered a seemingly natural polarity of coinciding opposites on an ontological level which indicated that life was fashioned by two forces of one power. The one power is divine love, *agape*, existing in a participated form in the individual himself. The self was where the two forces had to unfocus and then refocus; Barfield would say that the self had to move from original participation to final participation. The move is from unawakened innocence to innocence regained by (often painful) choice of the good. We might say that for Lewis every individual has to experience personally *being redeemed* or restored to inner unity. The two forces within the self are the Masculine (the uncreated, supernatural gift of healing and edifying agapic love) and the Feminine (created being which lives on borrowed life and which is sustained in life only by its obediential potency to receive the begetting Masculine).

The triadic pattern of life is presented in the fiction in terms of the Perelandrian archetype of gender—the outward-gazing, vigilant Malacandra, and the inward-gazing, life-bearing Perelandra. Together they become the servants of the distinctively *human*; when Maleldil became *human* on Thulcandra, the cosmic effect was that the human species itself became the elected species.

In Lewis's Myth of Deep Heaven the Masculine and the Feminine were separated until Maleldil became Man. Maleldil supports the whole Masculine-Feminine-Marriage (union) triad: by becoming Man, the Masculine had to become Feminine *without intermeddling* the two. There are two halves of the self because the archetypal "case" for humanity is the hypostatic union of the two natures in the person of Jesus, as enunciated by the Council of Chalcedon. For Lewis, the pattern is first in God the Creator, then in creation. In this pattern the polar opposition between Creator and creation means that the Masculine is Masculine because it is in *relation* to the Feminine, and the Feminine is Feminine because it is placed in *relation* to the Masculine. Thus the bottom line for Lewis is that suffering has to be the main mode of transposition for both the

Masculine and the Feminine. The Creator is a *tragic* Creator and Redeemer because He had to *relate*, submit to creation and suffer out of love (just as Eros had to suffer the loss of Psyche in order to gain her back). Without submission creation could not receive the Masculine. Likewise, unless the Feminine submits to the Masculine in obedience, its own ability to share in the qualities of the Masculine, of begetting and bearing, would never result.

Thus, for Lewis, creation, male and female together, is the Feminine. God Himself is the Masculine. But Lewis believed in angels and in creation being delegated to a hierarchy of beings, as he says in *Letters to Malcolm*. Thus Malacandra represents the Masculine per se in a delegated and participated way and not by way of proper identity. We see in *That Hideous Strength* that when the Glund-Oyarsa descends he is called "King of Kings." He is not Christ but Lewis says that God has dealt out that being which dwells in Himself to such a degree that some aspects of creation can appear to be Him. This self-giving on the part of God is also the source of idolatry. When creation usurps and appropriates to itself the qualities of the Masculine, it also tries to replace Him. The right order of things is for the Feminine to enjoy and participate in the Masculine without appropriation: this is the source of holiness that the Feminine should receive and give created life to the uncreated Masculine. Lewis says as much in *The Pilgrim's Regress*, speaking of Mary, the mother of Jesus:

> It was a special case because it was the archetypal case. Has no one told you that that Lady spoke and acted for all that bears, in the presence of all that begets: for this country as against the things East and West: for matter as against form and patiency against agency? Is not the very word Mother akin to Matter? Be sure that the whole of this land, with all its warmth and wetness and fecundity, with all the dark and the heavy and the multitudinous for which you are too dainty, spoke through her lips when she said that He had regarded the lowliness of His handmaiden. And if that Lady was a maid though a mother, you need not doubt that the nature which is, to human sense, impure, is also pure. [p. 184]

In summary we can say that Lewis discovered the triadic pattern as the universal pattern for what might be called the central man. Lewis's vision recovers for us the power of obedience, which alone empowers human choice to be truly free. We get a glimpse of this in the eldils' antiphony of praise in *Perelandra*, which precedes Dr. Ransom's vision of the sacred marriage between Creator and creation. In Him we live, move, and have our being before revelation provides us with His Name. When we come to know who He is, we find that He has already transposed our humanity by assuming it into His divinity.

The same triad of human love—*delight: pain: fruit*, which Father History taught John in *The Pilgrim's Regress* and which began his search for real faith as a Christian—surfaces at the end of Lewis's life, but now the transformation of grieved love has ransomed Lewis and he is free to sing his praise to God:

> Praise is the mode of love which always has some element of joy in it. Praise in due order; of Him as the giver, of her as the gift. Don't we in praise somehow enjoy what we praise, however far we are from it? I must do more of this. I have lost the fruition I once had of H[elen]. And I am far, far away in the valley of my unlikeness, from the fruition which, if His mercies are infinite, I may some time have of God. But by praising I can still, in some degree, enjoy her, and already, in some degree, enjoy Him.[16]

Janice Witherspoon Neuleib

The Creative Act: Lewis on God and Art

IN one of his *Letters to Malcolm* Lewis says "One of the purposes for which God instituted prayer may have been to bear witness that the course of events is not governed like a state but created like a work of art to which every being makes its contribution and (in prayer) a conscious contribution, and in which every being is both an end and a means" [pp. 55-56]. Lewis's God is the great artist forming the universe in a gigantic eternal pattern that "was made for the sake of all it does ánd is, down to the curve of every wave and the flight of every insect" [p. 56]. Because of this interpretation of the Divine as artist, Lewis was able to deal consistently and effectively with the question of free will and predestination in his art, as well as in his nonfictional prose. It thus was possible for Lewis to deliver a religious "message" without didactic overtones because he "made" his fiction in such a way that the medium became the message.

Devout Lewis enthusiasts may perhaps object to the application of the McLuhan title to one so conscientiously old-fashioned as Lewis. No phrase, however, could pinpoint more accurately Lewis's art and his ideas. It was very important to Lewis that God be understood as existing in eternity. The concepts of past, present, and future are concepts that are accurate only for those of us who live in time. For God there is no time; there is only the gigantic picture of the whole. About the question of the afterlife and about salvation, Lewis said in one of his letters, "the Timeless God chooses the timeless soul timelessly. . . . I believe the saved soul always (timelessly) chooses Him. And the reprobate soul in like manner always rejects him. This response of rejection in fact *is* the soul. The good and bad deeds done on earth are the appearance (in Time) of its willed nature."[1] The insistence that God is not in time is certainly not new with Lewis, but he did apply that concept in a practical way. At the same time, he did, of course, see that there were problems with his interpretation. God is still the artist, and the artist is in some sense responsible for his characters' blessed or cursed natures. Lewis chose to explain the "how" but admitted that he could not explain the "why." He solved the dilemma by instructing Mr. Lennox in the above quoted letter that one is "not to *worry*."

Any reader who knows Lewis at all will want to smile at that last admonition. It is so characteristic. There is a huge problem that has been debated for centuries. Lewis gives his interpretation of the answer, admits the difficulties, and then cautions the reader that he is not to worry. Perhaps Lewis can be a carefree comforter because as artist he is able to explain the "why" that was left unanswered in his persuasive arguments.

Since Greek times artists have been defending their work with the argument that their art imitates nature and by the analogy that they themselves in some way imitate the creator. Lewis, in the latter part of his career, extended the image to make it clear that the artist offers a means of understanding the ways of God. This conviction he imbedded in his later works: the Ransom trilogy, the Chronicles of Narnia, and *Till We Have Faces*. The troublesome problems of God's will versus man's will and free will versus predestination are dealt with in these works not as philosophical questions but as artistic building blocks which strengthen the creations and make them more subtle and impressive in their structures.

Blending theology, philosophy, and art is not an easy task for any author. To combine all three with what might be called a "popular art form" might seem a less than modest undertaking, but such is exactly the task of Lewis the creator in the trilogy. In these three novels Lewis deals with the fall of man, including all the implied questions about the responsibility of God for evil and about His seemingly inevitable control over the events of men's lives.

In the first novel of the trilogy the main character Ransom is set quite literally spinning on an adventure to the planet Mars, or Malacandra. Within the first few pages, questions arise about Ransom's free will. The man hardly plans to be walking down a country road at dusk, or to be captured by two ruffian scientists who bundle him into a Wellsian space vehicle and whisk him out of earth's domain. Upon his arrival on the red planet, Ransom is running wildly from his captors when he meets the gentle Hyoi and begins to be changed by the life and attitudes of an unspoiled planet. In both aspects of the plot, events that appear to the character to be random occurrences turn out to be for the reader, who stands outside the frame of the whole, events which must lead to some preset climax—else why write a novel?

More importantly, since Ransom is a character who is to appear in the two later volumes of the trilogy as hero and saviour, those events which to him seem to be so much happenstance are central to the thread of, as Lewis would call it, "the whole show." For the reader of the entire trilogy it is important to have at all times the conviction that the characters are acting of their own wills in a game in which the stakes really matter and in which something is to be won and lost. No one would read the trilogy if this apparent approximation of human action were not there. At the same time, there must also be the feeling that there is purpose in action. Even more importantly, we want to be assured that the artist is back there somewhere guiding the action so that it has order as well as apparent freedom. And we want to be able to do both things without being aware that anything more is happening to us than the excitement of the story itself.

Lewis manages to incorporate our well-learned faith in the artist into the texture of his own artistic creation. When at the end of *Out of the Silent Planet* the Oyarsa says that he expects to see Ransom again and that "it is not without the wisdom of Maleldil that we have met now" [p. 143], the reader is willing to accept both the control of the artist and of the divine Maleldil. Both are behind the action of the story. Of course, no sensible reader is going to identify consciously the real artist with the imagined God figure, but the technique serves to suggest its own purpose. So much does this technique work its special suggestiveness that by the time one turns to the second volume of the trilogy, he or she is ready to face the perplexing question of man's apparent freedom to sin in a world which is controlled by God. No heavy discussion of Arminianism versus Calvinism is offered in *Perelandra*; rather, Lewis shows a perfect and an imperfect creature, each making significant decisions.

This portrayal of the process of salvation as it works itself out in life is the technique of *Perelandra*. The reader, having finished the novel, looks at the whole and says it must have been so, but the character within the frame of the picture sees choice and freedom. The advantage of a good creative work is that one may reread it; a second reading provides the opportunity to experience both the controlled whole and the chosen moment. A second reading offers one a chance to experience time as the Divine nature might, viewing the entire panorama as one grand scene.

Previous critical opinion has seen *Perelandra* as a statement in myth of the essential weakness of human nature, the revolt of the personal will against God's will.[2] Certainly it is that. There is no way, however, that one could trace a dialectic on the issue through the novel. Rather it is the process of the telling that conveys the message about the human and the Divine natures. One first sees Ransom taking off for outer space again, but this time he goes of his own will, or so it appears. The coffinlike thing in which he travels is a symbol for a kind of death to his former personal existence. His new or renewed experience on the planet unfolds slowly. There are all sorts of exotic plants and creatures which cause Ransom to speculate about both philosophy and art. The bubble trees cause him to ask himself if evil is the willed repetition of experience, in defiance of obvious Divine direction. The dragon, too, makes Ransom ask whether myth as pictured in art reflects reality elsewhere in God's creation. Such speculations may serve to make the reader question previous assumptions, but I think not. What they certainly do, however, is to suggest the artistic control behind apparent reality. Ransom is able to see for the first time the flow of the universe, to appreciate the variety and breadth of possible created forms and events. In fact, for the first time, he begins to see events as created rather than experienced. The unfolding of the created event is the essence of *Perelandra*.

Joy in the God-given experience as well as in the God-given object is what the Green Lady learns early in her conversations with Ransom. Not only is she a physical creature, she is also being created spiritually and may participate in that creation. " 'I thought,' she said, 'that I was carried in the will of Him I love, but now I see that I walk with it' " [p. 69]. She sees that she is able to form herself to fit Maleldil's will or to defy that will if she chooses. Of course, from the reader's point of view, her decision conforms to the plot and theme of the novel as well as to Maleldil's will. There is dissonance between her apparent freedom to choose and her actual suspension within the motion of the novel's plot. That dissonance establishes the artistic consistency of *Perelandra*. Intellectually and in retrospect the discrepancy is apparent to the reader. At the moment and in the process of reading the novel, that reader is enmeshed in the implied comparison of artist and Maleldil. Lewis does not have to go out of his way to remind his reader that the Green Lady is a character in a novel. The reader knows, but he is aware only of Divine control, not, of course, of artistic. Lewis, not being a Divine creator, cannot offer her the Divine paradox, to be created, controlled, and free at once.

Neither does he offer it to Ransom, but Ransom's choices are more difficult than the Lady's. Ransom's dark night of the soul is much closer to an artist-persona struggling with the demands of the world he has created. Maleldil does not talk to him as He does to the Lady, nor does He reveal His will explicitly. Not until Ransom struggles through a dialogue half with the Divine and half with his own conscience does he see that he is destined to act a part that he would never choose. His decision is to go willingly into the created event though his every fiber rejects what he knows is to come. Lewis, the artist, describes Ransom's attitude after the moment of decision so: "The thing was going to be done. There was going to arrive, in the course of time, a moment at which he would have done it. The future act stood there, fixed and unaltered as if he had already performed it. It was a mere irrelevant detail that it happened to occupy the position we call future instead of that which we call past. . . . Predestination and freedom were apparently identical. He could no longer see any meaning in the many arguments he had heard on this subject" [p. 149].

Again the reader is asked to be convinced not on the basis of argued reason but on the basis of the feelings of a character. The created being sees his own relationship to the divine will as both his own decision and as a set of circumstances already stretched out on the painted canvas of eternity. He sees no conflict, nor does Lewis offer the reader an opportunity to construct one. In the next few pages Ransom meets the Un-man in battle and is able to save the green planet. By the time the issue of "What would have happened if. . ." arises, Ransom is safe with the Lady and her King and all conjecture seems unlikely, as any guess about a different past always does. The novel's end is near and all has been accomplished. Speculation only causes the pattern as it is to seem more vivid because the Divine artist, as well as the mortal artist, is given credit for the picture.

In the last book of the trilogy a woman is the focus of the struggle—not, however, in the same way as the Green Lady.[3] The Lady was a walking myth whose submission was made believable because of her superior ability to communicate with the Creator.[4] Jane Studdock, on the other hand, is a very modern young woman who has the Divine plan imposed upon her life in a way that she cannot ignore. She is forced to make a decision for or against Maleldil despite a desire to withdraw from cosmic conflict and live her own life. Jane is probably more appealing to many modern readers because of this desire to be a private person; she is also, therefore, the ideal character to show how no one can be indifferent to the Creator. Again, Lewis's technique is perfect. He creates a story that works on the reader in much the same way that the events in the novel work on the main character.

Jane is impressive. She is a good person who tries to be a modern scholar and to be a woman at the same time. Her self-reliance and her individuality make her the ideal heroine for the typical modern novel (assuming, of course, that there is such a thing). She is so sensible that it is impossible not to be sympathetic when she starts to have nightmares. One is also inclined to sympathize with her frustration when her friends cannot offer her any relief from the nightly intrusions into her privacy. In Jane's case, it is not as if the Divine has chosen her; it is as if the Divine has barged in and permanently settled itself in her life without asking leave at all. Lewis presents her indignation as being exactly appropriate. That is why it is such a jolt to the reader when this independent Jane comes face to face with the reborn Ransom and is immediately undone.

One must recall that, in the first two novels, Ransom was about as sensible and ordinary as Jane herself. His metamorphosis is spectacular, as Jane discovers when she walks into a room and meets a man who looks like a Greek god and who is able to change her life at a glance. The phrase used to describe this change is "her world was unmade" [p. 143]. Even so, Jane resists the test for a while, still planning to avoid all the irrational nonsense involved in strange men and stranger dreams. Not until she meets the Fairy, a female secret police officer, does she run toward the fate that has apparently been pursuing her throughout the novel. From Jane's point of view, it seems clear that she has made the best decision and made it none too soon. If one steps outside the novel, however, it becomes apparent that there was little choice. The Divine seemed to be relentlessly pursuing the good that was in Jane. The author also seems to have created a situation for her that could move in only one direction. She is free, and yet she is trapped in a stream of events. Thus, here in the novel that is set on earth, the panorama of the created work illustrating the form and freedom of the created universe as displayed in the Ransom trilogy is completed.

Although the trilogy talks of Maleldil, he never is described or given the dimension offered to characters portrayed in the text.[5] In the Chronicles of Narnia, however, Divinity takes on incarnate form in the person of the great lion, Aslan. Both the Divine creator and the artistic creator appear within the pages of these books, albeit the authorial intrusions of Lewis's persona are limited to such advice as the firm warning that one must never step into and close a wardrobe. Still, he does remind the reader that he is there and that he will keep a firm hand on the story. Aslan does more. He makes it clear from the beginning that he is in command of all events which occur in Narnia and that he is the chosen embodiment of his Father, sent to create life forms and events in the country of animals. Lewis, the narrator, says of Aslan, "People who have not been in Narnia sometimes think that a thing cannot be good and terrible at the same time. If the children had ever thought so, they were cured of it now" [*The Lion, the Witch and the Wardrobe*, p. 123]. The great lion produces the awe due both to his lordly animal nature and to his Divine nature. In the first of the Chronicles this marvellous beast dies a terrible death in exchange for the life of a treacherous child. Not only is the description of Aslan's death powerful, it also serves to associate for the reader the great lion Aslan with the Lion of Judah.

In the sixth book, *The Magician's Nephew*, Lewis shows Aslan creating Narnia. The scene identifies the Divine act of creation with the artistic act of creation. Rather than move a magic wand or do any of a number of things a creator might do, Aslan sings the land of Narnia into existence. Through an artistic act, he creates the world of talking animals and living trees. Lewis says of Digory's response to the singing that "it was so beautiful he could hardly bear it" [p. 99]. That one voice is soon joined by the music of the stars which he is creating and then by all the beings of the planet as it springs to life. Lewis makes the music of creation into a literal scene. All this description helps to show the artistic whole that is the world of Narnia. In fact, the last book of the Chronicles gives exactly as powerful a description of the unmaking of Narnia as the preceding description of its making. In the end, all turns cold at Aslan's command as the land is devoured and the nothingness of the void returns. Aslan's final command is that Peter shut the door on the barren darkness [*The Last Battle*, p. 157]. Lewis cannot, of course, leave the portrait so; this is the world of the eternal creator with no finite limits. Thus, the final book ends with all the characters going up and into an infinite number of pictured frames of both Narnia and of England, "like an onion," says Mr. Tumnus, "except that as you continue to go in and in, each circle is larger than the last" [p. 180].

Lewis has given a closed picture of a world that begins and ends within the supposed time scheme of what would be only fifty years or so by earth time. By doing this, he is able to establish the sense of freedom and control that I have been illustrating. Aslan creates and rules what is very clearly an artistic unit, yet within the bounds of that unit there are seven adventure stories, all of which deal with numerous moral choices on the parts of the young adventurers. From their points of view there is certainly freedom, perhaps more than some of them would prefer. From the viewpoint of the creators, leonine and human, the character's lives are constantly controlled. From the point of view of the reader, both are true at the same time. In these Chronicles of Narnia Lewis closed the circle of his art even more firmly than he had done in the more familiar worlds of Maleldil.

The Chronicles of Narnia completed, Lewis wrote his last work of fiction. Whereas the two earlier sets of books are future fantasy or parallel universe fantasy, *Till We Have Faces* is the modern retelling of an ancient myth. At first glance, it might seem that this novel deals very specifically with free will and leaves the question of Predestination completely untouched. If one looks carefully at the ending, however, it becomes clear that Orual's lesson is precisely the lesson about the Divine nature that only art can illustrate. At first, she curses the gods for tricking her and ruining her life by hiding from her at the most crucial moments. After many years as queen and after a challenge to the gods, she makes the amazing discovery that the evil in her life was her own doing, called on herself precisely because she refused to accept the Divine nature. Not until she sees her sister, Psyche, journey into Hell, taunted by all Orual's demands, does this unhappy queen admit her own guilt in refusing to realize the Divine control of life and to see the ultimate benevolence behind that control [pp. 303-04]. In this tale Lewis is able to emphasize the importance of the creative nature of the Divine. Wisdom comes to the main character when she, the artist of her own life's story, is able to recognize the beauty in the whole story, ugly as the parts may have seemed.

So Lewis ended his career as writer of fiction, insisting that beauty was to be found in the pattern of the divine will. The corollary is that the artist can see the illustration of that will in his own creation. Though it is impossible to see the whole picture of eternity as God sees it, man can certainly see the pattern of a work of fiction as the artist presents it. If the Divine nature is incorporated into the novel, then the reader is able to see both the freedom of the characters and the control of both artist and God. This use of the most perplexing paradox thus becomes a building block for a skillfully executed work of art in which the form perfectly illustrates the theme and the artist is able to teach and delight in one purposeful act of creation.

II: THE RANSOM TRILOGY

Wayne Shumaker

The Cosmic Trilogy of C. S. Lewis

UNTIL the late 1930s C. S. Lewis, Oxford don and converted atheist, was known to persons interested in literature chiefly as the author of a much-admired work of medieval scholarship entitled *The Allegory of Love.* He had written other things, among them two small volumes of poetry, a Christian allegory called *The Pilgrim's Regress,* and, with E. M. W. Tillyard, a pamphlet of literary controversy named *The Personal Heresy*; but his reputation had hardly spread beyond academic circles, and among scholars he must have seemed noteworthy mainly because of the liveliness of his style, his boldness in translating Old French verse into Middle English, and his luck in finding an especially good subject for research. In the late 1930s and 1940s, however, he burst suddenly into an extraordinary activity. He not only began to pour out books at an enormous rate but appeared in new and unexpected roles: as a Christian propagandist who lectured on the radio, at military camps, and in churches; as a serious theologian; and as a prolific writer of creative fiction. It is in the third of these roles that I wish to consider him in the present essay. My attention will be confined, however, almost entirely to a trilogy of fantastic novels—*Out of the Silent Planet, Perelandra,* and *That Hideous Strength*—which received a fairly good press as they appeared but have not been given the critical notice they deserve as a group. Whether the plan of the trilogy grew on Lewis as he wrote or was blocked out before he began I do not know; but in what follows I shall assume that all three volumes were the products of a single creative urge.

Reprinted by permission from *The Hudson Review*, Volume VIII, No. 2 (Summer 1955). Copyright © 1955 by The Hudson Review, Inc.

It is essential from the outset to realize that the three novels were intended to render both intellectually and emotionally attractive a whole complex of ideas which pre-existed them. Other novelists may have forged meanings in the smithies of their souls as they wrote, but not Lewis. His meanings were firmly enough grasped to be capable of expression in ratiocinative prose as well as in fictive images, and, indeed, were soon to be so expressed in a whole series of lucid volumes. What made his mastery of the ideas relatively easy and confident was that they were not new. They had been fitted together powerfully in discursive structures by Augustine and Aquinas, among others, and in imaginal structures by such poets as Dante, Chaucer, Spenser, and Milton. They were viable, cohesive, and extensional. If, as the notions of orthodox Christian theology, they were not ideally fitted to prosper in the existent climate of literary opinion, they nevertheless had behind them the pressure of a long tradition. Moreover, Lewis was not the man to be deterred from a creative purpose by the sensing of a hostile atmosphere. "In his own subject," he wrote in *The Problem of Pain*, "every man knows that all discoveries are made and all errors corrected by those who ignore the 'climate of opinion'" [p. 134]. Behind him also, as experience, was the manipulation of similar ideas in *The Pilgrim's Regress*, a narrative of allegorical vision; and he had an intimate and loving acquaintance with the Christian novels and fantasies of his acknowledged nineteenth-century master, George MacDonald. The problem was not, therefore, that of discovering meanings in the process of fitting together images representative of directly sensed human experience. It was rather that of finding a fictive analogue for a prepared world view—an analogue, this time, which would have at least a semi-realistic credibility, for his purpose was to write not dream-fantasies but novels.

The heart of the problem lay in the difficulty of bringing within the range of normal human perceptions what really was outside normal experience. In one of his broadcast talks Lewis said, "If there was a controlling power outside the universe, it could not show itself to us as one of the facts inside the universe—no more than the architect of a house could actually be a wall or staircase or fireplace in that house."[1] Ultimate reality is timeless and perhaps spaceless. Novels, however, are impregnated with time and space as allegory and vision are not. In *The Pilgrim's Regress* it had been possible to set a representative young man named John talking with allegorical abstractions named The Landlord, Mr. Vertue, Reason, and Mother Kirk. In *The Great Divorce* Lewis was to dream his way into Hell and Heaven and see last things, or some fictive metaphor of them, with direct eyes. But in novels, as distinct from visions, there must be "real" people, not mere abstractions or ghosts; and the world must be a "real" world—contemporary China, possibly, or twelfth-century France, but not Puritania or Heaven. It was necessary somehow to bridge the gap between a nonsensory reality and the limitations of normal sense organs.

The solution, so obvious once seized upon that in the actual process of composition it may have preceded the recognition of a problem, was space fiction. The fictive universe could be extended beyond the limits of ordinary human perception without compromising the decision to rely mainly on normal modes of cognition. On Mars, on Venus, in space or Deep Heaven, anything is possible. No one could tell what might or might not be sensed outside terrestrial boundaries if only an ordinary human being could get there. And arranging that someone should get there was not much of a trick. Waiting to be scooped up, by an easy sweep of the imagination, was the device of the spaceship. Let the ordinary human beings, with their ordinary sensory equipment, be taken away from the familiar Earth, and there was hardly any limit to what they might experience. The novels might then be fantastic without becoming vision or allegory.

The longer this general plan was scrutinized the more apt it must have appeared. If space travel was unusual, it had ceased to be thought impossible. Moreover, as Lewis was to point out in *Miracles*, the unusual is permissible if it is what is being written *about*, and an artistic crime only if dragged in to get the writer out of a hole [p. 101]. A crucial advantage was that if life was imagined on a distant planet, it would not have to be imagined as similar to life on Earth. H. G. Wells had set one sort of precedent—"Bulbous eyes, grinning jaws, horns, stings, mandibles"[*Out of the Silent Planet*, p. 35]—but it was equally feasible to imagine a better kind of rational animal than man, a humanity unfallen and still, in some degree, in direct communication with the Eternal. And Lewis wanted such creatures, since by setting them in contrast with self-divided, self-exiled, diseased Tellurians he could dramatize the meaning of alienation from the Divine Will. The method had been recommended long ago by Aristotle: "To find out what is natural, we must study specimens which retain their nature and not those which have been corrupted."[2] In due time attention could be recalled to the Earth, which would then appear to the reader's sharpened perceptions in its true character, as the battleground of a fight to the death between good and evil.[3]

By some such train of thought the basic plan of the trilogy must have been determined. The fundamental difference between Mars and Venus, as the plan developed, came to be that on the former the *hnau*, or rational creatures, had never fallen and could be seen in prelapsarian happiness and security, whereas on the latter a yet-unfallen Eve was to be caught trembling between choices that would permit her world to remain all good, like Mars, or plunge it into misery and conflict, like that on Earth. Other differences flowed easily from the premises. Mars, as an old world associated by tradition with war, could be shown as frosty, austere, *mar*tial; Venus, as a young world associated by tradition with love, could be warm, richly sensuous, enchanting. Again, since rational life might be supposed to have been created first on Mars and last on Venus, on Mars the *hnau* might be conceived to have pre-Earthly or partly inhuman bodies, but on Venus, in consequence of the dignifying of the Earthly body by the Incarnation, intelligence could be placed in forms different from the familiar Earthly ones chiefly by greater beauty, strength, and dignity. The situations in the three worlds could also be interestingly varied. In the first volume dramatic tension could arise from the hazards of space travel, dissensions among the travelers, unnecessary fear of the Martians, and perhaps also some adventurous sport proper for a warlike people living in perpetual peace. On Venus the narrative center would be the temptation of Eve—a sufficiently perilous matter to dominate the whole volume, since on its outcome would depend the fate of a world. About the central drama, however, might be clustered other peripheral conflicts: for example, a physical struggle between an Earthly visitor and the diabolical tempter. On Earth the obvious antagonists were a small group of God-centered Christians and a much larger group of irreligious men backed by all the power of atheistic science. There was ample opportunity for thematic permutation, for the making of the same point three times and yet, since the volumes were to be organically connected, once only on three levels. The result, if all went well, would be the placing of Earthly experience in a context of cosmic purpose, hence the diminution of the two greatest hindrances to spiritual health, a feeling of individual self-sufficiency, on the one hand, or of spiritual isolation, on the other. What better means to the end than the removal of the reader to a distance from Earth at which the familiar world would appear no larger than a half-crown? "Come out," Lewis was later to say to persons who hold that Nature is the ultimate reality, "look back, and then you will see" [*Miracles*, p. 67].

Such, very briefly, was the fable devised by Lewis as a vehicle for his intended meanings. On the whole, its limitations were those necessarily arising from the transposition of eternal truth into sensory symbols. The sensory objects in the trilogy would not, of course, be ideally representative of their spiritual referenda. For example, inorganic spirit is almost by definition something which cannot enter into the sensory field of an organic consciousness. When the *eldila*, or angels, are seen as columns of faint light and are heard to speak in bloodless, inorganic voices which sound like instruments being played, we must understand that we have been offered an image, not the very truth. We must remember, however, that all theology, even when not overtly fictionized, is a tissue of similar approximations. "To know God as he really is," wrote Milton in a treatise with which Lewis was certainly acquainted, "far transcends the powers of man's thoughts, much more of his perception."[4] Other aspects of ultimate reality are almost equally opaque to human thought. Indeed, Lewis is willing to admit that the whole of Christian truth is rather myth than actuality. In *The Pilgrim's Regress* the central character, in the very midst of an act symbolizing baptism, hears the voice of a former friend, Wisdom, muttering that all the discoveries are figurative. Thereupon another voice speaks behind the protagonist, saying, "Child, if you will, it *is* mythology. It is but truth, not fact: an image, not the very real. But then it is My mythology. The words of Wisdom are also myth and metaphor: but since they do not know themselves for what they are, in them the hidden myth is master, where it should be servant" [p. 171]. The objection to Lewis's symbols, if objection there is to be, must accordingly be grounded not on the distance between the symbols and objective reality, but rather on the distance between these symbols and the other less concrete and sensory symbols of discursive theology; and even this distance, to be significant, must be a distance in meaning. By that standard, the columns of faint light and the tinkling inorganic voices can pass muster.

Let us look more closely at a representative series of details, all having to do with the way in which the universe is shown to be permeated with mind. The demonstration of the permeation was the most basic part of Lewis's total purpose, since his world view rests on a conviction that behind the apparently mechanical processes of the universe are both Divine awareness and Divine purpose. The Empirical Bogey ("the great myth of our century with its gases and galaxies, its light years and evolutions, its nightmare perspectives of simple arithmetic" [*Perelandra*, p. 164]) had to be overborne by images with contrary implications. But how image Divine Mind, which, although totally present at every point in space and therefore immanent in every setting and event,[5] is nonmaterial and therefore nonsensory?

There were several stages in the process Lewis adopted to meet the problem. In the first, the reader had to be made to feel a Presence which it would not be tactful explicitly to assert. Thus Ransom, Lewis's Earthly protagonist, once shanghaied by unscrupulous scientists into a spaceship, was made to feel extremely well and to look out with pleasure from the ship's dark side, where he could see "planets of unbelievable majesty, and constellations undreamed of . . . celestial sapphires, rubies, emeralds and pinpricks of burning gold." As the nights passed he found his former assumption that beyond the Earth's atmosphere was only cold, black vacuity rapidly disappearing. Instead, it seemed to him more and more difficult to disbelieve in the old astrology: "Almost he felt, wholly he imagined, 'sweet influence' pouring or even stabbing into his surrendered body." Despite the danger of meteorites hinted by the constant tinkling of small particles of world-stuff on the outside of the hollow shell, fear was impossible. On the side of the ship flooded by the sun he was "totally immersed in a bath of pure ethereal colour and of unrelenting though unwounding brightness" and lay "stretched his full length and with eyes half closed in the strange chariot that bore them, faintly quivering, through depth after depth of tranquillity," feeling his mind and body "daily rubbed and scoured and filled with new vitality." Gradually he came to realize that the word

"Space" [was] a blasphemous libel for this empyrean ocean of radiance in which they swam. He could not call it "dead"; he felt life pouring into him from it every moment. How indeed should it be otherwise, since out of this ocean the worlds and all their life had come? He had thought it barren: he saw now that it was the womb of worlds, whose blazing and innumerable offspring looked down nightly even upon the earth with so many eyes—and here, with how many more! No: Space was the wrong name. Older thinkers had been wiser when they named it simply the heavens—the heavens which declared the glory [of God]. [*Out of the Silent Planet*, p. 32]

There is a joyous lift about this—and only a little of it can be quoted here—which makes Ransom's sensations credible by successfully evoking them in the reader. What more likely than that the sensations of a space traveler would be unexpected? And if unexpected, why not as well these as others? So strong is the illusion that when, in arriving on Mars, the ship ceases to be "a chariot gliding in the fields of heaven" and becomes "a dark steel box dimly lighted by a slit of window, and falling . . . out of the heaven, into a world," we are astonished, if we pause to think about the matter, that our interest in space has become so intense as to make the arrival on a planet seem anticlimactic and depressing and the planet itself appear a half-obscene lump inferior to the space it displaces.

In the second stage the planet also is redeemed by the disclosure that it is informed with friendly spirit exactly as space had been. Gradually, as Ransom's grotesque expectations are corrected by experience, he learns that the organic life of Mars is observed by hundreds or thousands of almost-invisible eldila. The recognition culminates in an audience with the Oyarsa, or planetary intelligence, who informs him, in a sweet, remote, and unshaken voice, that he and his two evil companions have been watched since long before their spaceship entered the thin Martian atmosphere. There has been no time when he was alone, no place where his actions were secret. "I cannot understand," he says. "Have you servants out in the heavens?" "Where else?" comes the answer. "There is nowhere else. . . . Malacandra, like all worlds, floats in heaven. And I am not 'here' altogether as you are, Ransom of Thulcandra. Creatures of your kind must drop out of heaven into a world; for us the worlds are places in heaven. . . . I and my servants are even now in heaven" [p. 120]. Only the Earth—Thulcandra, the Silent Planet, whither the Bent Oyarsa, Satan, was driven after great war in heaven—does not throng with intelligent and friendly spirits. Elsewhere in the universe mortal beings can sense vitality in the apparently empty spaces about them.

The discovery is borne out on the return trip to Earth, during which Ransom perceives that the space surrounding the ship is more really vital than the air within it. Because the ship swims in intense light he can see no eldila; but "he heard, or thought he heard, all kinds of delicate sound, or vibrations akin to sound, mixed with the tinkling rain of meteorites, and often the sense of unseen presences even within the space-ship became irresistible. . . . He and all his race showed small and ephemeral against a background of such immeasurable fullness. His brain reeled at the thought of the true population of the universe, the three-dimensional infinitude of their territory, and the unchronicled æons of their past; but his heart became steadier than it had ever been" [pp. 146-47]. The permeation of space by Maleldil, Very God, has not yet been fictionally demonstrated; but as long as the fictive spell is on us we shall accept the old philosophical doctrine of plenitude.

The third and final step is taken in the second volume, *Perelandra*. In the first chapter we are given another view of an eldil, this time through the consciousness of a man who has taken no journey through space and therefore is unprepared for the appearance by earlier surprises. The sensation now most strongly insisted on is that of pressure. "I felt sure that the creature was what we call 'good,' but I wasn't sure whether I liked 'goodness' so much as I had supposed. . . . Here at last was a bit of that world from beyond the world, which I had always supposed that I loved and desired, breaking through and appearing to my senses: and I didn't like it, I wanted it to go away. I wanted every possible distance, gulf, curtain, blanket, and barrier to be placed between it and me" [p. 19]. There is a direct connection between this description and Lewis's assertion in *Miracles* that "If we must have a mental picture to symbolise Spirit, we should represent it as something *heavier* than matter" [p. 95]. The vitality of pure spirit expresses itself to human senses as weight. This weightiness is picked up and insisted on again and again in *Perelandra*; and it grows enormously, for on Venus there are no eldila except only the Oyarsa, and the spirit which talks to Ransom is Deity Itself.

The first experience of Maleldil's presence comes during one of Ransom's early conversations with Tinidril, the Venusian Eve. "How do you know that?" he asks in astonishment at one of her statements. "Maleldil is telling me," she replies; and at the same moment Ransom feels a difference in the landscape: "The light was dim, the air gentle, and all Ransom's body was bathed in bliss, but the garden world where he stood seemed to be packed quite full, and as if an unendurable pressure had been laid upon his shoulders, his legs failed him and he half sank, half fell, into a sitting position" [p. 61]. The remainder of the conversation is difficult, and after it he falls into an exhausted sleep.

The sense of being in Someone's presence does not disappear when Ransom is alone. On the contrary, it increases until there seems to be "no *room*." It is intolerable, however, "only at certain moments—at just those moments in fact (symbolised by his impulse to smoke and to put his hands in his pockets) when a man asserts his independence and feels that now at last he's on his own." At such times the "very air seemed too crowded to breathe"; but when he yielded to the pressure there was no burden to be borne. "It became not a load but a medium, a sort of splendour as of eatable, drinkable, breathable gold, which fed and carried you and not only poured into you but out from you as well. Taken the wrong way, it suffocated; taken the right way, it made terrestrial life seem, by comparison, a vacuum" [p. 72]. The experience culminates in the thick darkness of a Perelandrian night, when the Presence, which Ransom now realizes has never been absent even though he has sometimes succeeded in ignoring it, simply flings back in his face, almost impatiently, all the evasions by which he attempts to escape the horrible necessity of physical combat with the Un-man who has been tempting the Lady to disobedience. The silence becomes "more and more like a face, a face not without sadness, that looks upon you while you are telling lies, and never interrupts, but gradually you know that it knows, and falter, and contradict yourself, and lapse into silence" [p. 144]. Then the Presence becomes a voice, though a voice that speaks without noise; and at last, when Ransom no longer fights, the pressure ceases, and he falls again into sleep. But from that time forward he knows, though sometimes in pain or fatigue he may forget, that the consciousness of Maleldil is everywhere.

Thus, in brief, does Lewis meet one of the thornier problems involved in the fictionizing of a theology. In the hands of a lesser writer the purpose might have generated long stretches of dreary exposition. In the trilogy, as in all novels, there is some exposition. Characters talk, and they cannot always be forbidden to talk rationally. The chief vehicle of meaning, however, is sensory impressions which carry a metaphorical burden and add up, as a series, to myth. The qualities of mind that enabled Lewis to write dream allegories and allegorical fairy tales permitted him to show more meanings than he explained even in his quasi-realistic fiction, and thus relieved him, to a rather astonishing degree, from the necessity of arguing.

The practice of showing instead of explaining reaches down into the details, so that what at first appears to be a realistic description of a house, a person, or a landscape is recognized later to have rich symbolic overtones. Symbolism in the parts (I use the word in a rather extended sense) is not only methodologically and tonally compatible with myth in the whole but is indeed the same thing on a smaller scale: elements are fitted together in such a way as to stand for more than they picture. The difficulty was that the symbolical content always had to be adjusted to the realistic appearance; for it was essential that credibility not be sacrificed to doctrine. The views to be recommended in the trilogy were to have relevance not only to a life beyond life but also to the situations in which men find themselves daily.

An illustration of how the technique works can be found in the first and second chapters of the trilogy, where methodological precedents are set for all three volumes. In pursuance of an accepted duty, Ransom goes to a place called The Rise, where he is to inquire into the failure of a hired boy to return home. The gate is locked, and it is necessary for Ransom to force his way through a hedge that proves unexpectedly thick and prickly. Once on the other side, he finds himself on a drive which has two branches, that on the right leading across a neglected lawn to the front door, the other, which is churned into deep ruts as if by trucks, leading towards the back premises, where he can see a column of smoke issuing from a chimney that reminds him of a factory or laundry. The house itself shows no light. Some of the windows are shuttered, the rest are without either shutter or curtain, and all are lifeless and inhospitable. Drawn to the back premises by shouts and the noise of a scuffle, he has the impression of outhouses, a low door full of red firelight, and a domed shape that we learn in due time is the space ship. Inside the house is a mixture of luxury and squalor. Two costly arm chairs stand on an uncarpeted floor strewn with litter; the wallpaper shows stains left by furniture and pictures; on the table are empty champagne bottles, cigar and cigarette-ends, opened sardine tins, and the like. In this room Ransom is presently drugged and the adventurous action of the trilogy begins.

One need not, obviously, read this description with close attention to details. On the surface it presents merely an untidy and rather unattractive house occupied by a scientist and his partner-assistant. And this is enough. Lewis does not want the scientist's way of life to appear humanly satisfying, but he does not, I suppose, insist that the passage be intensively scrutinized. Anyone who chooses to scrutinize it will discover, however, that it is full of symbolic suggestions about two cultural patterns, one decayed, the other dominant. The intellectual soundness of the older humanistic culture is hinted by the light we can easily imagine once to have issued from the now darkened windows, and the amenities encouraged by the humanistic value system are implicit in the neglected lawn, the right-hand path leading in a gentle sweep to the front door and a hospitable porch, and the missing pictures, furniture, and carpet. The dominant scientific culture is characterized by the barred gate, the disfigured and commercialized left-hand path, the absence of light, the concentration of activity in back premises, the red glare of the furnace, the contrast of two luxurious arm-chairs with the surrounding litter, and the artificial and unappetizing nourishment. There is significance, too, in the hedge through which Ransom must pass in order to gain access to the house: it is the initial obstacle to the performance of any unpleasant duty, beyond which one's way becomes clearer ("it was lighter on the drive than it had been under the trees"). Comprehension of these and other similar implications is necessary neither to the absorbed following of the surface narrative of adventure nor to an appreciative understanding of Lewis's basic meanings in the trilogy. If not fully understood, the suggestions will work on the reader unconsciously, through tonality. If searched for, they fall immediately into order and subtilize the impressions which come through the senses.

The technique is used again and again in the three volumes; indeed, it is one of the pervasive elements of method. Another instance is the description of a man significantly named Wither, who is head of an atheistic institution called the Institute of Coordinated Experiments. Wither is a white-haired old man (evil has been active in Earthly affairs since the Fall) with a courtly manner (which disguises his real spitefulness and makes it superficially attractive). His face is very large (evil is everywhere), his eyes watery (evil can't stand the light), and his expression vague (evil is slippery, refuses to make unconditional commitments). When he talks, he does not appear to give interlocutors his full attention (evil is self-centered, self-seeking).[6] Everywhere significance is carried down into the details; but it is always possible to hurry over minutiae without sacrificing either the fundamental meanings or the coherence. As in *Paradise Lost*, with which there are many points of contact, the deepest meanings are unmistakable. What is gained from repeated and more intensive readings is not something qualitatively different but a denser and technically more exciting version of the same thing. Unlike many recent novelists, Lewis does not demand that his readers be clever; but if they are clever he rewards them. On one level only or on many, the trilogy succeeds in communicating.

I should like, before concluding, to suggest in still another way Lewis's ability to present meanings without rational explication. In the descriptions of Tinidril, the Venusian Eve, it was necessary to portray a creature without much experience of life but endowed with enormous intellectual power—in the theological phrase, with Right Reason. Milton's Eve fails often to convince us that she has just been made from a "Rib with cordial spirits warme." All too frequently her behavior lends color to Taine's objection that she is really the wife of some seventeenth-century Colonel Hutchinson. Not so Tinidril, who is indeed "Simplicitie and spotless innocence." Let us observe how she is kept both mentally and physically young.

The trick is turned without recourse to elaborate artifice: Lewis merely keeps steadily in mind that in experience Tinidril is a child. When we first see her she is looking at Ransom, "her feet together, her arms hanging at her sides, her stare level and unafraid," like a child intent on some entrancing novelty. "I am from another world," Ransom begins in the Old Solar tongue, which he has learned on Mars; whereupon, with the emotional volatility of a child, Tinidril begins suddenly to laugh, "Peal upon peal of laughter till her whole body shook with it, till she bent almost double, with her hands resting on her knees, still laughing and repeatedly pointing at him." The cause of her merriment, we learn, is that Ransom's naked body has been made parti-colored by one-sided exposure to the sun during his trip to Venus—cause enough, surely, for innocent amusement. This mood too changes quickly. The Lady disappears for a moment, carried out of sight by an alteration in the shape of her floating island; and when Ransom sees her again she is sitting "with her legs trailing in the sea, half unconsciously caressing a gazelle-like creature which had thrust its soft nose under her arm. It was difficult to believe that she had ever laughed, ever done anything but sit on the shore of her floating isle. Never had Ransom seen a face so calm, and so unearthly, despite the full humanity of every feature." Our first impression, accordingly, is of a gloriously beautiful young woman with the mind and emotions of a child.

The impression is modified by a conversation held the next day, when it becomes evident that the calmness of Tinidril's expression is the calmness not of idiocy but of innocence. "I was young yesterday," she explains to Ransom, "when I laughed at you. Now I know that the people in your world do not like to be laughed at." To this explanation Ransom's very natural response is a question: "Are you not young to-day also?" Tinidril is startled, and falls into so deep a study that some blue flowers drop unnoticed from her hand. "I see it now," she replies at last. "It is very strange to say one is young at the moment one is speaking. But to-morrow I shall be older. And then I shall say I was young to-day." She is puzzled, however, by the necessity of considering time objectively instead of regarding it as a series of moments during which she is occupied in doing something. "I see that you come from a wise world . . . if this is wise. I have never done it before—stepping out of life into the Alongside and looking at oneself living as if one were not alive." The impression produced by these and other similar speeches is exactly what Lewis wants it to be: that of a quick and penetrating mind to which almost every item of experience is new. Within eight pages of first meeting Tinidril we are convinced both of her intelligence and of her almost complete lack of a past.[7]

From this point on there is no flaw, no jolt, only development. At one moment her inexperience is in the foreground, at another the dignity and authority that accompany her possession of Right Reason. The wonder is that Lewis can pass so smoothly from one to the other. For example, when Tinidril learns that Ransom is not, as she had naively supposed, the Earthly equivalent of her own missing King, but only one of a king's many children, her attitude toward him changes at once, but so gently that there is no break in the narrative texture. " 'Greet your Lady and Mother well from me when you return to your own world,' said the Green Woman. And now for the first time there was a note of deliberate courtesy, even of ceremony, in her speech" [p. 67]—a note given irony, but not made ridiculous, by the reader's awareness that Ransom's Mother and Lady has been dead for thousands of years. So skillful, indeed, is Lewis's handling of this very difficult person that we are at once charmed, amused, and awed. Ransom himself is sometimes so awed by Tinidril that he can hardly look steadily at her: "He knew now what the old painters were trying to represent when they invented the halo. Gaiety and gravity together, a splendour as of martyrdom yet with no pain in it at all, seemed to pour from her countenance" [p. 68]. Yet she misunderstands, is puzzled by the most ordinary facial expressions, attends as courteously to the tempter as to her defender, and in other ways shows clearly the limitations due to her inexperience. One mark of Lewis's control appears in the reader's tardy recollection that although a naked man and a beautiful naked woman have been made to spend many nights together on a tropical island, no suspicion of sexual adventure has been permitted to arise. It is a curious achievement, and not one which every writer would be able to keep his audience from regretting.

In such ways as those that have been described Lewis succeeds in making a body of reasoned theological doctrine perceptually available in quasi-realistic fiction. By embodying the doctrines in meaningful situations which coalesce as myth (something that in recent years has been much talked about by critics but almost never achieved by creative artists), he has contrived to transpose his opinions into images and thus to resist a temptation to which many propaganda novelists succumb, the urge to drive every perception home by logical assertion. Moreover, except towards the end of *That Hideous Strength*, where disembodied spirit is permitted to take matters out of the hands of human agents, the situations are steadily credible on their own terms. (The exception, unfortunately, is serious, for it is not on Mars or Venus, but on Earth, that the real test of the Christian world view must come.)

No doubt the trilogy is not for everybody. The congenitally unimaginative reader will find it dizzying and perhaps absurd. The de-converted Christian may resist actively and effectively the pull of renounced affections. Writers who like to imagine that they have the power to create, instead of an opportunity to perceive, a cosmos may be repelled by Lewis's assumptions. Yet the volumes are capable of delighting, not once but many times, more readers than they have reached; and to serious students of fiction they can suggest that the formal complexity so prized nowadays by a perceptive minority need not always entail the sacrifice of meaning for the less perceptive majority.

The Reeducation of the Fearful Pilgrim

WHEN C. S. Lewis turned to science fiction in *Out of the Silent Planet*, he did not have to invent the genre or establish its traditions and conventions. A long line of worthy predecessors, some most frequently published in luridly illustrated magazines and others available in dignified hard covers, had done the pioneer work. Lewis could function in a world that had already been mapped out. I remember a former student of mine, Frank Robinson—who later helped create the scenario of *The Towering Inferno*—explaining these matters to me when he was at Beloit College. He pointed out that by long established tradition, Mars is an old planet, in process of desiccation, whereas Venus is usually warm and sensuous, with something of a Polynesian lifestyle. These comments were decades ago, before anyone knew how tropical Venus actually is.

C. S. Lewis, a traditionalist in so many things, was not a rebel against the great tradition of science fiction when he wrote the tale of Ransom's forced visit to Malacandra and his adventures and experiences there. As any science-fiction reader would expect, Ransom finds a network of artificial channels, and soon recognizes that the planet is slowly dying from lack of water, warmth, and air. The very colors that gently engage his eyes—lavender and pale green and pale rose—have a subdued quality, as though anything flamboyant would be out of place on a planet which has long since passed through the stages of its youth.

Lewis's faithfulness to the tradition of science fiction can lead at times to apparent symbolism which may be nothing more than obedience to a well-established literary convention. Take, for instance, the vertical quality of the Malacandran landscapes. Its inhabitants are elongated, the mountains rise at impossible angles, and slender vegetables soar higher than earthly trees. Some have seen in these details a symbology of spiritual aspiration and ascent, contrasting with the more eathbound landscape of Tellus. Possibly, but probably not. One of the canons of science fiction is to treat with respect whatever scientific knowledge is available at the moment, or at least the share that has somehow reached the writer at his desk. Lewis knew that Mars has low gravity.

Out of the Silent Planet is science fiction before it is anything else, but in the house of science fiction there are many mansions, not all equally interesting as dwelling places. Some science-fiction stories are simply adventure tales, replete with interplanetary marvels; these can be as innocent of philosophic and metaphysical resonance as many literary fairy tales or the more routine expressions of the Wild West myth. But there is another kind of science fiction in which life on other planets illumines by contrast life on this. These are the stories that pose, and sometimes imaginatively rc olve, the great philosophic, religious, and metaphysical questions that will not be shamed or intimidated into disappearing.

Clarke's *Childhood's End*, with its vision of mankind as a way station toward cosmic being, is one example; another is Stapledon's *Last and First Men*, which presents the epic sweep of evolution until its culmination and extinction in "eighteenth man." Lindsay's *Voyage to Arcturus*, which Lewis greatly admired, is a cosmic novel of metaphysical adventures. It is the occasional books like these (and not routine science fiction) that create the genre-within-a-genre to which *Out of the Silent Planet* belongs.

One parallel between Lewis's space trilogy and the Narnia tales instantly leaps to mind. Many a child and some adults have read the Narnia stories and enjoyed them wholeheartedly on their first level, without paying much conscious attention to the religious themes that run through the seven books. In the same way it is possible to read the trilogy and enjoy it simply for the exciting adventures that are recounted. To do this is not an error in itself; the adventures are indeed enthralling. But it is obvious that from the beginning Lewis intended more than mere adventure.

In a fuller treatment, the three novels of the trilogy would have to be considered as a unit. The overall plot is the struggle between divine and demonic powers, not just on this fallen planet, but in the cosmos. A suitable scriptural text would be Ephesians 6:11-12: "Put on the whole armour of God, that ye may be able to stand against the wiles of the devil. For we wrestle not against flesh and blood, but against principalities, against powers, against the rulers of the darkness of this world, against spiritual wickedness in high places." Or as the New English Bible puts it in language more akin to science fiction: "Put on all the armour which God provides, so that you may be able to stand firm against the devices of the devil. For our fight is not against human foes, but against cosmic powers, against the authorities and potentates of this dark world, against the superhuman forces of evil in the heavens."

The trilogy is a three-act drama. In Act One, Malacandra is threatened by a greedy gold seeker and a half-demented scientist. Both are ready to subjugate or destroy the native inhabitants to win gold, or to conquer additional *Lebensraum* for the human race. Ransom, the Cambridge philologist with an evocative name, finds himself in a position where he can ally himself with the Martians and help them frustrate earth's imperialist designs. In *Perelandra* a fresh-made world, gleaming from the hands of God, is in danger of falling into disobedience and suffering the sad, alienated fate of the earth. Here again Ransom is a key figure in saving the beauty and innocence of the new creation. Finally, Ransom plays a central role in defeating the all-out assault of the powers of darkness against Tellus in the concluding volume, *That Hideous Strength*.

The cosmic drama runs through all three books, but it is possible to take *Out of the Silent Planet* by itself and to discern a subplot —the gradual reeducation of Ransom, as he is taught by his adventures and his contacts with various varieties of *hnau* whom he encounters on Malacandra.

When we first meet Ransom, he is a bachelor don, in early middle age, a philologist. He is pious in a quiet way; when expecting death on Malacandra he says his prayers, and at one point he worries about whether he should impart some elements of revealed religion to the Martians—who turn out to be worrying about the same question in reverse.

Ransom is one of the "new men" whom Lewis discusses in *Mere Christianity*. Basically, he is already on the side of God, but there is some further progress he needs to make. In particular, he is fearful. He doubts his own uncertain courage and his mind is filled with an appalling vision of space as void, dead, threatening. When he does think about the possibility of life on Mars, his science-fiction reading and fearful imagination conjure up "various incompatible monstrosities—bulbous eyes, grinning jaws, horns, stings, mandibles. Loathing of insects, loathing of snakes, loathing of things that squashed and squelched, all played their horrible symphonies over his nerves. But the reality would be worse: it would be an extra-terrestrial Otherness—something one had never thought of, never could have thought of" [p. 35].

A fearful man (but one who turns out braver than he expects to be) and an academic slightly vain about his scholarship, Ransom is addicted at most to venial sins. He is about as "unbent" as a mortal can hope to be in this life. Fundamentally he is on the side of the divine forces of the universe; for his perfection he needs merely to lose his fears, which stem from an imperfectly vivid awareness that the cosmos belongs to God and is therefore not to be feared.

One explicit symbol that figures prominently in the book is that of birth or rebirth. At the beginning, Ransom is hiking a lonely English road, seeking a place to lay his head, but the hotel in the little village is full. After Ransom is kidnapped by Weston and Devine and taken into their spacecraft, the birth images multiply. The inside of the craft is shaped remarkably like a womb. The cloying heat compels him to strip himself naked. He is within the local womb, but all around him is the creative womb of space:

> The very name "Space" seemed a blasphemous libel for this empyrean ocean of radiance in which they swam. He could not call it "dead"; he felt life pouring into him from it every moment. How indeed should it be otherwise, since out of this ocean the worlds and all their life had come? He had thought it barren: he saw now that it was the womb of worlds. [p. 32]

Ransom himself is both expectant mother and fetus. He was mother when he knocked at the hotel on earth and found it full. He experiences the sensations of a pregnant woman when the spacecraft approaches Mars: "It was explained to him that their bodies, in response to the planet that had caught them in its field, were actually gaining weight every minute and doubling in weight with every twenty-four hours. They had the experiences of a pregnant woman, but magnified almost beyond endurance" [p. 38]. The exit from the spaceship, after it lands on Malacandra, also fits the birth motif—whether Lewis consciously intended it or not—when Ransom pushes his head and shoulders through the manhole [p. 41], to the colder air outside. A newborn uncertainty of vision afflicts Ransom: "He saw nothing but colours—colours that refused to form themselves into things. Moreover, he knew nothing yet well enough to see it: you cannot see things till you know roughly what they are. His first impression was of a bright, pale world—a water-colour world out of a child's paint-box" [p. 42].

Ransom has been born or reborn to life on Malacandra. But more important is the reeducation that lies ahead. Stumbling and childlike as his first responses to the planet may be, there are forces there that mean him well and which will combine to lead him deeper into the divine mysteries.

It is not that Ransom's reeducation begins strictly at the moment he sets foot on the mysterious planet. Some of it has been prenatal. Inside the spaceship he came to a new vision of space, as we have seen, and recognized that it is the planets that are dark spots in the teeming radiance of space. While yet in the craft he also lost a little of his fearfulness. He took the imperfect but real step of resolving to commit suicide before he could be turned over to the mercies of the imagined sorns. Later, he will grow strong enough to face the sorns without the fallback of possible suicide, but for the moment the knife he conceals is a sign of his progress.

This progress toward conquest of fear—another way of saying it is toward trust in God—ends abruptly soon after the landing, when Ransom catches his first glimpse of sorns and struggles to escape from Devine's clutch. In the midst of their combat, a *hnakra* is suddenly sighted and in the confusion Ransom makes his escape, without having resolved his terror of the sorns; he still believes his captors have brought him along to be given as a human sacrifice to the gaunt half-manlike creatures. The fear, of course, is based on the genuine intentions of Weston and Devine, but the latter have misunderstood the Martians, whom they had encountered on a previous trip to the planet. As Ransom wanders the strange landscape, his fear of the sorns soon subsides, though he is not eager to seek them out. At least, they no longer seem science-fiction horrors; they are more like "spooks on stilts" or "surrealistic bogymen with their long faces" [p. 47]. He abandons the thought of suicide and moves toward a sturdy intention to defend himself and survive: "He was determined to back his luck to the end. He prayed, and he felt his knife." Not a bad beginning for one so recently arrived from another world.

His more fundamental reeducation begins when he encounters a *hross* and they become friends across the linguistic and biological barriers. He is made welcome in their village. Bit by bit, their way of life clarifies his own thinking, the very set of his emotions. He learns, for example, that the *hrossa* do not fear death. It comes at its appointed time, the age of 160; it is as though a senior were looking to the special day when he will graduate. Death is predictable, but any *hross* knows it is the door of rebirth into a spiritual existence with Maleldil. All this is explained matter-of-factly by the *hrossa*, who marvel that any *hnau* should not know it already.

The religious faith that Ransom brought with him, including trust in God, is everyday folk wisdom on Malacandra, not convictions arrived at with great spiritual toil and contrary to the assumptions dominant on Tellus. Another bit of wisdom Ransom learns is that *hnau*—rational beings—can actually live by reason.

Malacandra might easily have a population problem, but does not; the *hrossa* voluntarily limit themselves to a couple of offspring. They cannot think of sex apart from procreation; it is all one totality. When their breeding days are over, they compose songs about the experience and spend their years reliving in memory the moments of love, but they would be horrified at the suggestion they should literally repeat the act.

Ransom also learns that there is an objective, indeed theocratic, order on Malacandra. Oyarsa serves directly under Maleldil as his viceroy. Subject to his orders are the *eldila* who appear to human eyes as faint flecks of light, if they are seen at all. The will of Maleldil, mediated down the chain of command from Oyarsa to *eldila* to *hnau*, is not subject to human quibbling. Ransom is instructed by an *eldil* to journey to Meldilorn, but delays. He argues with a *hross*:

> "But that will leave the bent *hmãna* here. They may do more harm."
> "They will not set on the *hrossa*. You have said they are afraid. It is more likely that we will come upon them. Never fear—they will not see us or hear us. We will take them to Oyarsa. But you must go now, as the *eldil* said."
> "Your people will think I have run away because I am afraid to look in their faces after Hyoi's death."
> "It is not a question of thinking but of what an *eldil* says. This is cubs' talk." [p. 83]

The most dramatic reeducation of Ransom takes place a little before the last conversation. It is the episode where he sets out with an expedition of *hrossa* in little boats, to intercept *hnakra* swimming down from the melting polar ice cap. Ransom, as the esteemed visitor from another planet, is given the place of honor, at the front of the fleet. "A short time ago, in England, nothing would have seemed more impossible to Ransom than to accept the post of honour and danger in an attack upon an unknown but certainly deadly aquatic monster" [p. 77], but Malacandra is making a new man of him. "Whatever happened, he must show that the human species also were *hnau*. . . . He felt an unwonted assurance that somehow or other he would be able to go through with it. It was necessary, and the necessary was always possible."

When Ransom strikes the mortal blow and is acclaimed as *hnakrapunt* (*hnakra*-slayer), he enters a new spiritual state, though he does not put it that way to himself. By braving the fearsome monster, he has passed through death and beyond and can now act with freedom and spontaneity. He has overcome his anxieties sufficiently so that he is even willing to turn himself over to Weston

and Devine, if that will persuade the two men to leave the Martians
alone. He is also liberated from constant, subjective misgivings. He
learns, with some help from the *hrossa*, to disregard the state of
his emotions. True, his old fears leap out of the storehouse of archetypes once in a while as he travels toward the land of the sorns,
on the way to Meldilorn, but he brushes these terrors aside. He
has resolved to go to Meldilorn; he will go. And he has been
assured that Oyarsa will protect him along the way; he trusts in
the promise. So Ransom steadfastly seeks the very sorns he had
so frantically tried earlier to avoid. He seeks and finds them and,
eventually, in a flash of true vision, recognizes that their elongated
faces are not spooky but "august."

Ransom, citizen of a distant and fallen planet, where truth can
establish only such costly bridgeheads as a Socrates given the
hemlock or a Jesus on the cross, has seen spiritual reality as it is
without the obscuring pollution of sin. On Malacandra all is clarity.
Like a well-organized army, physical and spiritual beings exist
in mutual love and harmony, all under the benign rule of Maleldil.
There is nothing to fear. There is no need for inner agonizing.
Obey and trust Maleldil, and all will be well. This is all mere common sense to the Martians, but they live on an unfallen planet.
In their environment, an earthling like Ransom can achieve similar
clarity of vision. But Ransom was basically on the side of truth and
life before he came. The completely "broken" Devine and badly
"bent" Weston undergo no spiritual awakening on Malacandra;
their ignorance is invincible.

Ransom has favorable conditions for his reeducation. All around
him are the three native species, illustrating by their daily lives
what true life can be. He is also safer than he at first realizes.
Oyarsa, the agent of Maleldil, is aware of his presence on the
planet from the beginning, and mobilizes *eldila* to safeguard him.
On such a planet, loss of fear and growth in grace come easy.
There is, however, a price. Malacandra is a planned society, and
the safeguards against the fallen powers of the universe are so
systematically worked out that neither an individual nor society
as a whole has much chance to launch a rebellion. Oyarsa's *eldila*
could be regarded as a kind of benevolent C.I.A., on the lookout
for subversive movements. And Oyarsa's unbodying rod is at the
ready, in the event of a major emergency.

In any event, when Ransom returns to earth, walks into a pub, and
orders a pint of bitter (the messianic banquet?), he is a far different man from the one who had been dragged into the spacecraft
and sent on the terrifying voyage to Malacandra. He now *knows* the
truths he once believed as an heroic act of faith. Never again will

he listen to the Enemy's chatter about "cold, dead space." Never again will he blaspheme against the meaningfulness of God's universe.

The trilogy, however, is one vast myth, not three completely self-contained novels. Ransom is destined for further reeducation. The second stage is when he travels yet again through space, supernaturally transported by *eldila* to Perelandra. There he truly earns the name of Ransom, as he enacts the role of a kind of savior, a little Christ, in rescuing that virgin planet from the downfall that Tellus suffered. Everything has come to a sharper point in Perelandra. Malacandra had many safeguards built into its way of life; Perelandra is more like the earth before Adam and Eve listened to the bent Oyarsa of their planet. The new Adam and Eve are free to fall; there is no indication that heavenly hosts of *eldila* will attempt a last-minute blocking action. By comparison with Perelandra, Malacandra has something of the organization and discipline of a benign boarding school.

Good and evil confront Ransom more nakedly on Perelandra. Weston, who in the earlier book was badly bent but not completely broken (he still had some fellow feeling for his species, at least in the abstract), is now the Un-man, indwelt by the fallen Oyarsa. Obedient to his master, he is intent on tempting the new Eve into disobedience against God, with all the predictable consequences. A battle of words between the two men turns into a battle of bodies, and Ransom at last ransoms the new paradise by slaying the demonic Weston.

Eternally youthful from his stay on the blessed and unfallen planet, Ransom is summoned back to earth in *That Hideous Strength* to help lead the forces of good in their struggle against the diabolic powers striving for total and final victory on earth. The man who long ago, in the midst of his fumbling and fearful faith, was in principle already a "new man," now plays his full role as a "little Christ," for the salvation of his native planet.

The main structure of *Out of the Silent Planet* is now clear. By itself, it can be considered a tale of science-fiction adventures. But it is a tale in which religious and metaphysical realities are as important as marvels and strange adventures; indeed the two categories cannot really be separated. The central plot is the reeducation of Ransom under the influence of an unfallen way of life. The book, however, does not stand by itself. It is one installment of a myth that demands three installments. And in each of these further volumes, the reeducation of Ransom continues, as he steadily becomes more attuned to the Maleldil who reigns over the solar system and indeed the entire cosmos.

As we have seen, *Out of the Silent Planet* is like a series of
concentric circles, each with a greater diameter than the last.
There is the science-fiction tale (the smallest circle). Then
Ransom's reeducation, and new knowledge of the relation of God
to *hnau*. Finally, the biggest circle, the cosmic drama that begins
for us readers on Malacandra but does not end there. That smallest
circle is crucial. By telling a superbly convincing science-fiction
story, Lewis makes us willing to believe in, and explore, the ever-
widening circles that issue from the narrative of Ransom's adventures.

Margaret P. Hannay

A Preface to *Perelandra*

THOUGH C. S. Lewis has emerged as a champion of Milton against those who would make him a heretic and those who would limit his verse to a sonorous "organ music" of proper names, Lewis believed Milton had made some significant mistakes in his portrayal of the Edenic myth. It is a fascinating study to note that those things which disappointed Lewis in *Paradise Lost* have been altered in Lewis's own Edenic myth, *Perelandra*; those elements which he most approved in Milton he has sought to emulate. Therefore, approaching the novel through Lewis's Miltonic criticism significantly clarifies its themes and techniques.

The areas of disagreement with Milton may be conveniently divided into the familiar categories of Satan, God, and Mankind. Because Lewis objects to the grandeur of Milton's Satan, his own Satan figure is made wholly contemptible. Because he disapproves of the Olympic tradition of bringing God directly onto the stage, he makes his own Maleldil the source of all power and glory; we are shown only the shadow of the glory, and are never brought face to face with the One whose nature is beyond our comprehension. And because Lewis is convinced that Milton erred in presenting the prelapsarian sexuality, he carefully avoids that problem, but inadvertently creates a less appealing Adam. The major differences in plot occur at the end of the novel, when the Lady is saved from further temptation after weeks of withstanding the wiles of the Un-man, the King refuses to put his wife before obedience to Maleldil, and the unfallen pair are invested with the rulership of their planet after they have proven their worth by obedience.

73

In *A Preface to Paradise Lost* Lewis defended Milton against the Satanist critics, demonstrating that Satan was gradually degraded from the grandeur of his initial appearance. Yet Lewis believed that Milton erred by making Satan so attractive in the opening of the poem that he could be mistaken as the hero of the epic. If one were to say that Lewis wrote most of his adult fiction to counteract the pernicious image of Milton's Satan, one would not be far wrong.

Milton deliberately displays the heroic qualities of the fallen archangel in order to demonstrate the progressive nature of sin; the devil is never quite so completely heroic as the Romantics would claim, and by Book IV is beginning his rapid descent toward mere evil. Lewis, having attempted to combat the Satanist reading of Milton, is not so subtle. Lewis attempts to demonstrate the disgusting nature of evil, divorced from all good qualities. In *The Allegory of Love* Lewis had contrasted the portrayal of evil in Milton and Deguileville:

> Milton's or Dante's hell, superior as they are by innumerable degrees in art, yet do not come so near to the worst we can imagine. There we have grandeur, fortitude, even beauty; but Deguileville's vision is of the last evil—of something almost omnipotent yet wholly mean; an ultimate deformity.[1]

Lewis's Satan figure is characterized by imbecility, unprovoked and even disinterested cruelty, and by petty obscenities: "It had a whole repertory of obscenities to perform with its own—or rather with Weston's—body: and the mere silliness of them was almost worse than the dirtiness" [p. 129]. Lewis is striving for Deguileville's effect of producing nausea, not admiration, for evil. The Un-man is actually an embodiment of Williams's assertion that Pride leads to idiocy and then to hell. For occasionally Weston's personality would reappear, in a whining list of the indignities to his self-esteem. Injured merit is the cause of Weston's initial discontent, as is clearly revealed in his disjointed monologue:

> They won't let me see my press cuttings. So then I went and told him that if they didn't want me in the first Fifteen they could jolly well do without me, see. We'll tell that young whelp it's an insult to the examiners to show up this kind of work. What I want to know is why I should pay for a first-class ticket and then be crowded out like this. It's not fair. [pp. 129-30]

"It's not fair" was the theme of Weston's decaying personality. Lewis is doing the same thing he found Milton doing, making the devil ridiculous by showing him in that "well known state of mind which we can all study in domestic animals, children, film-stars, politicians, or minor poets."[2] Lewis has simply made the absurdity of Pride more obvious by making Weston less attractive, more whining, than the Satan of *Paradise Lost*.

Lewis's basic objection to Milton's presentation is that in Milton evil is shown as having will and energy. Even Comus is "spritely and virile."[3] Lewis far prefers the treatment of Spenser who shows good as energy, while temptation is frequently portrayed as lassitude. *Paradise Lost* is quoted by Lewis to demonstrate that "evil is portrayed as involving immense concentrations of will":

> What though the field be lost?
> All is not lost; the unconquerable Will,
> And study of revenge, immortal hate,
> And courage never to submit or yield.
>   [I.105-08][4]

In Milton as in Marlowe and Shakespeare, Lewis says, evil "appears as *energy*—lawless and rebellious energy, no doubt, but nevertheless energy, abounding and upsurging." This energetic evil is the reason for the poet's difficulty "in making the good a fit antagonist for the evil . . . [the reason] why Milton's God has a popularity rating lower than his Satan" [*Spenser's Images*, p. 66].

Lewis's Un-man has no such heroic resolution. His reason is merely a weapon and not an attribute; in his "off hours" he was no more interested in Reason than in courtesy or justice. Though there is no explicit motive given for the attempt to bring sin into Perelandra, the Un-man remembers the first-century Aramaic of Christ's cry of desolation upon the cross; the attack is apparently one of conquest and revenge.[5] The history of Weston, the man who lost his humanity, is carefully presented in the trilogy. In *Out of the Silent Planet* he is a cruel scientist totally dedicated to the attempt to promote the progress of Mankind by destroying other intelligent species on other planets.[6] When Weston arrives on Perelandra he informs Ransom that his former ideas were rather naive, that the real thing is the Life-Force. To support his new spiritualism, he paraphrases the arguments of Blake in *The Marriage of Heaven and Hell*: "*Your* Devil and *your* God . . . are both pictures of the same Force" [p. 93].[7] Weston calls upon that Force to overtake him completely; Weston's body then becomes the foothold for evil on sinless Perelandra. The division between Weston and the Un-man is revealed immediately. The scientist went into convulsions, then lay completely still. Ransom, attempting to help, offered brandy. "To his consternation the teeth opened, closed on the neck of the bottle and bit it through. No glass was spat out. . . . The face suggested that either he was in no pain or in pain beyond all human comprehension" [p. 96]. Weston had left the realm of humanity; his body became the Un-man.

There has been criticism of this impersonification of evil. Dabney Hart charges that Weston was ineffective because he never was a real person.[8] Lewis would probably have appreciated that comment, since his primary purpose was to demonstrate how evil destroys personality. However, Hart is assuredly correct that the contrast between Weston and the Un-man would have been far more effective if Weston had been a fully rounded character. As the trilogy stands, Weston is a two-dimensional representation of the immoral scientist, rather than a distinct individual. Hart continues to note that the use of the Un-man is at times "expressed with imaginative force; but in general the use of the pronoun 'it' to distinguish the Un-man from Weston seems contrived." Although Hart may be correct in a technical analysis of the form of the novel, the impersonal pronoun demonstrates the principal difference between the devil of Milton and the devil of Lewis. Milton always presents Satan as "he," a being with real personality, a being who started out with equal potential for good or evil. Lewis presents the Un-man as a body controlled by pure evil; he has no human characteristics left (not even the need for sleep) and has become incapable of independent choice between good and evil. "He does all my thinking for me," Weston said in one of his rare appearances [p. 129]. Reason, that prime attribute of humanity for both Milton and Lewis, has been destroyed.

Lewis and Milton differ in their portrayal of the nature of evil primarily in the fact that Satan loses his good qualities gradually, so gradually that it is imperceptible to many critics; the emergence of the Un-man in the body of Weston precludes any good qualities. But both Milton and Lewis perceive evil as good qualities perverted to the wrong end. Energy is *never* actually an attribute of evil, although the good quality of energy may be utilized as a tool of evil, like intelligence or beauty. Because Satan's early magnificence has blinded many critics to the end to which Satan devotes his courage, cunning, and eloquence, Lewis has presented a clearly despicable demon figure, whose reason is merely a weapon assumed for battle, whose cunning is merely a clever distortion of the truth, whose courage is maintained by passing the physical agony to the submerged consciousness of Weston. Lewis, knowing that the writer can no longer count on an audience which "still believed that there really was such a person as Satan, and that he was a liar" [*Preface*, p. 100], has abandoned subtlety.

Lewis's decision to alter the Satan of *Paradise Lost* in his own novel is conscious, deliberate, and emphasized in *Perelandra* itself, in a passage worth quoting at length:

> He did not dare to let the enemy out of his sight for a moment, and every day its society became more unendurable. He had full opportunity to learn the falsity of the maxim that the Prince of Darkness is a gentleman. Again and again he felt that a suave and subtle Mephistopheles with red cloak and rapier . . . or even a sombre tragic Satan out of *Paradise Lost*, would have been a welcome release from the thing he was actually doomed to watch. It was not like dealing with a wicked politician at all: it was much more like being set to guard an imbecile or a monkey or a very nasty child. . . . It showed plenty of subtlety and intelligence when talking to the Lady; but Ransom soon perceived that it regarded intelligence simply and solely as a weapon, which it had no more wish to employ in its off-duty hours than a soldier has to do bayonet practice when he is on leave. . . . It assumed reason as externally and inorganically as it had assumed Weston's body. The moment the Lady was out of sight it seemed to relapse. A great deal of his time was spent in protecting the animals from it. Whenever it got out of sight, or even a few yards ahead, it would make a grab at any beast or bird within its reach and pull out some fur or feathers. [pp. 128-29]

A romantic glorification of the Un-man is inconceivable.

Both Milton and Lewis find the key to the existence of evil in free will. In "Areopagitica" Milton exclaims "when God gave him reason, he gave him freedom to choose, for reason is but choosing; he had been else a mere artificial Adam" [*The Student's Milton*, p. 741]. In *Miracles* Lewis said almost the same thing:

> It is better for you and for everyone else in the long run that other people, including wicked ones, should exercise free will than that you should be protected from cruelty or treachery by turning the human race into automata. [p. 187]

There is no power that can impose evil on good; if evil exists, it must exist by choice. This is partly profound theology, and partly simple common sense. "You make a thing voluntary and then half the people do not do it. That is not what you willed, but your will has made it possible" [*Mere Christianity*, p. 37]. Both Lewis and Milton are dealing with the consequences of the decision to reject

God and embrace evil; Lewis, having struggled against the mis-
interpretation of Milton's Satan, is more blunt about the immediate
effect of that decision.[9]

Lewis, explaining why Satan is the best drawn of Milton's characters, pointed out that "to make a character worse than oneself it is
only necessary to release imaginatively from control some of the
bad passions which, in real life, are always straining at the leash."
The true difficulty comes in drawing the good characters, for "if
you try to draw a character better than yourself, all you can do is
to take the best moments you have had and to imagine them pro-
longed and more consistently embodied in action" [Preface, p. 100].
Portraying God Himself is to raise this difficulty to infinite propor-
tions.

Though C. S. Lewis was fully aware of the epic form of Paradise
Lost, and probably of the consequent necessity for "fitting" the
Christian God into the classical framework, the presentation of
God in Paradise Lost deeply disturbed him. Some of Milton's flaws
might be theological, he asserted, but they "would not be poetically
disastrous if only Milton had shown more poetical prudence. A
God, theologically speaking, much worse than Milton's, would
escape criticism if only He had been made sufficiently awful,
mysterious, and vague" [Preface, p. 130]. Lewis cites with approval the line "Dark with excessive bright thy skirts appeer" [III.
380], contrasting it with the ludicrous picture of the Son bowing
over His sceptre. The problem is, Lewis declares, that Milton has
failed to disentangle himself from "the bad tradition . . . of trying
to make Heaven too like Olympus" [Preface, p. 131—the epic
machinery could have been limited to the angels; there is no epic
necessity for bringing an anthropomorphic God on the stage].
Dante and the Hebrew prophets demonstrate that the Divine
laughter need not sound "merely spiteful and the Divine rebukes
querulous."[10]

Since Lewis is antipathetical to Milton's Olympic presentation
of God, he carefully follows Dante in removing Him beyond our
sight. In so doing, Lewis draws heavily on the medieval model
which, instead of showing Man standing "at the top of a stair whose
foot is lost in obscurity" as in modern evolutionary thought, shows
man "at the bottom of a stair whose top is invisible with light"
[The Discarded Image, pp. 74-75]. He presents God to us by con-
centrating all the glory which he is capable of describing upon
some lower creation, such as the Oyarsa of Glund, and then suddenly shooting us back in perspective to see how far God is above
all that we can visualize.

Lewis also presents God through the praise of His creation. The most hauntingly beautiful of Lewis's images of God is given in the Great Dance of praise at the close of *Perelandra*. (There is an amazing amount of doctrinal content in the hymns; it would be a useful exercise to analyze their theology, though unfortunately beyond the scope of this study.) One such hymn deals directly with the nature of God and with evil as negation:

> Where Maleldil is, there is the centre. He is in every place. Not some of Him in one place and some in another, but in each place the whole Maleldil, even in the smallness beyond thought. There is no way out of the centre save into the Bent Will which casts itself into the Nowhere. Blessed be He! [p. 216][11]

Though Milton is incomparably the greater artist, Lewis's God is more judiciously drawn than Milton's, because He is less completely drawn; when infinity is being portrayed finitely, it is better to be certain that the reader cannot mistake the portrait for the reality. Both men firmly believed in the doctrine of accommodated truth, but Milton was overly optimistic in assuming that the reader could abstract from the anthropomorphism a picture of the Truth. Lewis imitates the method of Dante and the Hebrew prophets in leaving God "sufficiently awful, mysterious, and vague"; Milton, writing in the epic tradition, apparently cannot escape making God occasionally appear rather petulant and arbitrary as he attempts to fit Him into the Olympic mold. In this case, at least, Form has been allowed to determine Content. Peter Kreeft concludes that "few writers of fiction *or* apologetics, and far fewer writers of both, have portrayed as compellingly attractive a God as Lewis has dared to portray."[12]

As Lewis has avoided the somewhat Homeric presentation of God, so he alters the Olympian aspect of the angels. The eldila are corporeal, like Milton's angels, but their bodies differ from planetary animals. They are apparently made of, or at least perceived as, light. The eldila can be perceived by Ransom only at the periphery of his vision; when he faces one, it is invisible to him. This quality is true to the spirit of Milton. Raphael is apparent to unfallen Adam, but when Michael comes to fallen Adam, "doubt and carnal fear" dim his eyes.

Lewis is very explicit that the eldila do not die and do not breed [pp. 9, 82]. He is the more careful because of the embarrassment caused by what More called "the amorous propension" of Milton's angels [cited in *Preface*, p. 112]. Lewis has completely rejected the humanoid body of Miltonic angels (except when

Malacandra and Perelandra deliberately "put on" human appearance to do honor to the young King and Queen). Actually Milton
is explicit that the human shapes of his angels are assumed rather
than inherent:

> For Spirits when they please
> Can either Sex assume, or both; so soft
> And uncompounded is their Essence pure, . . .
>   but in what shape they choose
> Dilated or condens't, bright or obscure,
> Can execute their aerie purposes.
>
> [I.423-30]

But because Milton's angels are presented in human form, the
reader tends to forget that he is seeing merely an appearance;
Lewis limits the humanoid appearance to a single scene.

Lewis finds the War in Heaven to be one of the weaker portions
of *Paradise Lost*, so he carefully avoids involving his eldila in direct
warfare. We know that Malacandra has the power to decompose
the elements of a body, so if he were involved in a war, it would
not be an undignified battle of swords and cannon.

Lewis consistently attempts to substitute the mysterious, the
vague, the incomprehensible, for the Homeric directness of Milton.
But it cannot be too greatly stressed that it is a difference of
artistic presentation, not theology. Milton is, as we have seen, quite
emphatic that God is not corporeal, and his Spirits, like Lewis's
eldila, are capable of assuming any form.

The story of Mankind is, in the Christian doctrine, the story of
original innocence, temptation, and fall. Lewis has given himself
great freedom by not recreating the Edenic myth precisely; it is
instead reenacted on a different planet, and may therefore be pre-
sumed to have a different outcome.

William Norwood has listed some of the differences between
the myth as told by Milton and as told by Lewis: the time and place
have been radically altered; Adam and Eve are colored green,
probably to show a lack of relationship with the people of earth;
eldila replace angels; Ransom, rather than angels, serves as God's
representative; evil is personified in a human body rather than in a
serpent's body; and, most importantly, Paradise is retained rather
than lost.[13]

One of the most rudimentary changes Lewis makes in the actual
temptation myth is separating the King and Queen, from the beginning of the novel to near the end. This is an economical and rather

subtle method of avoiding what Lewis considered one of Milton's worst mistakes—attempting to portray an unfallen sexuality. Milton defied Augustine's warning that sexuality can now be presented only "in the likeness of the turbid lust we have tried and not of the tranquil volition we conjecture" [cited in *Preface*, p. 122]. Lewis declares that "it is dangerous to attempt a poetical representation of something which is unimaginable, not in the sense of raising no images, but in the more disastrous sense of inevitably raising the wrong ones" [p. 122]. He complains that Milton thinks throwing in the word "mysterious" a few times will solve the problem. "The trouble is that the poet hardly seems to be aware of the magnitude of his own undertaking" [p. 124]. That difficulty is emphasized in the necessity for presenting a totally different type of sexuality after the Fall. Lewis solves this problem by avoiding it; he keeps the King and Queen separate until the triumphal celebration at the close of Ransom's stay, when they appear (metaphorically) in their robes of state. There is no attempt whatever to portray their personal relationship; the only direct hint that they have any physical intimacy is an oblique reference to children. Lewis does, however, manage to convey indirectly a great deal of the radiant sexuality of the two as he contemplates, through Ransom's eyes, their physical perfection. Ransom falls down before them begging, "Do not move away, do not raise me up. . . . I have never before seen a man or a woman. I have lived all my life among shadows and broken images" [p. 205]. Since this follows Lewis's statement on the cosmic implications of gender, and since the Paradisal couple are fittingly naked, their physical perfection must imply sexuality. But nothing is directly presented. This wise caution is proof of Lewis's statement that "a little man may sometimes avoid some single error made by a great one."[14] However, the avoidance of this error leads him into problems with the characterization of the King, as we shall see later.

Lewis thoroughly approves of Milton's presentation of the majesty of Adam and Eve: "They are people with whom modern critics would be well advised not to take liberties." Indeed, "no useful criticism of the Miltonic Adam is possible until the last trace of the *naif*, simple, childlike Adam has been removed from our imaginations" [*Preface*, p. 118]. The problem, as Lewis saw it, was not "that of recovering the freshness and simplicity of mere nature" (Rousseau's "noble savage") but the far more difficult task "of drawing someone who, in his solitude and nakedness, shall *really be* what Solomon and Charlemagne and Haroun-al-Raschid and Louis XIV lamely and unsuccessfully strove to imitate on thrones of ivory between lanes of drawn swords and under jeweled baldachins" [Preface, p. 118]. Lewis strives to emulate this achievement. Note, for example, his description of the King and Queen at the close of Perelandra:

> For as the light reached its perfection and settled itself, as it were, like a lord upon his throne or like wine in a bowl, and filled the whole flowery cup of the mountain top, every cranny, with its purity, the holy thing, Paradise itself in its two Persons, Paradise walking hand in hand, its two bodies shining in the light like emeralds yet not themselves too bright to look at, came in sight in the cleft between two peaks, and stood a moment with its male right hand lifted in regal and pontifical benediction, and they walked down and stood on the far side of the water. And the gods kneeled and bowed their huge bodies before the small forms of that young King and Queen. [p. 204]

This is Lewis's attempt to capture the awe Milton created with his description of the pair:

> Two of far nobler shape erect and tall,
> Godlike erect, with native Honour clad
> In naked Majestie seemd Lords of all,
> And worthie seemd, for in thir looks Divine
> The image of thir glorious Maker shon,
> Truth, Wisdome, Sanctitude severe and pure.
> [IV.288-93]

Lewis reminds us that Eve is humble only in comparison with the grandeur of Adam; she is far beyond any fallen mortal, male or female. We must remember that she speaks to Adam as "a lover to a lover, a wife to a husband, the Queen of earth to the King" [Preface, p. 120]. This humility toward her husband Lewis finds most becoming, since he is a firm believer in divinely ordained hierarchy, including that of husband over wife, man over woman. Lewis approves Adam's lectures to his wife, and has his own King deliver a similar lecture to his wife when he finally is united with her.

But Lewis is less successful than Milton in imparting majesty to his Eve; she is innocent, serene, intelligent, loving, but hardly regal. The closing ceremony gives opportunity for emphasizing a majesty that might not be apparent in a more casual setting, but Lewis instead concentrates his energies on demonstrating the superiority of the King. He is presumably attempting to do for his Adam what he did for his God—giving all the admirable qualities to a lesser being, and then projecting greatness beyond that. In this case, unfortunately, the method fails dismally. In a completely gratuituous

scene the King gives "a great laugh" at the woman's ignorance for
not knowing about arches and images [p. 211], matters he has
apparently learned by direct revelation in comfort while she was
busy resisting temptation; in this tale, the King is never directly
tempted.

It was obvious to Lewis that Milton meant Adam's sin to be less
ignoble than Eve's; while she sought self-advancement, he put
the secondary good of conjugal love above the primary good of
obedience to God. "If the reader finds it hard to look upon
Adam's action as a sin at all, that is because he is not really
granting Milton's premises," Lewis declares [*Preface*, p. 127].[15]
Adam could do nothing for Eve by joining her in sin. We do not
know what would have happened if Adam had "scolded or even
chastised Eve and then interceded with God on her behalf." We
do not know what would have happened because Milton did not
know; according to the Genesis account, Adam fell also. We know
only that the situation " '*seemd* remediless' " [*Preface*, p. 127].
In *Perelandra* Lewis has speculated as to what would have happened, for in his Eden, the Adam makes the other choice:

> Though a man were to be torn in two halves . . . though half of him
> turned into earth. . . . The living half must still follow Maleldil. For
> if it also lay down and became earth, what hope would there be for
> the whole? But while one half lived, through it He might send life
> back into the other. . . . He gave me no assurance. No fixed land.
> Always one must throw oneself into the wave. [p. 210—the first two
> ellipses are in the original]

Though Lewis neatly avoided the problem of sexuality in Paradise,
and though he showed his Adam choosing responsibility, the Adam
of Milton is far more appealing. Perhaps it is because Lewis has
not convinced the reader that the King really loves his wife at all;
he is quite cheerfully separated from her, sees her ordeal from a
comfortable distance, quickly decides to repudiate her if she falls,
offers no praise for her resistance to temptation, and corrects her
ignorance on trivial matters when they are finally rejoined. Yet
according to Lewis he is far superior to the Lady. Perhaps Lewis
is the victim of his own strategy in withholding this character
until the end of the novel; there is no time or space to make the King
come alive, to demonstrate his superiority. But whatever the reason for Lewis's failure with the King, he, like Arthegall, does not
emerge as a figure worthy of his Lady.

In any reworking of the myth of the Fall of Man, the temptation
must necessarily be the climax of the story. The most obvious
(and superficial) difference between the temptation scenes of

Milton and Lewis is their length. Victor Hamm contrasts the two accounts, rather too much to the advantage of Lewis:

> Mr. Lewis would disclaim the compliment, but I think anyone who compares his presentation of the scene with Milton's will conclude that he has here excelled the poet. Milton has not sufficiently centered the temptation, the pivotal detail in the whole picture of man's disobedience, and has not labored to make the drama of the seduction subtle and rich enough. In less than 250 lines of his epic of over 10,000 lines, Eve is approached, tempted, and conquered, in spite of Raphael's elaborate warning (which, incidentally, is spread over more than three books—more than 2000 lines). And the Miltonic Satan's methods are those of the mere rationalist-sophist: there is none of the gradual, indirect approach; there is no hint of days consumed in the process, nothing of insinuation. Eve falls like a ripe plum.[16]

Milton's Eve is still a bit less credulous than the Eve of Genesis, who does not seem at all surprised when the serpent asks her a question. In *Paradise Lost* the serpent has to work hard to catch her attention with his exaggerated admiration in pantomime before he ventures verbal flattery. Eve accepts the flattery, but is sensibly amazed that the creature can speak [IX.551-52]. Her questioning gives opportunity for the serpent to attribute his powers of speech to the magical properties of the fruit. Because Milton's Satan has given a reason for the serpent's power of speech, the Genesis assertion "Ye shall not surely die" can be expanded into the powerful testimony of the serpent himself:

> Look on mee,
> Mee who have touch'd and tasted, yet both live,
> And life more perfet have attaind then Fate
> Meant mee, by ventring higher then my Lot.
> [IX.687-90]

Eve, ignorant of the fact that Satan has immeasurably debased his archangelic nature by becoming a serpent, rather than raising a serpent to human rationality, apparently accepts this as conclusive proof [IX. 764-66].

Milton's serpent throws in an extra fillip which, as we shall see, becomes the crux of the argument in Lewis's treatment—God will not be angry, but will actually praise your courage in denouncing Death. Eve does not perceive the verbal acrobatics in the claims that she will not die, and yet will win praise for flaunting Death. Satan also draws on the argument for knowledge that Milton had used in "Areopagitica," uses false analogies and false syllogisms to

prove the impossibility of judgement, questions God's role in creation, redefines death to mean putting on a divine nature, and ends
with the sensory appeal to taste. The sensory appeal is apparently
uppermost in Eve's mind, for her reflection in lines 735-43 mentions all five senses. This passage is a direct use of Genesis: "And
when the woman saw that the tree was good for food, and that it
was pleasant to the eyes, and a tree desired to make one wise, she
. . . did eat" [3:6].

Lewis, like Milton, emphasizes the role of free will in the Fall.
Milton's God asks the rhetorical question, whose fault was the Fall?

> Whose but his own? ingrate, he had of mee
> All he could have; I made him just and right,
> Sufficient to have stood, though free to fall.
> [III.97-99]

On Perelandra, Ransom came to the realization that "If the issue
lay in Maleldil's hands, Ransom and the Lady *were* those hands.
The fate of a world really depended on how they behaved in the
next few hours" [p. 142]. (This is probably an instance of sound
doctrine marred by the petulance of Milton's anthropomorphic deity.
However, Lewis and Milton express the same doctrine.)

Both poets precede the actual temptation with an appeal to the
imagination. Satan introduced into Eve's dream

> At least distemperd, discontented thoughts,
> Vain hopes, vain aimes, inordinate desires
> Blown up with high conceits ingendring pride.
> [IV.807-09]

Though Millicent Bell is surely wrong that Eve had already fallen
in the dream[17] (even in IX.659, Milton calls her "*Eve* yet sinless"),
Eve did become dissatisfied with her place in the hierarchy, and
was ripe for the temptation to Pride. It is after this seed of evil has
been planted in Eve's imagination that Raphael comes to warn of
the impending danger:

> That thou art happie, owe to God;
> That thou continu'st such, owe to thy self,
> That is, to thy obedience. . . .
> God made thee perfet, not immutable;
> And good he made thee, but to persevere
> He left it in thy power.
> [V.520-26]

Lewis also makes it very clear that the Lady may fall. After some time under the Un-man's temptation, Ransom noted a change in her expression, "the hint of something precarious had increased" [p. 113]. Later "she was still in her innocence. No evil intention had been formed in her mind. But if her will was uncorrupted, half her imagination was already filled with bright, poisonous shapes" [p. 134]. Lewis, like Milton, believes that evil appeared first to the imagination, and then to the will.

Lewis, however, leaves out the whole element of sensual temptation. It is the good places in the novel, the floating islands and the mountain of glory, that have soft breezes wafting fragrance of flowering trees, heraldic animals gamboling around a beautiful woman, warm nights, and luscious fruits. The Forbidden Land, the object of the temptation, is cold, barren, and uncomfortable. Lewis is taking no chances on making the temptation beguile the *reader*, probably because of his own battle against the misunderstanding of Acrasia's bower in *The Faerie Queene*.

Also, *Perelandra* does not focus on a fruit as the object of temptation, but on the Fixed Land. Norwood says that "contemporary readers would too quickly reject . . . a magic apple," and so Lewis changed the myth.[18] This is surely an oversimplification; Milton did not believe the fruit had any "magic" either. Nor did Lewis believe that the fruit was important in itself; it assumed its importance from the situation, as did Desdemona's handkerchief. The Fixed Land has been given various interpretations. Clyde S. Kilby is probably correct when he says that the islands symbolize the "Christian's abandonment to God's direction," and the Fixed Land legality, man's will rather than God's.[19] The Lady had no possessions and no control over her own life whatever; her island floated with her across the seas according to Maleldil's will, not her own. The Green Lady is therefore tempted to stay on the Fixed Land so that she can keep things and know where to find them, so that she will not have to be separated from the King, so that she can depend on her own will rather than the will of Maleldil. (Notice here that Lewis has reversed Milton's strategy. Eve is tempted by her desire to be separated from Adam; the Lady is tempted through her desire to be reunited with the King.)

When Ransom first arrives, the Lady has no concept of herself as a separate entity. Ransom asks her if she is alone, and, as Phelan says, her answer "speaks a whole world of innocence and contact with God: 'What is "alone"?' "[20] Ransom soon understands that her peace is not a permanent thing. It is fragile and could be shattered. It is a balance maintained by the mind, not a state of being. Yet Ransom inadvertently leads her perilously close to the brink himself, in suggesting that there are some things sent by Maleldil that one would seek to avoid if one could—like her separation from the King. For when she first saw Ransom, she was disappointed that he was not the King. She quickly pushed aside the temptation to discontent, but Ransom shows her that she could have "rejected the wave."

Weston initiated the actual temptation by questioning Maleldil's command as Satan had questioned God's. He wanted her to make up a story about living on the Fixed Land, appealing first to her imagination as the dream had appealed to Eve's. Though she could not understand why she should make a story about something which cannot be, Weston had thereby implanted a seed of desire for security in her mind. Next he questioned the hierarchy. "Do you not think the King must sometimes be tired of being the older? Would he not love you more if you were wiser than he?" [p. 105]. The Lady's motives here are somewhat more noble than Eve's, but it is the same temptation—to be above her husband in the hierarchy, an unforgiveable sin to Milton and to Lewis.

Next, Weston taught the Lady that Maleldil was letting go of her hand, letting her walk alone. It was just one step further to say that the command was given so that she could demonstrate her independence by breaking it. Maleldil cannot tell her to break His command, for then she would not be making her own choice. The Un-man, a sophist like the Satan of *Paradise Regained*, tells her "the wrong kind of obeying itself can be a disobeying" [p. 115]. This echoes Satan's argument that God will praise "your dauntless vertue, whom the pain / Of Death denounc't" [IX.694-95]. God *wants* you to assert your independence by disobeying Him, they are told.

Ransom was able to answer this argument. The command is given so that there *could* be obedience; all the other commands are things she would choose to do anyway. And the Green Lady again is older than the men of earth:

> Oh, how well I see it! We cannot walk out of Maleldil's will: but He has given us a way to walk out of *our* will. And there could be no such way except a command like this. . . . I knew there was joy in looking upon the Fixed Island and laying down all thought of ever living there, but I did not till now understand. [p. 118]

The Green Lady here echoes Milton's statement in *De Doctrina* that "it was necessary that something should be forbidden or commanded as a test of fidelity"—something which he would not do without a command. For Adam would have given no "proof of obedience by the performance of works to which he was led by a natural impulse, independently of the divine command" [*The Student's Milton*, p. 986].

The Un-man then attempted a third approach, raising in her mind the idea of Duty and trying to convince the Lady that this disobedience of Maleldil was a great deed that needed to be done for her husband and for the children which she would bear. By telling her stories of noble women and urging her to imitate them, the Un-man raised in her a hint of theatricality, the barest trace of veiled egotism. (Lewis, of course, can draw on human history in his temptation scenes; Milton, writing of the beginning, could not.) Weston robed her like a tragedy queen, awakening her vanity only to awaken her notion of her great soul. The scene which involves a mirror for the trying on of the robe probably owes much to Milton's picture of Eve looking at her face in a pool; both women are sinless, but something which could lead to vanity has been awakened.[21]

Although the Lady had at first instinctively rejected temptation by falling asleep from boredom [pp. 120-21], she is now passionately concerned about her responsibility to choose; her new self-awareness has increased her vulnerability. It is at this point that Ransom knew the temptation had to be stopped, realizing finally that it was up to him to stop it with physical combat. The story ends in triumph because an escape is provided for the Lady. This is the crucial difference between the two accounts, a difference made explicit within the novel:

> Up to this point the Lady had repelled her assailant. She was shaken and weary, and there were some stains perhaps in her imagination, but she had stood. In that respect the story already differed from anything that he certainly knew about the mother of our own race. He did not know whether Eve had resisted at all, or if so, for how long. Still less did he know how the story would have ended if she had. If the "serpent" had been foiled, and returned the next day, and the next . . . what then? Would the trial have lasted for ever? How would Maleldil have stopped it? [p. 145—ellipsis in the original]

Charles Marriott, reviewing *Perelandra*, says that Lewis cheated. He "loads the dice rather heavily for his own Eve. Quite obviously, left alone, she would not have overcome Satan."[22]

This is Lewis's point exactly. Would the temptation have lasted infinitely? Perhaps, but such an outcome is impractical for a novel. She must either give in, as Eve did, or finally be rescued, as the Green Lady was. Ransom's attempts to find an answer in Genesis were futile, for there is never an answer to the question "What would have happened if . . . ." Ransom knew that "here in Perelandra the temptation would be stopped by Ransom, or it would not be stopped at all" [p. 146]. For the triumphal ending of *Perelandra*, Lewis takes his cue from the Miltonic projection of what would have happened if they had not fallen:

> This had been
> Perhaps thy Capital Seate, from whence had spred
> All generations, and had hither come
> From all the ends of th' Earth, to celebrate
> And reverence thee thir great Progenitor.
>
> [XI.342-46]

Eve did not need to try her virtue; the fact that she had lived that long in the garden without disobeying was *itself* a trial of her virtue. Milton at least hints that this would have been the first of many tests, that Adam and Eve would have ascended in the hierarchy as they proved their worth. In effect, they failed the first round of examinations.

The Lady of Perelandra has stood; they have passed the test. At the close of *Perelandra* there is a magnificent scene where the Oyarsa gives up her authority to the unfallen humanity, to the King and Queen of their race. They are on solid ground for the ceremony, so Ransom begins to wonder how they will reach the islands before nightfall. But no one answers his questions "for somehow he knew perfectly well that *this* island had never been forbidden them, and that one purpose in forbidding the other had been to lead them to this their destined throne" [pp. 203-04]. In a sense Tor and Tinidril have not merely retained their Paradise, but by passing the test, have gained it. Tor speaks of what will happen—they will have children, teach the beasts wisdom and speech, and then "it is Maleldil's purpose to make us free of Deep Heaven. Our bodies will be changed, but not all changed. We shall be as the eldila, but not all as eldila" [p. 211]. This is almost a direct parallel of Raphael's statement "Your bodies may at last turn all to Spirit, / . . . and wingd ascend / Ethereal, as wee, or may at choice / Here or in Heav'nly Paradises dwell" [V.497-500]. The condition is "If ye be found obedient." Adam and Eve were not; Tor and Tinidril were. Tor and Tinidril will ascend to a higher level of being; Adam and Eve descend to a lower.

Adam and Eve ate of the Tree of Knowledge of Good and Evil, and learned "of Good lost, and Evil got" [XI.87]. The King and Queen on Perelandra also learn of evil "though not as the Evil

One wished us to learn. . . . There is an ignorance of evil that comes from being young: there is a darker ignorance that comes from doing it, as men by sleeping lose the knowledge of sleep. . . . Maleldil has brought us out of the one ignorance, and we have not entered the other" [p. 209]. Lewis has completed his myth with the "alternate ending" suggested by Milton. Paradise is retained, Adam and Eve ascend to a higher level of being as a result of passing the test of obedience. We all know what has happened as a result of Sin and, if we did not, we could learn from Books XI and XII of *Paradise Lost*. Lewis has therefore chosen to give the reader a glimpse of the glory of a sinless world.

Approaching *Perelandra* through Lewis's work on Milton clarifies the themes and techniques of the novel. It becomes clear that Lewis rejected those aspects of Milton's Edenic myth which he found distasteful—the magnificent Satan, the anthropomorphic deity, the undignified corporeality of the angels, the mistaken attempt to describe prelapsarian sexuality. Lewis praises the magnificence of Adam and Eve, striving to emulate Milton's achievement. Lewis agrees with Milton that Eve is inferior to Adam (though far above any unfallen person), and attempts to demonstrate the superior knowledge of the King. Lewis, like Milton, gives the man special revelation the wife does not hear. Lewis agrees with Milton that the problem of the Fall is the problem of free will, and emphasizes individual choices. Lewis believed that Milton's Eve fell through Pride; his own Eve is tempted to take her destiny into her own hands, to set herself up as her own god. Both Eves are separated from their husbands when the temptation comes. This is traditional; however, there is no indication in Genesis that Adam was not standing beside his wife during the temptation. The major departures from *Paradise Lost* come toward the end of *Perelandra*. The Lady is saved by outside intervention, freeing Lewis to follow through with Milton's hint of the glorious future of unfallen mankind.

Lewis's *A Preface to Paradise Lost* provides an excellent introduction to the epic. But many students have found that *Perelandra*, by reworking many of the same motifs, provides at least as good a door into the world of *Paradise Lost*. The reverse is also true. Close attention to Lewis's Milton criticism results in a richer understanding of his own Edenic myth, *Perelandra*.

Richard L. Purtill

That Hideous Strength: A Double Story

THERE are two cities, said St. Augustine, a city of God founded on love of God and our fellow man, and a city of man founded on love of self. That is the matter of C. S. Lewis's *That Hideous Strength*; the opposition between the society at the Manor at St. Anne's, founded on love and fellowship, and the group at the mansion at Belbury, founded on self-aggrandizement, treachery, and fear. But the manner of telling the story is also based on opposition and contrast; the dialectic of the theme is echoed by the dialectic of the tale. This is obvious enough in the larger structure of the story, the alternation of scenes in which Jane Studdock takes a part and those in which her husband Mark plays a role. But the finer structure of the story also displays an intricate and detailed opposition of scenes and characters; it is this opposition, and the ideas on which it rests, that I wish to examine in what follows.

The opposition begins with the situation of the two protagonists. Jane Studdock is a person who has fled from making a real commitment of herself, either in her marriage or in other areas of her life. She has made her scholarship an excuse not to have children and not to fully share her life with her husband: "She had always intended to continue her own career as a scholar after she was married: that was one of the reasons why they were to have no children, at any rate for a long time yet" [p. 14]. But she has no real commitment to her scholarship, although she tries to make herself believe that "if she got out all her notebooks and editions and really sat down to the job, she could force herself back into her lost enthusiasm" [p. 14].

Mark Studdock's problem is not lack of commitment; he has made an "almost heroic sacrifice of nearly every person and thing he ac-

91

tually enjoyed" [p. 246]. But his commitment has been to an ideal essentially base and trivial—the desire to be an "insider," to be in the "inner ring." Lewis has written of this desire in an essay: "The lust for the esoteric, the longing to be inside, take many forms. . . . We hope, no doubt, for tangible profits from every Inner Ring we penetrate: power, money, liberty to break rules. . . . But all these would not satisfy us if we did not get in addition the delicious sense of secret intimacy. . . . This desire is one of the great permanent mainsprings of human action."[1] Mark's problem, then, is a wrong commitment as his wife's is a wrong lack of commitment.

In the dialectic of the story, both Mark and Jane eventually free themselves from their ruling vice; but they must first display in their actions what this vice is. Jane's lack of commitment to her marriage is hinted at by her interaction with Mark early in the story. After one of her frightening dreams (which as the story develops are seen to be a sort of vision or "second sight"), Jane meets Mark on his return home frightened and sobbing: "There was a quality in the very muscles of his wife's body which took him by surprise. A certain indefinable defensiveness had momentarily deserted her. He had known such occasions before, but they were rare. They were already becoming rarer. And they tended, in his experience, to be followed next day by inexplicable quarrels" [p. 44].

Similarly, Mark's desire to be an insider is adumbrated in the first few scenes in which he figures. He has newly become a member of the Progressive Element, the "Inner Ring" of his college: "You would never have guessed from the tone of Studdock's reply what intense pleasure he derived from Curry's use of the pronoun 'we.' So very recently he had been an outsider, watching the proceedings of what he then called 'Curry and his gang' with awe. . . . Now he was inside and 'Curry and his gang' had become 'we' or 'the Progressive Element in College.' It had all happened quite suddenly and was still sweet in the mouth" [p. 17]. The loss of real friendship which this involves is also suggested in this early scene: "He did not always like Curry either. His pleasure in being with him was not that sort of pleasure" [p. 18].

As the plot develops, Jane's attitude towards Mark and towards her marriage is developed by contrast with the marriages of others —the Dimbles, the Dennisons, Ivy Maggs and her husband. Mark moves from Bracton to Belbury and into the innermost ring at Belbury; at each stage we are shown something of what he has lost and where he is going.

As the action of the story begins, both Jane and Mark encounter people who have been involved in their past lives and who introduce them to a next, crucial, stage in their lives. Jane encounters a former teacher, Dr. Dimble, and his wife, "Mother" Dimble, who had become fond of Jane while Jane was Dimble's pupil. Through the Dimbles, Jane is sent to the Manor at St. Anne's for the next stage of her spiritual journey. Mark encounters Lord Feverstone, not a man he had known well but, as Curry reveals in an early scene, the man who had been influential in getting Mark his fellowship at Bracton. It is through Feverstone that Mark goes to Belbury.

As it turns out both the group at St. Anne's and the group at Belbury would like to make use of Jane's gift of "seeing" or "vision." The difference in their tactics is revealing: Jane is sent to St. Anne's by the Dimbles, who are fond of her. Once there, her gift and its dangers are explained to her and she is invited freely to become one of the company at St. Anne's. This first invitation she refuses and she returns home as freely as she came.

The Belbury group, on the other hand, try to get Jane in their power by first getting Mark. As Wither says on one occasion, "If a mere arrest could have secured the—er—good will and collaboration of Mrs. Studdock, we should hardly have embarrassed ourselves with the presence of her husband" [p. 161]. Once having secured Mark they attempt to make use of him in various ways, but the initial reason for getting him to Belbury is as part of a complicated plot to get Jane's cooperation, as the quote above makes clear. Lord Feverstone has no regard for Mark; when the tormented young man says, "I thought you at least were my friend," Feverstone's reply is, "Incurable romantic!" [p. 112].

Even our early glimpses of the Dimble's on the one hand and Feverstone on the other give us something of their very different atmosphere. Dimble is a conscientious teacher. " 'There is my dullest pupil just ringing the bell,' he said. 'I must go to the study, and listen to an essay on Swift beginning, "Swift was born." Must try to keep my mind on it, too, which won't be easy' " [p. 33]. His wife "appeared to like all Dr. Dimble's pupils of both sexes and the Dimbles' house, away on the far side of the river, was a kind of noisy *salon* all the term. She had been particularly fond of Jane" [p. 29].

When we first meet Feverstone he baits Curry, his host and ally, then derides him to Mark after Curry has left to go to a meeting. His conversation reveals that he is on the side of Belbury not because he believes in the publicly proclaimed ideals of the N.I.C.E. (National Institute of Co-ordinated Experiments) but because he wants power. His appeal to Mark is, "Man has got to take charge of Man. That means, remember, that some men have got to take charge of the rest. . . . You and I want to be the people who do the taking charge, not the ones who are taken charge of" [p. 42]. The next day Feverstone drives Mark to Belbury and his driving gives another clue to his character: "The speed of the car, even in the narrow streets of Edgestow, was impressive, and so were the laconic criticisms of Feverstone on other drivers and pedestrians. Once over the level crossing . . . their speed became so great that even on a rather empty road the inexcusably bad drivers, the manifestly half-witted pedestrians and men with horses, the hen that they actually ran over and the dogs and hens that Feverstone pronounced 'damned lucky,' seemed to follow one another almost without intermission. . . . Mark, drunk with air and at once fascinated and repelled by the insolence of Feverstone's driving sat saying, 'Yes,' and 'Quite,' and 'It was *their* fault' " [p. 49]. Once at Belbury, Feverstone abandons Mark to the psychological softening up by Wither and the other powers of Belbury.

Jane's first meeting at St. Anne's is with Camilla Denniston, to whom she takes a liking, but her important contact is with Grace Ironwood, whom she finds stern and unsympathetic. This is one of the few instances, incidentally, where Lewis has painted himself into a corner from a literary point of view. He wanted to show the initial face of Belbury as pleasant and amiable, the initial face of St. Anne's as seemingly repellent. There is a sound tradition behind this move—the straight and narrow path of virtue as opposed to the broad and flowery path to destruction, the stern visage of duty as opposed to the smiling face of vice. But in order to give St. Anne's this initially unsympathetic face, Lewis created a somewhat unsympathetic character, Grace Ironwood, who is a slight embarrassment to him in later scenes. She is absent, on a slight pretext or none, from most of the later scenes involving friendship and companionship. Lewis could, of course, have shown an initially unsympathetic character becoming more sympathetic, but given the many other things he had to do in the book he may be forgiven for having sidestepped the problem by first using Grace Ironwood and then retiring her to the background.

Even the gardens at St. Anne's and at Belbury help the contrast between the two spiritual atmospheres. Jane, even on her first visit apprehensive and somewhat hostile, finds the garden at St. Anne's delightful: "It was like the garden in *Peter Rabbit*. Or was it like the garden in the *Romance of the Rose*? No, not in the least like really. Or like Klingsor's garden? Or the garden in *Alice*?" [pp. 61-62]. For Mark, on the other hand, the garden at Belbury is just another of its torments: "They were not the sort of grounds that anyone could walk in for pleasure. The Edwardian millionaire who had built Belbury had enclosed about twenty acres with a low brick wall surmounted by an iron railing, and laid it all out in what his contractor called Ornamental Pleasure Grounds. There were trees dotted about and winding paths covered so thickly with round white pebbles that you could hardly walk on them. . . . There were plantations—slabs would be almost a better word—of that kind of laurel which looks as if it were made of cleverly painted and varnished metal. . . . The whole effect was like that of a municipal cemetery" [p. 101].

This contrast between the gardens may seem purely adventitious, something "dragged in" to darken Belbury and highlight St. Anne's. But Lewis is using the two gardens as a metaphor for the anti-life attitude of Belbury and the pro-life attitude of St. Anne's. All of the St. Anne's people are connected with traditional "natural" activities in some way: MacPhee and Grace Ironwood work in the garden at St. Anne's; the Dimbles' garden at their home is famous for its beauty. Camilla and Arthur Denniston share a taste for weather and nature. Ivy Maggs has a sort of *rapport* with Bultitude the bear; Ransom has a power over animals gained by his sojourn on Perelandra.

Belbury's attitude is made explicit by Filostrato: "We do not want the world any longer furred over with organic life, like what you call the blue mould—all sprouting and budding and breeding and decaying. We must get rid of it. By little and little, of course. Slowly we learn how. Learn to make our brains live with less and less body: learn to build our bodies directly with chemicals, no longer have to stuff them full of dead brutes and weeds" [p. 173]. Earlier Feverstone had suggested the same idea: "The second problem is our rivals on this planet. I don't mean only insects and bacteria. There's far too much life of every kind about, animal and vegetable. We haven't really cleared the place yet" [p. 42].

The theory behind the St. Anne's attitude towards nature is the idea of man as a link between the animal and the spiritual. Man should not sink to a purely animal level but it is equally fatal for man to attempt to live as if he were a pure spirit, to attempt to sever his links with the organic. Man's place, as Ransom says, is "between the angels who are our elder brothers and the beasts who are our jesters, servants and playfellows" [p. 378]. The image of the world which Belbury wants to make is the cold sterile moon, imagined as inhabited by a race which has denied its organic component, which feeds and even procreates by artificial means. The image of the world which St. Anne's wants is the Venus of Lewis's earlier book *Perelandra*, envisioned as an Eden where the humanlike inhabitants live in harmony with nature and in partnership with the angelic intelligences who have prepared the planet for their coming.

Interestingly enough, though, Filostrato is a stranger to the full
scope and purpose of Belbury, for he knows nothing of the evil
angels who are the real force behind its plans and purposes: "He
was not an initiate, he knew nothing of the dark eldils. He believed that his skill had really kept Alcasan's brain alive" [p. 354].
But Filostrato's dedication to an anti-natural ideal of science makes
him a natural tool for the demonic forces who rule Belbury.

MacPhee at St. Anne's is also a partial stranger to the full mission of Ransom's Fellowship. He apparently believes in God (though
his model, Lewis's old tutor Kirkpatrick, did not). But he seems not
to be a Christian and maintains a sceptical attitude toward the eldils
and even towards Ransom's account of his adventures on Mars and
Venus. But his concern for truth and his appreciation of Ransom's
goodness make him as much a natural ally of St. Anne's as Filostrato is of Belbury. Notice also that Hingest, who is a chemist of
international reputation and an agnostic, rejects Belbury as soon as
he sees what it is like, because he has his own standards both of
science and of personal conduct: "There *are* no sciences like Sociology. And if I found chemistry beginning to fit in with a secret
police run by a middle-aged virago who doesn't wear corsets and a
scheme for taking away his farm and his shop and his children
from every Englishman, I'd let chemistry go to the devil and take up
gardening again" [pp. 70-71]. The intellectual pride of the physical scientist is well hit off ("There *are* no sciences like Sociology")
but so is Hingest's concern for the ordinary man (and gardening is
again a symbol for a pro-life attitude).

The key point here is one which goes very deep in Lewis's thinking. It is the idea that any real and unselfish devotion to an ideal
outside oneself leads to God and away from evil, whereas any ideal,
no matter how apparently noble, leads away from God and goodness if pursued for the wrong reasons or by the wrong means.
(Filostrato's ambition is not to serve science but to become one of
the "chosen heads" who will rule the earth, and he will kill and
betray to gain his end.)

To return to the adventures of Jane and Mark, we see Mark
leave Belbury temporarily and return; on his return he is introduced
to the Head, the severed head of Alcasan through which the evil
eldils speak. Jane also returns home after her first visit to St.
Anne's; on her second visit she meets Ransom, the Director of St.
Anne's, and has a momentary experience of the power and strangeness of the good eldils who are the allies of St. Anne's. Mark's experience is terrifying and literally nauseating and as a result of it
he is willing to sacrifice Jane to the aims of Belbury: "Apparently
he would *have* to bring her to Belbury. His mind had made this

decision for him at some moment he did not remember. He must get her, to save his life. . . . The first hint of a real threat to his bodily life knocked him sprawling" [p. 185].

Jane, however, has had an experience of great joy and awe: "Her world was unmade; . . . anything might happen now" [p. 143]. On her trip home "she was in the sphere of Jove, amid light and music and festal pomp, brimmed with life and radiant in health, jocund and clothed in shining garments" [p. 151]. And this experience, though focused on the person of the Director, gives her "new feelings about Mark, feelings of guilt and pity. . . . It was Mark who had made the fatal mistake; she must, must, must be 'nice' to Mark. . . . There arose, clouded with some undefined emotion, a resolution to give Mark much more than she had ever given him before" [p. 151].

In the intricate dialectic of the plot Jane on this return to Edgestow meets a representative of Belbury, "Fairy" Hardcastle, and Mark soon leaves Belbury again to return to Edgestow and meet Dimble, a representative of St. Anne's. Hardcastle tortures Jane and tries to take her back to Belbury; Jane escapes only by accident. Mark finds his meeting with Dimble unpleasant, but only because Dimble shows Mark to himself as he has become: " 'Studdock,' said Dimble. 'This is not a time for foolery, or compliments. . . . I don't trust you. Why should I? You are (at least in some degree) the accomplice of the worst men in the world. . . . They have corrupted better men than you or me before now. Straik was a good man once. Filostrato was at least a great genius. . . . Who are you to be exempt?' " [p. 222]. Despite this, Dimble offers to help Mark leave Belbury, knowing that Mark's coming may be a trap, knowing he risks his own life and even the mission of St. Anne's.

It is worth noting the intricate pattern made by the movement of the two Studdocks, a pattern too orderly to be accidental. Jane and Mark each leave home on the same day; Jane goes to St. Anne's, Mark to Belbury. They each return and meet each other. At this stage Mark is happy and confident, Jane worried and apprehensive. Mark returns to Belbury, Jane to St. Anne's; each there meets the real authority of the place. Jane on her second departure from St. Anne's leaves reluctantly; Mark is running in fear on his second departure from Belbury. Their positions are now reversed: Jane is happy, Mark afraid. As we have seen, each meets a representative of the other side, then returns. Jane goes back to St. Anne's gladly, fleeing from "Fairy" Hardcastle's persecution and finding St. Anne's a place of refuge and peace. Mark returns to Belbury a prisoner, afraid and beginning to reject what Belbury stands for. At the end of the book Jane and Mark are united again both physically and spiritually. In one way the question of the book has always been, "Will Jane join Mark at Belbury, to their mutual destruction, or will Mark join Jane at St. Anne's, to their mutual salvation?" And it is by staying at St. Anne's that Jane plays her part in the events which lead to the freeing of Mark.

The story here moves on several levels. On one level it is merely the stock adventure of romance—lovers are separated; will they get back together? At another level it is about the adventures of any soul and the different ways in which it may choose good or evil. But on an intermediate level it is a parable of what happens when two people in a relationship begin to go different ways. Jane must not lightly leave Mark; Ransom sends her back to plead with Mark to leave Belbury. But she must not go to him if this means *her* destruction; there is no question of her staying with Hardcastle in order to be reunited with Mark. Her mission of going to plead with Mark is frustrated; she never meets him until all is decided. But her effort bears fruit in unexpected ways: she is tortured by Hardcastle and the knowledge of this fact probably plays a part in Mark's turnaround.

After the returns to St. Anne's and Belbury, each of the Studdocks faces danger and each has to face up to the thought of death. Jane meets the real Merlin and the forces he unleashes and does not much like the experience. Mark meets the false Merlin and likes him; without knowing it he finds the right kind of "inner ring" based on friendship and shared danger. Each learns from the experience: Jane is further jolted out of her smug contemporary outfit of ideas and Mark's friendship with the tramp is another point of strength in his growing resistance to Belbury. Both Jane and Mark are offered an opportunity to become more a part of the group which they have joined: Jane goes out on the search for the awakened Merlin and later shares with the others in the "side effects" produced by the descent of the eldils on St. Anne's. After her dismaying experience with the dwarves and the terrestrial Venus, she has a true mystical experience, a sort of brief union with God for which perhaps her gifts as a "seer" especially prepare her. Mark is offered the opportunity to become an "initiate," one of those wholly possessed by the evil eldils who rule Belbury. It is the last and most terrible form of his old temptation to be in the "inner ring": "For here, surely at last (so his desire whispered to him) was the true inner circle of all, the circle whose centre was outside the human race—the ultimate secret, the supreme power, the last initiation. The fact that it was almost completely horrible did not in the least diminish its attraction" [pp. 259-60]. But

Mark is strengthened by his memory of Jane, by his friendship with the tramp, by his realization (brought on by facing the seeming certainty of death) of how he has wasted his life. Mark resists. He begins to fight back.

In all this, in the eventual defeat of their attempt to control England, in the failure of their attempt to control Mark, the powers of Belbury are the unwitting agents of their own defeat. In trying to invade Perelandra the evil eldils have broken a sort of treaty which prevented the good eldils from acting directly on earth; the treaty once broken, the eldils can use Merlin as a channel for their power and destroy the evil at Belbury and Edgestow. But even in small things Belbury's own attitudes and methods work against its purposes.

A minor villain named Cosser tries to make use of Mark to do some work which is really Cosser's job: visiting and writing a report on a village which is to be wiped out by one of Belbury's schemes. But the village reminds Mark of happy holidays when he was young and an old aunt he was fond of. (The aunt was one of the very type of people Belbury now wants to eliminate.) The visit sows some of Mark's first doubts about Belbury. Cosser's petty bit of meanness, trying to trick Mark into doing some work for him, is on a smaller scale just what the higher-ups at Belbury are trying to do: use Mark for their own purposes. But since people are not tools, attempts to use them for our purposes can backfire, as they do in Mark's case. Belbury, by treating people only as tools, does not even get the best out of them as tools.

St. Anne's, by enlisting the free cooperation first of Jane and then of Merlin, gains two formidable allies, but also two additions to its circle of friends and companions. By getting to know Merlin, both Ransom and Dimble gain an incomparable insight into Arthurian Britain; one cannot imagine Wither or Frost getting to know Merlin in this way or caring about what they can learn from him if it does not help their schemes. By treating Jane merely as an object for her sadistic impulses, "Fairy" Hardcastle frightens her and ensures that she will run straight back to St. Anne's; but each of the people at St. Anne's (except Grace Ironwood) befriends Jane in some way and, though they mainly seem to be giving to her, helping her, they also inevitably gain something in the exchange. Ivy Maggs, for instance, gains at least the knowledge that Jane's situation is worse than her own, for Fred Maggs though in prison is not on the side of Belbury. Mother Dimble perhaps finds in Jane the daughter she never had.

Most important for all those at St. Anne's is the fact that they have the opportunity to help someone come closer to goodness, to

God. For the really essential struggle between Belbury and St. Anne's is the struggle for souls. As Frost says, "One must guard against the error of supposing that the political and economic dominance of England by the N.I.C.E. is more than a subordinate object: it is individuals that we are really concerned with. A hard unchangeable core of individuals really devoted to the same cause as ourselves—that is what we need and what, indeed, we are under orders to supply" [p. 242]. Lewis supposes here, as he does in *The Screwtape Letters*, that the damned want fresh recruits in order to feed on them in some way or absorb them; as Wither says in the same scene, "Any fresh individual brought into that unity would be a source of the most intense satisfaction to—ah—all concerned. I desire the closest possible bond. I would welcome an interpenetration of personalities so close, so irrevocable, that it almost transcends individuality. You need not doubt that I would open my arms to receive—to absorb—to assimilate this young man" [p. 243].

This bond of "assimilation" among the lost is a sort of infernal parody of the unity of Christian love; even some of the same terms can be used, though with terribly different meanings. So also Wither is a sort of infernal parody of Ransom. Ransom is the Director of St. Anne's, his own man, freely obeying the will of God as shown to him by the eldils. Wither, significantly, is the *Deputy* Director of the N.I.C.E., the puppet of the real ruler of Belbury, Alcasan's severed head through which the evil eldils speak. Wither uses speech to confuse, to bewilder, to mislead. Ransom is a poet and linguist, a lover and respectful user of language. After first bamboozling Mark to get him to stay at Belbury, Wither constantly terrifies and degrades him (for example, by pretending to forget his name); his attitude towards him is a cold dislike. Ransom's attitude toward Jane is consistently friendly and interested; he talks to her about books, shows her the mice which pick up the crumbs, talks with her about the problems in her marriage. Indeed Ransom seems alive to and interested in everything, whereas Wither "had learned to withdraw most of his consciousness from the task of living, to conduct business, even, with only a quarter of his mind. Colours, tastes, smells, and tactual sensations no doubt bombarded his physical senses in the normal manner: they did not now reach his ego" [p. 250].

This last contrast between Wither and Ransom may seem exaggerated; surely a man can be very evil and yet be alive to the world around him and appreciative of it. But Lewis intends Wither to be a picture of man in the last stages of separation from God, and one of Lewis's most basic convictions is that ultimately separation from God is separation from everything good. Insofar as a man still has an appreciation of any good thing, whether it be art or nature or other people, that man is not wholly lost. Insofar, on the other hand, as a man is wholly separated from God he loses his appreciation of all good things, which may have first started him on the path away from God. *Any* good thing taken apart from God loses its goodness; it is not a question of God or this good, for without God "this good" will no longer *be* good.

At this stage, if not long before, the reader not in sympathy, or not entirely in sympathy, with Lewis's theology may find himself rejecting *That Hideous Strength* as a work of fiction. Is it not, he may ask, on my own showing a work of propaganda rather than a work of art, designed to influence the reader by putting a certain way of life or set of values in a good light and the opposing way of life or set of values in a bad light? Is there not, the critic may ask, more to be said for Belbury than Lewis allows, more to be criticised in St. Anne's than Lewis allows us to see?

If the critic merely means that there is more to be said for science, or sociology, or even for scientific planning as applied to society than Lewis allows, then the criticism rests on a misunderstanding. Belbury really cares nothing for science or for human society; it uses its pretended concern for these things as a cloak for its real aims. Nor is Lewis attacking these values as such. As he points out in an essay, he is saying "not 'scientific planning will certainly lead to Hell,' but 'Under modern conditions any effective invitation to Hell will certainly appear in the guise of scientific planning'—as Hitler's régime in fact did. Every tyrant must begin by claiming to have what his victims respect and to give what they want. The majority in most modern countries respect science and want to be planned. And, therefore, almost by definition, if any man or group wishes to enslave us it will of course describe itself as 'scientific planned democracy.' It may be true that any real salvation must equally, though by hypothesis truthfully, describe itself as 'scientific planned democracy.' All the more reason to look very carefully at anything which bears that label."[2]

If not science or scientific planning, what is Lewis writing against when he pictures Belbury? Just what we have seen: the real face and not the mask of Belbury. And what is this real face? It is seen in the cruelty of "Fairy" Hardcastle, in Filostrato's rejection of nature, in Wither's use of language to confuse and deceive, in Frost's "objectivity" which is a rejection of personhood. It is a rejection of the love of God and our neighbor, ultimately a rejection of anything outside ourselves. We sometimes call it, as Augustine does, "self-love." But ultimately it is a hatred of all selves, including oneself. It is saying "*my* will, not Thine, be done" even when my will being done leads and can be seen to lead to loss and destruction. The true face of Belbury is Frost's face as he dies: "The nearest thing to a human passion which still existed in him was a sort of cold fury against all who believed in the mind. There was no tolerating such an illusion. There were not, and must not be, such things as men" [p. 357]. As Frost dies, "Escape for the soul, if not for the body, was offered him. He became able to know (and simultaneously refused the knowledge) that he had been wrong from the beginning, that souls and personal responsibility existed. He half saw: he wholly hated. The physical torture of the burning was not fiercer than his hatred of that. With one supreme effort he flung himself back into his illusion. In that attitude eternity overtook him as sunrise in old tales overtakes [trolls] and turns them into unchangeable stone" [p. 358].

It is against this hatred of the human, this abolition of man, that Lewis writes. If his book is propaganda it is propaganda against that. It is not argument; the arguments are to be found in his non-fiction, especially in *The Abolition of Man*. Nor is the book propaganda if by propaganda is meant an attempt to sway the emotions by exaggeration and by the selection and suppression of facts. But that it is propaganda in an older sense, *Propaganda fide—* preaching, Lewis would not, I think, deny. *That Hideous Strength* is, if you like, a sermon, preached against certain dangers of our times. It is more than that—it is a fairy tale, a satire on academic life, a commentary on marriage and modern mores. But among all of these things it is also a sermon, and like all sermons its purpose is to make us repent and change our ways. That it is addressed to our condition is proved by the kind of opposition it has aroused. If we do not take warning from Lewis's tale, it may before long be truth and not fiction that "the shadow of one dark wing is over all Tellus. . . . The Hideous Strength holds all this Earth in its fist to squeeze as it wishes" [p. 293].

III: THE CHRONICLES OF NARNIA

Walter Hooper

Narnia: The Author, the Critics, and the Tale

BEFORE the recent revival of fairy tales got fully under way, C. S. Lewis's seven Chronicles of Narnia were treated a little like "hand-me-down" clothes, which are passed down from big to little children and are immediately given up when the little ones outgrow them. Now that people are returning to the old distinction between stories which can only be read by children and those which can be enjoyed by people of all ages, the Narnian books occupy a position on something like a "Jacob's Ladder" and are continually being passed up and down from young to old, from old to young, depending on which member of the family discovers them first. Of the million copies of the Chronicles sold in England and the United States last year (1973), about half were bought by college students.

Professor Tolkien's *Hobbit* and *Lord of the Rings* grew out of the stories he told his children, but Lewis, who was a bachelor for most of his life and knew little about children, wrote fairy tales simply because he liked them himself and because he found them the best art form for what he had to say. As scholars of the past, both men knew that the association of fairy tales and fantasy with children is very recent and accidental. Fairy tales gravitated to the nursery when they became unfashionable with adults. It surely marks an important recovery that they are coming back—indeed *are* back—into fashion with whoever likes them of whatever age.

Asked how he came to write the first Chronicle of Narnia—*The Lion, the Witch and the Wardrobe*—Lewis said: "All my seven Narnian books, and my three science fiction books, began with

Reprinted from *Children's Literature*, Volume III (1974), by permission of the Temple University Press. Copyright © 1974 by Francelia Butler.

seeing pictures in my head. At first they were not a story, just pictures. The *Lion* all began with a picture of a Faun carrying an umbrella and parcels in a snowy wood. This picture had been in my mind since I was about sixteen. Then one day, when I was about forty, I said to myself: 'Let's try to make a story about it.' "[1]

Though Lewis had probably forgotten it, there is some evidence which would seem to indicate that the initial impetus behind his Narnian stories came from real children.

In the autumn of 1939 four schoolgirls were evacuated from London to Lewis's home on the outskirts of Oxford. It was his adopted "mother," Mrs. Moore, who mainly looked after the evacuees, but Lewis shared the responsibility of entertaining the young visitors. On the back of another book he was writing at the time, I found what I believe to be the germinal passage of the first story of Narnia—*The Lion, the Witch and the Wardrobe*. It says: "This book is about four children whose names were Ann, Martin, Rose and Peter. But it is most about Peter who was the youngest. They all had to go away from London suddenly because of the Air Raids, and because Father, who was in the army, had gone off to the War and Mother was doing some kind of war work. They were sent to stay with a relation of Mother's who was a very old Professor who lived by himself in the country."

I've been told by a neighbor who used to see them across her back fence that the schoolgirls did not remain very long in Oxford, and I've never been able to discover whether Lewis wrote any more of the story at this time. The next we hear of the books is from Chad Walsh who says that, when he visited Lewis in the summer of 1948, he talked "vaguely of completing a children's book which he [had] begun 'in the tradition of E. Nesbit.' "[2] Then, on the 10th of March 1949, Lewis read the first two chapters of *The Lion, the Witch and the Wardrobe* to his friend, Roger Lancelyn Green, who is the only person to read all seven stories in manuscript. Spurred on by Lancelyn Green's encouragement, *The Lion* was completed by the end of the month. More "pictures" or mental images—which Lewis said were his only means of inspiration—began forming in his head and the next two stories, *Prince Caspian* and *The Voyage of the "Dawn Treader,"* were completed by the end of February 1950. Before the year was out he had written *The Silver Chair* and *The Horse and His Boy* and made a start on *The Magician's Nephew*. The final installment, *The Last Battle*, was written two years later.

Lewis is generally thought to have been the best-read man of his time. Though this, in itself, would not insure readable books, the combination of his vast learning, his superior abilities as a prose-stylist, and his rich and vivid imagination have resulted in the Narnian books being first, though not foremost, extremely well-written adventure stories. What has led people to read the stories over and over again—what I'd say is the foremost reason for their success—is, I think, quite simply their "meaning." Before going into this, however, I should glance at the unpleasant reactions of some adults to the Narnian books.

Objections to the books are rare. When they've come, it's usually been from schoolmistresses and professional educators for whom the delicate unreality which they call the "whole child" seems to bear little resemblance to the children most of us meet. They claim that the Narnian battles and wicked characters frighten children and give them nightmares. I believe there is no better answer to these charges than that given by Lewis himself in his defense of fairy tales in his essay "On Three Ways of Writing for Children." While agreeing that we must not do anything (1) "likely to give the child those haunting, disabling, pathological fears against which ordinary courage is helpless," he was strongly opposed to the notion that we must keep out of the child's mind (2) "the knowledge that he is born into a world of death, violence, wounds, adventure, heroism and cowardice, good and evil":

> The second would indeed be to give children a false impression and feed them on escapism in the bad sense. There is something ludicrous in the idea of so educating a generation which is born to the Ogpu and the atomic bomb. Since it is so likely that they will meet cruel enemies, let them at least have heard of brave knights and heroic courage. Otherwise you are making their destiny not brighter but darker. Nor do most of us find that violence and bloodshed, in a story, produce any haunting dread in the minds of children. As far as that goes, I side impenitently with the human race against the modern reformer. Let there be wicked kings and beheadings, battles and dungeons, giants and dragons, and let villains be soundly killed at the end of the book. Nothing will persuade me that this causes an ordinary child any kind or degree of fear beyond what it wants, and needs, to feel. For, of course, it wants to be a little frightened.[3]

Another bit of adverse criticism comes from Mr. David Holbrook in his article "The Problem of C. S. Lewis" found in *Children's Literature in Education*, No. 10 (March 1973), pp. 3-25. The article is what booksellers call "Curious," and has convinced me that, though there is a problem, it is most certainly not Lewis's. Mr. Holbrook says:

Taking clues from the philosopher of surrealism, Gaston Bachelard, from psychoanalysis, and from my work on Sylvia Plath, I believe that C. S. Lewis's Narnia stories have their origins in the fact of his life that his mother died when he was a baby. I believe that this left him a psychic hunger—to be nurtured by the mother he had lost. It left him . . . needing to find his way *into the other world where the mother was*: the world of death.

How do we get there? Since we came into the world through mother's body, we could go back there, through her body: and the Wardrobe is her body (or, to be more specific, her birth passage). But also symbolized is the need *to be seen as ourselves* as we seek to *find ourselves in* the mother's eyes: in the front of the wardrobe is a mirror, and the path to "other worlds" is through reflecting pools. Going "through the mirror" (as in *Alice*, or in some of George MacDonald's stories) is *going through the mother's eyes* into the other world where the dead mother is, she who can help one to BE. This is, of course, a quest for *birth*. . . .

But now another problem arises. If we go into that other world of death where the mother is, we shall perhaps encounter a mother who has not been humanized by us, as a mother normally is, over the long years of knowing her as a child. She may be the all-bad, all-hate mother we were capable of phantasying as an infant. In Kleinian terms, she may be "bad breast" split off from wholeness. She may be what Melanie Klein called the "castrating mother."

Lewis never, of course, read this, but I recall a conversation we had about the same kind of thing. The difficulty, he said, about arguing with such Freud-ridden sheep is that *whatever* you say to the contrary, no matter how clear and obvious to a sensible man, the Freudian uses it to support what he's already decided to believe. Or, as Lewis says elsewhere, they argue in the same manner as a man who should say, "If there were an invisible cat in the chair, the chair would look empty; but the chair does look empty; therefore there is an invisible cat in it. A belief in invisible cats cannot be logically disproved, but it tells us a good deal about those who hold it."[4] I can find no chink in Mr. Holbrook's article whereby the light of reason might get through. As his sexual imagery goes on perpetuating itself, I have the sensation of observing a hydra that will go on sprouting heads whether you strike them off or not. Besides pointing out that Lewis was ten years old when his mother died—and so hardly a baby—the only thing I can say about Mr. Holbrook's article is that, were he given a lie-detector test to discover whether or not *he* believes what he's written, I feel sure he wouldn't pass.

Lewis was much gratified by the extraordinary success of the Narnian books. Of the many fan-letters he received, he seemed most pleased with those from children. Whereas adults usually wanted to know where he got his "ideas," children—not being required to write learned articles—let the stories act on them more directly.

To the many children who pleaded with him to write more stories, Lewis's answer was usually the same as that he gave me: "There are only two times at which you can stop a thing: one is before everyone is tired of it, and the other is after!" Almost all wrote of their love for Aslan, the Creator and ruler of Narnia. Last year an eleven-year old, Lucy Fryman, from Texas was so anxious to talk to someone who had known Lewis that she addressed the following words to his life-long friend, Owen Barfield:

> I have read Mr. Lewis's books. I got so envoveled [sic] in them all I did was eat, sleep, and read. I wanted to write to you and tell you I understand the books. I mean about the sy[m]bols and all. . . . I know that to me Aslan is God. And all the son's and daughter's of Adam and Eve are God's children. I have my own philosophies about the books. If it is possible I would like to meet you. None of my friends (well some of them) liked the books. I tried to explain to them but they don't understand about symbols. I never really did until I read the books.

I think it's an inaccuracy to say that most readers make the instant connection, as Lucy did, between Aslan and God. Lewis wanted it to happen naturally, or not at all. When another little girl asked what Aslan meant in the last chapter of The Voyage of the "Dawn Treader," when he tells the children that in their world they must learn to know him by "another name," Lewis answered:

> As to Aslan's other name, well, I want you to guess. Has there never been anyone in this world who (1) Arrived at the same time as Father Christmas (2) Said he was the Son of the Great Emperor (3) Gave himself up for someone else's fault to be jeered at and killed by wicked people (4) Came to life again (5) Is sometimes spoken of as a Lamb (at the end of the "Dawn Treader")? Don't you really know His name in this world?[5]

Lewis used a capital "H" in the "His" above because Aslan is Christ. In another place he explained the reason for his reticence in saying no more than this: "Why did one find it so hard to feel as one was told one ought to feel about God or about the sufferings of Christ? I thought the chief reason was that one was told one ought to. An obligation to feel can freeze feelings. . . . But supposing that by casting all these things into an imaginary world, stripping them of their stained-glass and Sunday school associations, one could make them for the first time appear in their real

potency? Could one not thus steal past those watchful dragons?
I thought one could."[6]

Professor Tolkien once told me that he thought the Christian
elements in the Narnian stories too "obvious." But I think this is
because he not only knew the Bible better than most of us, but
began by knowing what Lewis was "up to." Judging from what I
hear, only about half Lewis's readers guess that Aslan is meant to
be Christ—and that half is made up about equally of children and
adults. I side with Lewis in not wishing to attract the attention of
those "watchful dragons," but as the Narnian books are, whether
I like it or not, undergoing very detailed analysis, I offer the following comments about what I think the Christian elements in them
are. This requires, first of all, clearing up a linguistic difference
between Lewis and his readers.

It's about as natural as sneezing for moderns to call something
an "allegory" when it has a meaning slightly different from, or other
than, the one the author gives it. In this sense you can "allegorize"
practically anything. The reason why Lewis and Tolkien claimed
that their books are not allegories is that they were using the ancient
definition of the term: by allegory they meant the use of something real and tangible to stand for that which is real but intangible:
Love can be allegorized, patience can be allegorized, anything
immaterial can be allegorized or represented by feigned physical
objects. But Aslan and Gandalf are already physical objects. To try
to represent what Christ would be like in Narnia is to turn one
physical object into another (supposed) physical object—and that is
not, by Lewis and Tolkien's definition, an allegory.

There are those who consider Satan the "hero" of Milton's *Paradise Lost,* by which they mean, not that he is in any way good, but
that he's the best drawn character in the poem. Long before Lewis
wrote the Narnian stories, he explained in his *Preface to Paradise
Lost* (ch. xiii) why it is so much easier to draw a bad Satan than a
good God:

> To make a character worse than oneself it is only necessary to release
> imaginatively from control some of the bad passions which, in real life,
> are always straining at the leash; the Satan, the Iago, the Becky Sharp,
> within each of us, is always there and only too ready, the moment the
> leash is slipped, to come out and have in our books that holiday we
> try to deny them in our lives. But if you try to draw a character better
> than yourself, all you can do is to take the best moments you have had
> and to imagine them prolonged and more consistently embodied in
> action. But the real high virtues which we do not possess at all, we
> cannot depict except in a purely external fashion. We do not really
> know what it feels like to be a man much better than ourselves.

In talking with Lewis about his almost unbelievable success in picturing the divine Aslan—Who is a million times more interesting than any of his equally convincing bad characters—I found him reluctant to take any credit, pointing out that Aslan pushed His *own* way into the books. Not only has Aslan received the highest praise of anyone or anything in the books, but, perilous compliment though it may sound, I think most readers (of which I am one) have been unable to divorce Aslan from Christ. Though it is a contradiction in terms, some love Him even more than His Original. I'm reminded of a little boy here in Oxford who chopped through the back of his wardrobe and half-way through the bricks of the house to get to Him. Aslan is not a "reinterpretation" of Christ, as I think *Jesus Christ Superstar* is meant to be. He is, as Lewis says, "an invention giving an imaginary answer to the question, 'What might Christ become like, if there really were a world like Narnia and He chose to be incarnate and die and rise again in *that* world as He actually has done in ours?' " [*Letters*, p. 283]. But some of us, on meeting absolute goodness, discover it to be too strong for us. I remember Lewis reading an article in which the writer referred to Aslan as "smug," and I know this pained him. "Do you think Aslan 'smug'?" he asked. I think I replied that what would sound perfectly ordinary coming from God would sound deranged coming from a mere man. The humanitarians may think *us* unkind for holding clear and definite beliefs, but they can hardly expect the Creator of all worlds to qualify every statement with "so it seems to me" or "in my opinion."

The closest parallel between Aslan and Christ comes in *The Lion, the Witch and the Wardrobe* where Aslan offers His life to save Edmund. This is very similar to Christ's vicarious death on the cross, but if the analogy is pressed too closely it will be discovered that nowhere—not even here—does Lewis provide us with a geometrically perfect equivalent of anything in the Bible or Christian doctrine. Lewis hoped that by seeing Aslan die on the Stone Table we'd not only be better able to grasp the significance of what happened in the actual history of this world, but see that it was a very good thing in itself and in the context Lewis gave it.

Not only is "disguise" part of Lewis's intention, but it is also essential to see that what is in one book or world cannot be the same in another book or world. What "Miss T" eats does not remain as it was but *turns into* "Miss T." The instructions Aslan gives Eustace and Jill on how to discover Prince Rilian are meant, I think, to reinforce the importance of following Christ's commandments. On the other hand, if, while reading *The Silver Chair*, we're thinking only of Christ's instructions to the rich young man recounted in St. Mark 10: 17-21, we'll have missed what we are meant to be attending to in Narnia. It's afterwards, minutes or hours or perhaps even years afterwards, that the two worlds are to be joined in our minds. But even if that juncture *never* takes place, we will have benefited enormously from *The Silver Chair*, for it is part of the success of a great author that the sense of his book not depend on the reader's knowing the original source of its ingredients.

Is there any good to be had from source-hunting? My belief is that when teachers come across children who feel they have solved a "puzzle" by discovering that Narnia is the name of a place in Italy, that Arslan (which Lewis altered to Aslan) is the Turkish word for lion, the teacher should lead him away from the suspect realm of anthropology to true literary pleasures by showing him how one thing becomes a *different* thing in another book. For instance, it's not enough to say that the immediate source of Shakespeare's *Romeo and Juliet* is Arthur Brooke's extremely ugly *Tragical History of Romeus and Juliet*: we need to show him what a completely different use Shakespeare made of the story if we are to help him appreciate the latter's genius.

More than most books, the Narnian tales are specially rich hunting grounds for scholars. In chapter xiii of *The Voyage of the "Dawn Treader"* the children find three Lords of Narnia fast asleep under an enchantment, round a table spread with exotic foods supplied by a beautiful Princess. On the table is the cruel-looking knife with which the White Witch killed Aslan. The Princess's father, Ramandu, appears but is unable to speak until a bird lays a live coal on his lips. Among the many possible "sources" for these elements, other than Lewis's own imagination, are those we all know about. There is Rip Van Winkle; there is the passage in I Kings 17:6 which tells how ravens fed Elijah with "bread and flesh in the morning, and bread and flesh in the evening." The Knife recalls King Pelles's sword which struck the Dolorous Blow. The bird takes us back to Isaiah 6:6: "Then flew one of the seraphims unto me, having a live coal in his hand, which he had taken with the tongs from off the altar: and he laid it upon my mouth." It is inevitable that a man so widely read as Lewis should have known all these things—but they, neither collectively nor individually, are what *his* story is about.

Besides their obvious parallels, the Narnian books are suffused throughout with moral teaching of a quality which I don't believe anyone, whatever his beliefs, could fairly object to. The tales are not, as might be imagined, built around moral themes which were in the author's mind from the beginning, but grew out of the telling and are as much a part of the narrative as scent is to a flower.

I heard an expert on children's literature say the other day that writers are going back to moral themes—and cited "pollution" as the supreme example. None of us objects to a clean world, but the morality of Lewis's books goes far deeper and touches on levels of human understanding rarely attempted even by those who write for adults. An especially good example occurs in *The Voyage of the "Dawn Treader"* (ch. x). As Lucy searches the Magician's Book for the spell which will make the Dufflepuds visible, she comes across a spell which will let you know what your friends say about you. Not even wishing to avoid this dangerous thing, Lucy says the magical words and hears her good friend, Marjorie, say very unkind things about her to another person. Later, when Aslan discovers what poor heartbroken Lucy has done, He says, "Spying on people by magic is the same as spying on them in any other way. And you have misjudged your friend. She is weak, but she loves you. She was afraid of the older girl and said what she does not mean." "I don't think I'd ever be able to forget what I heard her say," answers Lucy. "No, you won't," replies Aslan.

Are there many of us who have not found, like Lucy, that such a dangerous course, once taken, forbids return? I've never seen the enormous difference between what our friends *say*, and what they really *think*, about us so unforgettably portrayed.

In *The Last Battle*, which won the Carnegie Medal for the best children's book of 1956, and is the most theological of all the books, Lewis uses a stable door as the way out of Narnia. Those familiar with Lewis's beliefs can understand how characteristic it is that he will not allow his readers to camp too long on any of his earthly creations. As we must, in reality, pass on, he will not write "and they lived happily ever after" till it is safe to do so. It is certainly not safe to do so at the beginning of *The Last Battle*, which is, in my opinion, the best written and the most sublime of all the Narnian stories, the crowning achievement of the whole Narnian creation. Everything else in all the other six stories finds its meaning in relation to this book. Not that one can't enjoy the other stories separately; but, as Lewis would say, you cannot possibly understand the play until you've seen it through to the end. Lewis insists on taking us to the end—and beyond.

If *The Last Battle* is reread less often than the other fairy tales this is probably because the first eleven chapters, which take place in the old, familiar Narnia, are so extremely painful to read. Almost everything we have come to love is, bit by bit, taken from us. Our sense of loss is made more excruciating because we are allowed—even encouraged—to believe that things will eventually get back to "normal." We feel certain that the King, at least, will not be deceived by Shift's trickery: but he is. When Eustace and Jill arrive we know it will only be a matter of time until all is put right. Yet, despite their willingness to help, there is so little they can do without the help of Aslan. And where, by the way, *is* He? Our hearts warm within us as Jewel the Unicorn recounts the centuries of past happiness in which every day and week in Narnia had been better than the last:

> And as he went on, the picture of all those happy years, all the thousands of them, piled up in Jill's mind till it was rather like looking down from a high hill onto a rich, lovely plain full of woods and waters and cornfields, which spread away and away till it got thin and misty from distance. And she said:
> "Oh, I do hope we can soon settle the Ape and get back to those good, ordinary times. And then I hope they'll go on for ever and ever and ever. *Our* world is going to have an end some day. Perhaps this one won't. Oh Jewel—wouldn't it be lovely if Narnia just went on and on—like what you said it has been?"
> "Nay, sister," answered Jewel, "all worlds draw to an end; except Aslan's own country."
> "Well, at least," said Jill, "I hope the end of this one is millions of millions of millions of years away." [ch. viii]

So do we all. Yet a few minutes later Farsight the Eagle brings word that Cair Paravel, the high seat of all the Kings of Narnia, has been taken by the Calormenes. And, as he lay dying, Roonwit the Centaur asked the King to remember that "all worlds draw to an end and that noble death is a treasure which no one is too poor to buy" [ch. viii].

Lewis's didactic purpose ought to be clear to those who are conversant with orthodox Christianity. He uses his own invented world to illustrate what the Church has been teaching since the beginning, but which is becoming more and more neglected or forgotten. Namely, that this world will come to an end; it was never meant to be our real home—that lies elsewhere; we do not know, we cannot possibly know, when the end will come; and the end will come, not from within, but from without.

Most of the events in *The Last Battle* are based on Our Lord's apocalyptic prophecies recorded in St. Matthew 24, St. Mark 13 and St. Luke 21. The treachery of Shift the Ape was suggested by the Dominical words found in St. Matthew 24:23-24:

> If any man shall say unto you, Lo, here is Christ, or there; believe it not. For there shall arise false Christs, and false prophets, and shall shew great signs and wonders; insomuch that, if it were possible, they shall deceive the very elect.

The Ape almost—almost—succeeds in deceiving even the most faithful followers of Aslan, first through trickery and, later, when he becomes the tool of Rishda Tarkaan and Ginger the Cat, in propounding his "new theology": the confusion of Aslan and the devil Tash as "Tashlan." As the monkey Shift is a parody of a man, so his "theology" is a parody of the truth. We are prepared for ordinary wickedness in an adventure story, but with the advent of the "new theology" we move into a new and dreadful dimension where ordinary courage seems helpless.

When it seems quite certain that Eustace and Jill will soon die fighting for Narnia, they speculate as to whether, at the moment of their death in Narnia, they will be found dead in England. Frightened by the idea, Jill begins a confession which she breaks off mid-sentence. "What were you going to say?" asks Eustace. She answers:

> I *was* going to say I wished we'd never come. But I don't, I don't, I don't. Even if we *are* killed. I'd rather be killed fighting for Narnia than grow old and stupid at home and perhaps go about in a bathchair and then die in the end just the same. [ch. ix]

From that point onwards Lewis lets go the full power of his imagination, and we are carried relentlessly forward into what is truly the *last* battle of Narnia, in front of the Stable. There the King, the children, and the remnant of faithful Narnians are either slain or make their way inside. The Stable has become none other than the way into Aslan's Country, and, drawing out this brilliant piece of symbolism, Lewis has Jill say in a moment of selfless appreciation: "In our world too, a Stable once had something inside it that was bigger than our whole world" [ch. xiii].

What is a little confusing, but which is partly explained in chapters iv and v, and fully cleared up in the last chapter, is that all (except one) of the "friends of Narnia"—Digory Kirke, Polly Plummer, Peter, Edmund and Lucy Pevensie, Eustace Scrubb, and Jill Pole—died together in a railway crash in England. They are reborn in glory and, inside the Stable, Eustace and Jill meet all the others. The exception is Susan Pevensie who, "no longer a friend of Narnia" [ch. xii], has drifted of her own free will into apostasy. Liberal clergymen and other "kind" but mistaken people, preferring the temporary passion of Pity to the eternal action of Pity, have found the absence of Susan a reason for calling Lewis "cruel." But they are well answered in *The Great Divorce* where, explaining why those who have chosen Hell shall not be allowed to veto the joys of Heaven, he says: "Every disease that submits to a cure shall be cured: but we will not call blue yellow to please those who

insist on still having jaundice, nor make a midden of the world's
garden for the sake of some who cannot abide the smell of roses"
[p. 121].

With a terrible beauty that almost makes the heart ache, and
which is perhaps only matched by Dante's *Paradiso*, Aslan goes to
the Stable door and holds His Last Judgement. Those who are
worthy pass in, the others turn away into darkness. Inside, the
children watch as Aslan, fulfilling the apocalyptic prophecies of
the New Testament, destroys Narnia by water and fire and closes
the Stable door upon it for ever.

After this dazzling feat of the imagination, one might reasonably
expect that Lewis could not help but let us down in "unwinding"
his story. He knew that the merest slip of the pen could have cast
a shadow of incredulity over all that went before, and he proceeded
very cautiously in opening the children's eyes to where they are.
The question was how do you portray Heaven? How make it
heavenly? How "unwind" *upwards*?

The answer lay in finding—and then trying to describe—the difference between the earthly and the eternal world. Years before,
writing about the difference between allegory and symbolism, he
said:

> The allegorist leaves the given—his own passions—to talk of that which
> is confessedly less real, which is a fiction. The symbolist leaves the
> given to find that which is more real. To put the difference in another
> way, for the symbolist it is we who are the allegory. We are the "frigid
> personifications"; the heavens above us are the "shadowy abstrac-
> tions"; the world which we mistake for reality is the flat outline of that
> which elsewhere veritably is in all the round of its unimaginable di-
> mensions.[7]

Symbolism, as described here, was not for Lewis a fanciful bit
of intellectualism. He believed that Heaven is the real thing of
which earth is an imperfect copy. His problem was not only of
finding some way to illustrate this, but to describe the heavenly
life in such a way that it would not seem a place of perpetual
negations. In his essay "Transposition," he suggests that we think
of a mother and son imprisoned in a dungeon. As the child has
never seen the outer world, his mother draws pencil sketches to illustrate what fields, rivers, mountains, cities and waves on a beach
are like:

> On the whole he gets on tolerably well until, one day, he says some-
> thing that gives his mother pause. For a minute or two they are at
> cross-purposes. Finally it dawns on her that he has, all these years,

lived under a misconception. "But," she gasps, "you didn't think that the real world was full of lines drawn in lead pencil?" "What?" says the boy. "No pencil-marks there?" And instantly his whole notion of the outer world becomes a blank. . . . So with us. "We know not what we shall be"; but we may be sure we shall be more, not less, than we were on earth.[8]

Lewis had a knack of making even the most difficult metaphysical concepts understandable and picturing the otherwise unpicturable. In order that his readers will feel as comfortable in the world beyond the Stable door as the children in the book, he brings in homely details such as the fact that Narnian clothes felt as well as looked beautiful and (I'll never forget how much Lewis disliked "dressing up") the even more pleasant fact that "there was no such thing as starch or flannel or elastic to be found from one end of the country to the other" [ch. xii]. Then, as the children and many of the animals they have come to love follow Aslan further into the country, their sense of strangeness wears off till it eventually dawns upon them that the reason why everything looks so familiar is because they are seeing for the first time the "real Narnia" of which the old one had only been a "copy." As they rejoice in this discovery, Lord Digory, whom we first met as old Professor Kirke in *The Lion, the Witch and the Wardrobe*, explains the difference between the two, adding, "It's all in Plato, all in Plato: bless me, what *do* they teach them at these schools!" [ch. xv]. He is referring, of course, to Plato's *Phaedo* in which he discusses immortality and the unchanging reality behind the changing forms.

One other little detail, overlooked perhaps by the majority of readers as it is blended so perfectly into the narrative, concerns the manner in which resurrected bodies differ from earthly ones. The children discover that they can scale waterfalls and run faster than an arrow flies. This is meant to be a parallel to the Gospel accounts of Christ's risen body: though still corporeal, He can move through a locked door [St. John 20:19] and ascend bodily into Heaven [St. Mark 16:19].

When the children reach the Mountain of Aslan they are joined by all the heroes of the other six books, Reepicheep the Mouse, Puddlegum the Marsh-wiggle, and a host of other old friends. Uneasy that their joy may yet be snatched from them, and that they may be sent back to earth, they turn to Aslan who answers the question in their minds: "Have you not guessed?" He says, "The term is over: the holidays have begun. The dream is ended: this is the morning."

After that we are told that "He no longer looked to them like a lion." Lewis is here referring to the passage in the Athanasian

Creed which states that Christ is both God and Man "not by conversion of the Godhead into flesh: but by taking of the Manhood
into God." This means that Aslan was transformed into a Man—
which Manhood He keeps for all time. "The things that began to
happen after that," says Lewis, "were so great and beautiful that I
cannot write them"—and, of course, neither can I or anyone else.

. There has never been a book written, I fancy, in which the assumptions of the author were not present, implicitly or explicitly.
Even the most blameless stories of child-life have at their base beliefs about something or the other. There is no such thing as not
believing *anything*. One who does not agree with Christianity must
agree with something else. Will it lead to better ends than those
prefigured in Lewis's books? I have read many modern works of
literature about which I am forced to say "I admire the workmanship, but deplore the sentiments"; but only of the Narnian Chronicles can I unhesitatingly say, "This is beautiful, and this is right."

Charles A. Huttar

C. S. Lewis's Narnia and the "Grand Design"

THIS paper is, of necessity, bifocal. One focus is C. S. Lewis's Chronicles of Narnia: I want to contribute to an understanding of Lewis's achievement in this work. My thesis is that the Chronicles must be seen as a literary whole. But how to label this whole I cannot discover in all the lexicon of literary structures. It is not epic, or novel, or any of the commonly known genres. Thus I must offer a new label, "scripture," and not only offer but explain and defend it—which accounts for the other focus.

In the present section I endeavor to explain the notion of "scripture" as a genre; the rest of the paper then may be seen as its defense—not directly, however, but in an effort to apply the notion to the Chronicles of Narnia. To the extent that my analysis "works" I will be able to claim validity for the genre "scripture."

"Scripture" might be taken to mean a canon of traditional utterances, held in especial reverence and embodying the wisdom and ideals of a culture. But this definition emphasizes the accidents of history and culture and has nothing to do with literary form; hence it would be, for our present purposes, misleading.

Let us single out from all the world's "scriptures" those most intimately related to our own culture, the Judeo-Christian sacred writings known as the Bible. Perhaps here we may find clues as to genre. Much recent study of "the Bible as literature" has been devoted to such inquiries. Recognizing that the Bible consists of many originally separate works, we might explore in some detail the distinctive literary qualities of its varied genres. Or, aware that literary influence results more from how a work is perceived than from what it actually is, we might inquire how our counterparts in earlier centuries perceived those literary qualities; an example would be the fascinating efforts in the sixteenth and seventeenth centuries to elaborate the principles of Hebrew poetics, before the now familiar concept of parallelism was enunciated.[1] We might also investigate the myriad transmutations of biblical archetype and narrative and doctrine and phrase into independent works of literature, all the way from the biblical idioms of *Piers Plowman* through the plot framework of Peele's *David and Bathsheba* and the symbolic patterns of *The Dunciad* to the elaboration of the Joseph story by Thomas Mann and the Pauline allegory of Christopher Fry's *A Phoenix Too Frequent*.[2] Another approach would be to study how the genres particularly associated with the Bible— psalm and parable and apocalypse, for example—have left their stamp on modern literary forms.

But none of these is what I have in mind. Beyond all the piecemeal study of the Bible's component parts it is possible to see the Bible as a whole in structural terms. It may seem strange to say this, when the word itself by derivation reminds us that it is a collection of materials widely separated in time, kind, intent, and sophistication. Yet it is certainly as a whole, more than as separate parts, that the Bible has had its greatest impact on the Western mind; may this be true not only of dogma but of literary form? I find literary justification for thinking of the Bible as a single work; it is not merely historical accident that compels us to do so. For this reason our choice of the Bible, out of all the world's "scriptures," is justified not merely because it is the most intimately related to our culture, but even more, because it is unique. Its uniqueness is a corollary of the unique Judeo-Christian incarnational view of history, in which Time is seen as linear and directional.

Surely the earliest biblical authors had no grand artistic scheme, shaping a massive outline for later writers to fill in. Still, the Bible *is* unified, by common strands of theme and imagery running throughout, and especially by the feature I have already mentioned, the idea of history as a meaningful succession of stages in a story that runs from the beginning of the world to its end. The later biblical writers saw themselves to be part of this ongoing process and deliberately wrote as continuers of a tradition; steeped in the older writings, they took traditional imagery and used it in a new way, unfolding its implicit meanings as the continuing process of history made these meanings become apparent.[3] The unity and structural arrangement of the Bible are matters of hindsight.

But it would be wrong to refer to the process of history as if it were something impersonal and mechanical. It is rather the concept of history as divine activity that imparts new depths of mean-

Ruoff, Gene W. "Romanticism." _The Grolier Electronic Encyclopedia_." CD-ROM. 1995 ed.

ing to the traditional images, and structure to the work as a whole. The underlying pattern of the Bible is not just discovered by its writers in the course of history: it *is* history. The beginning with Genesis and ending with Revelation and the basic division of Old and New Covenants illustrate how the whole structure is built on a foundation of history. Of course, the beginning recedes into prehistory and the end goes on into posthistory; both are necessarily mythographical. But if we think of "history" as the totality of events, and not limit it to events that have been recorded or might ever be recorded,[4] we shall see that Genesis and Revelation are not substantially different from the rest. Conceptually, the uniqueness of the Judeo-Christian scriptures lies in their refusal to draw a sharp line of demarcation between myth and history.

The beginning is light conquering darkness, the creative Word overcoming Chaos, followed quickly by the reappearance of the threat of Chaos in the Fall. The end is the final resurgence of Chaos, and then the destruction of destruction itself, and a new creation. In between, the whole story, reduced to its skeletal form, is redemption history. In this the Incarnation, Passion, and Resurrection of Christ are central and paradigmatic, but practically everything else is brought somehow into the pattern. The whole story is what Jonathan Edwards referred to as "the grand design of God"[5]— almost as if to designate God himself as the artist responsible for the original conception, which would mean that the basic structure of the scriptures is more something perceived by the human authors than something they invented; and that has deep implications for the nature of any artistic activity.

Be that as it may, the genre "scripture" in the sense that now concerns us seems to me to have these essential qualities: it is comprised of varied material loosely unified, it is a blend of mythography and realism, and its structure is that of the "grand design" —Creation and Fall, Redemption, and Eschatology.

How this genre has left its stamp on modern literary form is a question we might trace from the medieval cycle plays on down. Rather than taking that line now, let us look at a single recent work which strikingly reflects the characteristics just listed for the genre "scripture."

But some may wonder whether the Chronicles of Narnia can properly be thought of as a single work, especially as one deserving serious critical consideration. It has three strikes against it already. It came out in series form, and quite clearly the first book was written without any plan for a larger work; second, it is a collection of tales for children; and third, it has become immensely popular.

Nevertheless, Lewis's invention of Narnia has been hailed as a major achievement of the mythographic imagination, and some think that Lewis's place in history will owe as much to the Chronicles as to anything else he wrote. As for the unity, the example of the Bible shows us that retrospective structuring can convert what began as a loose collection into a literary whole.

Each of the seven books in the Chronicles of Narnia began, Lewis tells us, "with seeing pictures in my head." He wrote a few pages around the start of World War II but "at first . . . had very little idea how the story would go."[6] Lewis turned to other matters—indeed, to the most productive period in his life. The popular theological writings (*The Problem of Pain*, *The Screwtape Letters*, the books that were later to become *Mere Christianity*, and *Miracles*) all appeared in the period 1940-47. At the same time he was producing *Perelandra* and a nonfiction work closely related to it, *A Preface to Paradise Lost*; then *That Hideous Strength* and its companion, *The Abolition of Man*; and finally, in quick succession, *The Great Divorce*, the George MacDonald anthology, and the long essay "On Stories." To list the major themes of these works, and especially those they share in common, would be to anticipate what was preoccupying Lewis's mind during the period of writing the Chronicles of Narnia, 1949-53. Without seeming to claim for the Chronicles any exalted position beyond their due, we may say that in a way, all through this period, Lewis's mind was unconsciously preparing itself to return to the Pevensie children. By the late forties he was "talk[ing] vaguely of completing a children's book which he [had] begun."[7] Scarcely two years later, the first five books in the series were finished. What had happened? "Suddenly Aslan came bounding into it," he tells us. "Once He was there He pulled the whole story together"—this is the one that became *The Lion, the Witch and the Wardrobe*—"and soon He pulled the six other Narnian stories in after Him" [*Of Other Worlds*, p. 42].

But even this appears to me to be a highly condensed account of what the actual process must have been. We can infer from the meager surviving manuscripts that even after *The Lion, the Witch and the Wardrobe* Lewis didn't yet know where his inspiration was leading him.[8] During that intense period when the first five books were composed the scheme was growing in Lewis's mind, so that by the time publication of *Lion* was under way he was able to give the book's illustrator instructions for a map that contained references to *Prince Caspian* and *The Silver Chair*.[9] Further, these books occasionally cross-reference one another. Yet they still are more a series than a unified whole. Like the Bible, they contain material that is incidental to the main historical line: folktale (*The Horse and His Boy*) and voyage literature. The two books that frame the story of Narnia chronologically, *The Magician's Nephew* in which Narnia is created and *The Last Battle* in which it is destroyed, were the last to be written, and they didn't come as quickly as the others. After a year's work on *The Magician's Nephew* (among other things, of course, such as the *Oxford History of English Literature*), Lewis still was only three-quarters finished with it, and *The Last Battle* took him another year and a half. Only then could he sit down and write, for the record, a summary chronology of Narnian history from beginning to end[10]—not in itself evidence of literary unity, but still some indication of his interest in having the story of Narnia viewed as a whole. I conjecture it was mainly in late 1950 or early 1951, when all but the last two books in the series were completed, that the overall design of the Chronicles took firm shape in Lewis's mind. And it is these last two books that make of the whole collection a unified literary work, a panoramic survey of a world's entire existence, centering on the themes of creation, sin, redemption, and apocalypse: a sort of Bible for a Bibleless age.

In chapter viii of *The Magician's Nephew* four humans, a horse, and the witch Jadis find themselves in "an empty world" where there is no light, no wind, no sound. Then creation begins. There follows what must surely be one of Lewis's greatest achievements as a mythmaker. Those familiar with traditional accounts (I have chosen two for comparison, those in Genesis 1 and *Paradise Lost*) will notice a few echoes, and perhaps some hints as well of Lucretius or Ovid [*De rerum natura*, V.772-836; *Metamorphoses*, I.32-44, 69-75]; but on the whole, here is no scissors-and-paste job but a magnificently evocative new myth. The pagan critic Longinus had long since recognized the sublimity of Genesis, but the story is told there very rapidly, even summarily; indeed, the sublimity arises in part from the brevity. Milton offers considerably more detail—fascinating to follow, tracing out his classical and scientific and moralistic allusions. In Lewis we find both the detail and the sublimity, a sense of the numinous that Milton's Raphael, in his highly didactic conversation with Adam, is not permitted.

Two things account for the difference. First, Milton's description is almost entirely visual, while in Lewis, though visual imagery abounds, the other senses are also brought into play, and most of all the auditory. Second, Lewis is writing for children; therefore he need not stand on his dignity nor follow the grand style. He can risk a phrase such as "grassy land bubbling like water in a pot";

he can include "the first joke." For humor is no bar to true
"solemnity," as Lewis taught us in A Preface to Paradise Lost to
understand the word.[11] On the contrary, his evocation of the
numinous is aided by the recurring element of play, which is closely
allied to joy. Milton, taking a hint from Job 38:7, had the angelic
choirs celebrate the creation with song, both at the end of the first
day and again (accompanied by all the constellations in their
Pythagorean harmony) as the Son returned to heaven, his work of
creation complete. But such celebration fails to enter into his account of creation itself. Lewis, however, manages it. Traditionally
it is by God's *word* that creation is accomplished, as in Psalm
33:6 and in the first creation story in Genesis. By the time of
John 1:3 that Word has been identified as the second Person of
the Trinity. Lewis's imagination goes one step further, making
Aslan's creative voice a singing voice. Variations in the music
communicate his commands and call forth responses—from the
ground, life; from the spectators, fear, hatred, or joy. And when the
stars join in harmony, they too are a part of the creative activity.

When the animals burst full-grown from Narnian soil, Lewis
has several touches probably borrowed from Milton. In Lewis,
"the humps moved and swelled till they burst, and the crumbled
earth poured out of them, and from each hump there came out an
animal" [p. 113]. In Milton "the grassy clods now calved" [*Paradise Lost*, VII.463], and the great cats "the crumbled earth above
them threw / In hillocks" [468-69]. Lewis mentions specifically:
moles, dogs, stags ("at first Digory thought they were trees"—
p. 114), frogs (which immediately jumped into the river), panthers,
leopards "and things of that sort," birds, butterflies, bees, and an
elephant. In Milton's list, which follows in full, there are several
suggestive parallels: "the wild beast," cattle, lion, ounce, libbard,
tiger ("as the mole / Rising"), the stag (with "branching head"),
the elephant, the flocks, amphibious creatures (hippopotamus and
crocodile), insects, worms, ants, bees, serpents. Milton's lion is "paw-
ing to get free / His hinder parts"; Lewis's dogs are struggling as
if to get through a hedge, and his great cats "wash the loose earth
off their hind quarters." Milton's cattle fall at once to pasturing;
Lewis's dogs, frogs, panthers, and bees all begin immediately their
characteristic behavior. Most of these resemblances are far too
tenuous to support any assertion that Lewis consciously borrowed
from Milton, though doubtless the whole Miltonic passage was
stored in his mind somewhere, along with a great deal else, and
might have unconsciously furnished a detail here or there.

But the differences are much greater. Milton, of course, follows
the order of creation given in Genesis, which is why birds aren't

included in the passage just cited from *Paradise Lost*: they already existed. The traditional order of creation, you remember, was light, the firmament, dry land with grass and trees, the sun and moon and stars, fish and birds, animals, and finally man, whose creation is set apart stylistically and to whom is committed dominion over all the rest. Lewis has his visitors standing on dry land from the outset; when Aslan sings the stars appear first, all at once, and singing; then a light in the sky as of approaching dawn, against which the hills are silhouetted, together with a light wind (a suggestion of the divine spirit?); then the sun comes up, revealing a whole landscape, but without vegetation; then come the grass, trees, and flowers; and finally, the animals, including birds. Two steps in the process remain, the creation and the commissioning of man.

Man is already in Narnia and needs not to be created anew; in the light of what we shall soon observe regarding the Fall, it would be confusing if he were. The creation of man in Genesis is paralleled in Lewis by the elevation of selected animals to be Talking Beasts. At this moment, one of the climactic scenes in the whole Chronicles of Narnia, the stars burst forth again into song. With his breath and with "a swift flash like fire"—*two* symbols of the Holy Spirit—Aslan awakens the chosen animals to love, to think, to speak, to know. And he proceeds to appoint them a place in the hierarchy:

> Creatures, I give you yourselves. . . . I give to you forever this land of Narnia. I give you the woods, the fruits, the rivers. I give you the stars and I give you myself. The Dumb Beasts whom I have not chosen are yours also. Treat them gently and cherish them but do not go back to their ways lest you cease to be Talking Beasts. For out of them you were taken and into them you can return. [p. 118]

There are echoes here of two passages in Genesis—both things said to man: first, that all the plant kingdom has been given to him and to the beasts for food, and he is to have dominion over all the animal kingdom [1:28-30]; second, *after the Fall*, that man will "return unto the ground; for out of it wast thou taken; for dust thou art, and unto dust shalt thou return" [3:19].

Echoes—but just as important are the differences. The Talking Beasts do not fully occupy in Narnia the place given to man on Earth. Though man is not created in Narnia, he has a role there— a paradoxical role of rulership and service. Frank and Helen (for like Milton's Adam, who asks "In solitude / What happiness?" [*Paradise Lost*, VIII.364-65], the Cabby is allowed to send for his wife) are to be king and queen, but the reason is that "Adam's race shall help to heal" the harm brought into Narnia by humans. Their responsibilities are delineated. They are to name the animals, as Adam does in *Paradise Lost*, VIII.350, where they appear before him *two by two* (a detail Lewis incorporated earlier, when Aslan selected out the Talking Beasts). They have other responsibilities too, ones that would be inappropriate at the parallel place in Genesis, for that world was not yet fallen. They are to rule, do justice, protect from enemies, prevent oppression.

What are we to make of these differences? Is Lewis deliberately heterodox, is he simply enjoying imaginative freedom, or does he have reasons that lead him to deviate so much from the traditional creation myth? The form in which I have put the question hints strongly at my answer. In creating his mythical world of Narnia Lewis is consistent with principles he followed in his other imaginary worlds, in the space trilogy (published 1938-45). And these principles embody a theological point of no little importance.

Most of us take for granted the continuity of earthly experience with experience throughout the universe. Our age long ago adopted empiricism and uniformitarianism as working presuppositions, necessary to the endeavors we hold most valuable; the result by now, not surprisingly, has been to forget that they are no more than working presuppositions. Just as the speed of light and the atomic structure of silicon are constant throughout the universe, we easily assume that less tangible aspects of our own experience are constant as well—that our observations in the moral and spiritual realms are valid universally. It is a case, I think, of contemporary popular attitudes reduplicating those prevalent among professional thinkers a century ago. The professionals, meanwhile, have moved on. The Newtonian "law" of gravity may be adequate for mundane purposes, but ever since Einstein the world has been served notice that it may not simply project earthbound observation on a universal scale.[12] Such developments should prompt us to a certain skepticism about our assumptions, but they don't seem to have filtered down to the popular mind. Some scientists and some science-fiction writers may have the imagination to speculate of intelligent beings in other than human form, of whole life systems based on silicon instead of carbon; or, with even greater freedom, of a color spectrum or sense organs with no parallel in earthly biology, or social relationships following no human model. But such habits of thought are rare. Further, to imagine things outside our experience in the moral and spiritual realms is still more difficult.

As an example, let us consider the notion that only by a knowledge of evil can we fully appreciate the good. Since our whole experience bears witness to this obvious truth, it takes a great effort of the imagination, assisted perhaps by rigorous logic, to consider the possible existence of beings on this or any other world who might know and fully savor good per se, alone, by itself. Milton observed, in *Areopagitica*, how "involved and interwoven" is the knowledge of good with that of evil, and in how "many cunning resemblances hardly to be discerned." But then he went on to speculate that perhaps this was the meaning of the fruit of Adam's tree, the knowledge of good and evil: "That is to say, of knowing good by evil." For the central meaning of the Judeo-Christian doctrine of the Fall is that there are aspects of "human nature" as we have always experienced it that are at variance from "human nature" as it was meant to be and potentially is. When that idea is embodied in a myth which narrates that change actually taking place, it clashes head-on with the much more modern idea—equally mythical, in one sense of the word—of uniformitarianism.[13] But without the effort to get back behind Lyell and all he symbolizes, we shall miss the whole point of certain cruxes in *Paradise Lost*.

And we shall also fail to understand what Lewis was up to in the Chronicles of Narnia. For what Milton (and Christian tradition at large) saw as a radical break *within* the history of the human race,[14] Lewis projected into his imaginary worlds as a difference from earthly experience as we know it. His Malacandra is an unfallen world; realizing that fact is one of the major adjustments Ransom has to make when he visits it. Perelandra is also unfallen, differing, however, in that a temptation occurs there, but unsuccessfully. These two worlds differ also in the role played by humans. On Malacandra they are just visitors having no permanent impact, but on Perelandra they come to perform tasks that are crucial to overcoming the temptation; only then do they leave. How does Narnia compare with these worlds? The Fall is not a part of Narnian history; in this Narnia resembles Lewis's two imagined planets. Still, Narnia is in many ways like our fallen world. An evil force (a devil-figure) resides there permanently for most of Narnia's history; fallen children of Adam enter from time to time, some of them staying there and having descendants; and, for both these reasons, individual Narnians can fall (cf. Aslan's warning to the Talking Beasts quoted above, paralleled by a *post*lapsarian passage in Genesis). But there is no Fall as a racial event in Narnia, comparable to the Terran myth. The role of humans in the Chronicles needs to be described carefully. Unlike the otherworld visits in Lewis's space trilogy, the visits of humans to Narnia have no effect on earthly affairs, except insofar as they improve the character of a few children. But the converse is not true. Humans play an essential role in Narnian affairs: they are responsible for the entrance of evil in the very hour of creation, they influence the course of Narnian history with all their potential for both good and evil, and the true monarchs of Narnia are human.

This leads us to a further subtlety in Lewis's scheme. In addition to the truths he considered applicable only to Earth and its peculiar situation (the "silent planet" as he called it)—and the inability to know good per se is only a single example—he held to another class of principles, those truly universal. Two examples, especially germane to the part of the Chronicles presently under consideration, would be the principle of Hierarchy and that ultimate moral law which Lewis designated the "Tao."[15] Another would be the existence and the nature of God, including such attributes as his creative power, love, transcendence, and participation in human history. The high point of that participation is the Incarnation, which to Lewis meant a permanent union of the human with the divine.[16] Thus the humanity of God, though coming about through an event in mere earthly history, becomes a part of his nature and therefore of universal significance throughout all the worlds. It is for this reason that, though the intelligent life Ransom encounters on Malacandra has various bodily forms, on Perelandra, a younger planet, the King and Queen are in human shape. As the Green Lady explains, "Since our Beloved became a man, how should Reason in any world take on another form?" [*Perelandra*, p. 62].

To digress for a moment, we have now before us an interesting array of ways to view the universe. First there was the pre-Copernican view in which it all moved about Earth; this was sometimes accompanied by the anthropocentric idea that all the universe exists *for man's sake*. Concerning this idea two mistakes are often made: (1) that it is part of Christian theology,[17] (2) that it was stamped out when the new astronomy triumphed. On the contrary, it is still with us in a selfish, degenerate form today, and has borne fruit in our present ecological crisis. It also accounts in part for the energy with which space exploration has been pursued, and in this connection one of its most vigorous challengers has been C. S. Lewis. Furthermore, the scientific revolution quickly led in its turn, ironically enough, to a second kind of anthropocentricity, the attitude described above that human experience is the measure of all things. This too Lewis opposed, on the commonsense ground of Hamlet's remark to Horatio, "There are more things in heaven and earth . . . than are dreamt of in your philosophy." But his speculations on the subject, as we have seen, led him around to still a third sort of anthropocentric view, that it is both the glory and the tremendous burden of the human race to have been made the unique vehicle for God's identification of himself with his creatures.

Perhaps it would be well at this point to remind ourselves that these thoughts *were* speculations and that Lewis's other worlds are frankly imaginary. On the question whether other inhabited worlds actually exist he was (inevitably, one is tempted to add) agnostic. But if they should exist, he wanted to lay alongside the nineteenth-century anthropocentric view, which would in no case lack for champions, an alternative, perhaps an equal, possibility. Other "possibilities" may spring to mind as well: other *fallen* worlds; other, nonhuman, Incarnations. Presumably one might also build imaginative works on these speculations. Lewis was so habituated to using Occam's razor that he wasn't interested in doing so.

We now have the necessary framework for understanding Lewis's departures from Genesis in his Narnian creation. (1) According to Lewis's "Outline of Narnian History" the creation of Narnia took place A.D. 1900.[18] But the creation of the entire universe—the Genesis tradition—had obviously taken place long before; Lewis saw this as fact and, by definition, among those truths that have universal validity. The creation of Narnia, then, turns out to be quite a different sort of thing from the creation presented in Genesis. A major imaginative conception in Lewis is that of a world existing *in potentia* from the beginning, with land and water topography, but lifeless, waiting for the instant when it should be "turned on" —for that is the best way to describe the sudden appearance all at once of the stars, as the darkness and silence of this "empty world" in an instant give way to light and music. A similar effect is achieved in the sunrise which follows, as if the new world were set in motion at the flip of a switch, initiating the process (familiar to us) of the gradual coming of dawn. That "turning on" is not, strictly speaking, creation; all Aslan actually creates are the various forms of life on Narnia.

(2) Another difference is that the "breath of life" is imparted to beasts, not man. This is inconsistent not only with the Genesis tradition but with the principle Lewis set forth in *Perelandra* concerning Reason in human form. But Lewis had no choice: Talking Beasts are not only one of the hardiest conventions of children's literature, but they had also been a part of this world from the first book. This seems to support our conclusion that when he began the Chronicles Lewis did not anticipate the form it would finally take. Having given these chosen beasts Reason, Lewis must (in accord with another of his universal principles) find them a new place in the hierarchial Chain of Being. That is why they are given dominion over the dumb animals, which in Genesis is given to man.

(3) Still, man has a role in Narnia too. Ultimate rule (under Aslan) belongs to him. This is in keeping with the Green Lady's observation, and it holds true from the first book, where Sons of

Adam and Daughters of Eve are required in order to set matters right. But the humans who receive the throne are already fallen. That is why Aslan asks Frank, "Can you use a spade and a plough and raise food out of the earth?" So, too, things said to man before and after the Fall in Genesis are telescoped into this one scene at the finish of creation, concluding with the somewhat Abrahamic promise to Frank and Helen which ends chapter xi.

We must now try to rephrase more accurately the description of the Chronicles of Narnia as "a sort of Bible." The term is accurate enough as a label of the genre: a loose collection of varied material structured to highlight the climactic events of world history, beginning, middle, and end. But the history is not that of our world. If Lewis finally conceived of the Chronicles as a Bible, it is a Narnian Bible. Narnia's 2,555 years occupy less than half a century of human time and have no effect on human history. *Indirect* relationships may exist insofar as universal truths (e.g., hierarchy, moral law, the identities good/creation and evil/destruction, the interplay of transiency and permanence) produce similar situations in the two worlds. But in no way may the climactic events of Narnian history be equated with those of Earth. This is what Lewis meant by insisting that he was not writing allegory. Narnia's history resembles ours because the universe is truly a *uni*verse; when they differ, there is a reason—not some supposed allegory "breaking down."

The importance of this point becomes clear as we move to the next major biblical theme, how one man's disobedience "brought death into the world, and all our woe." In Narnia that does not happen. Nevertheless there are some points of tangency. For the concept of moral law, anywhere, implies the possibility of choice, and that in turn opens the door to temptation. Like Milton, and for the same reason just given, Lewis returned again and again in his writing to temptation scenes. The Chronicles of Narnia contains at least five, in which a number of significant biblical and Miltonic parallels may be noted. I do not propose to treat these in detail, offering instead just a list and some comments.

(1) Digory's temptation in Charn [*The Magician's Nephew*, ch. iv]. As in *Paradise Lost*, the man and woman quarrel and a part of the temptation's appeal—here, the major part—is to curiosity.

(2) Digory's temptation by the Witch [*The Magician's Nephew*, ch. xiii]. Here the parallels are numerous. There is a walled garden atop a lofty mountain [cf. *Paradise Lost*, IV.131-47]. The only proper access is through an eastern gate, though Jadis leaps over the wall instead [cf. 178-93]. The garden is deliciously fragrant

[cf. 156-66] and in the very center is a tree of life with silver fruit [cf. 218-20, golden fruit]. The Witch's attempt to persuade Digory to eat the fruit has much in common with the temptation of Eve in *Paradise Lost*, Book IX.

(3) Edmund's defection to the Witch [*The Lion, the Witch and the Wardrobe*, ch. iii-ix]. He is led astray first by greed—in this case, a boyish hunger for Turkish Delight—and then by appeals to his ego.

(4) Lucy reading the Magic book [*The Voyage of the "Dawn Treader*," ch. x]. The appeal is to forbidden knowledge.

(5) The temptations of Rilian and the others [*The Silver Chair*, ch. xi-xii]. The Prince's enchantment reminds us of the temptation scene in *Comus*. Both *Comus* and *Paradise Lost* are in the background of the next scene, in which a serpentine temptress of dubious parentage casts a rhetorical spell, obtruding false rules prankt in reason's garb.[19]

We may also note that when Digory returns from the garden, faithful to his promise, Aslan greets him with "Well done!"—the same greeting given Abdiel in *Paradise Lost* when he forsakes the rebel angels and returns to the camp of the faithful [VI.29]. Poggin the dwarf, who alone of the dwarfs fights on Tirian's side in *The Last Battle*, is also an Abdiel figure—a resister of temptation.

The next climactic event in human history is the Redemption. But like the Fall which made it necessary, this event is not universal but peculiar to Earth. There is no need to repeat in Narnia the full pattern of Christian redemption.

This will seem at first difficult to believe, there are so many obvious resemblances between Aslan and Christ. Each is the Son of the Highest and his emissary to the world; each possesses great power linked with immense self-control; each knows sorrow; each is killed as an innocent substitute for the guilty, and then returns to life.[20] But Aslan dies for Edmund alone, not for the whole world. The Atonement of mankind is a doctrine unique (so far as we may suppose) to Earth.

The principle of voluntary self-sacrifice on another's behalf, however, is one that is valid throughout the universe. Often it takes the form, in Narnian as well as in earthly myth, of a descent into the underworld, a journey to danger and death, to perform a rescue. Aslan, who submits silently to the Witch's knife, going for all he knows on a journey from which he will not return—this point is important[21]—is only one among many in the Chronicles who enact this archetypal descent. Lucy venturing into the Magician's room to free the Monopods from invisibility; Caspian sailing to the world's end to break the spell on the three sleeping lords; Jill and Eustace and Puddleglum journeying underground to rescue Prince

Rilian—all these also exemplify the pattern. Digory offers an example too, but with differences: he journeys to Paradise, not Hell, and does it in obedience to Aslan, and only secondarily to save his mother from death; but once there, he faces a temptation that threatens to destroy him. All these are Christ figures; but none mean the same thing to Narnia that Christ means to human history, because Narnia is not Earth.

In *The Last Battle* the history of Narnia comes to an end. Lewis's invented eschatology resembles these features of scriptural eschatology: Antichrist, Armageddon, final judgement, destruction of the world, the end of time, and the new paradisal creation.

It is all done, of course, as befits the audience, with a light touch. Puzzle, the lovable ass, dressed in a lionskin that he has fished out of the pool, is a far cry from the beast emerging from the sea in Revelation 13, with its ten crowned horns and seven heads marked with blasphemous titles. But the parallel is there. A false Aslan is set up—very pointedly, an anti-Christ—and all are made to worship him, all save a small remnant who are true to the old Narnia traditions. Compare Revelation 13:9-10: "If anyone has ears to hear, let him listen: Captivity for those who are destined for captivity; the sword for those who are to die by the sword. This is why the saints must have constancy and faith" [Jerusalem Bible]. The fate of the remnant reflects the persecution of Christians under Nero and his successors, as St. John identifies contemporary political evil with the unseen principalities that war against the faithful. It is in the spirit of this tradition that Lewis, in narrating the machinations of Ape and Cat to promote the false Aslan, attacks the demagoguery and false rationalism that characterize corrupt political activity in our own century.

Compared to the terrible image of Armageddon [Revelation 14: 18-20; 19:17-21], the last battle of Narnia doesn't amount to much; perhaps again we have what is suitable in a book for children. Yet the central importance of this scene is underscored by Lewis's choice of it for his book's title. And the next event in the scriptural eschatological vision is likewise paralleled in *The Last Battle*. In Revelation 20:12-13 the entire harvest of the dead comes before God to be judged. A fuller description of this impressive scene is found in Matthew 25:31-46, where the sheep and goats are separated for everlasting punishment or life eternal, according to the way they treated "the least of these my brethren." This passage has furnished many details for what is surely one of Lewis's most unforgettable scenes. The world of Narnia is coming to an end. Driven almost as in a stampede, all the Narnians pass before Aslan and, according to whether they can look upon him with desire or hatred, they go by on his right hand or his left. Even one devotee of the wicked god Tash finds himself in Aslan's country, thus proving the principle in the Matthew passage that God may be truly served even by those who do not know Him to call by name.

In the same discourse Matthew records Jesus as saying that "heaven and earth shall pass away" [24:35]. This is very much a part of New Testament apocalyptic tradition; we find it also in 2 Peter 3:10, which speaks of destruction by fire, and Revelation 20:11, where fire from heaven is part of the context but the immediate cause of heaven and earth ceasing to be is simply the removal from them of the divine sustaining power. This is closer to the way Lewis does it. Unhampered by any rainbow promise to Noah about how the earth will or will not end, Lewis has his "other world" overwhelmed by the rising sea: what was dry land becomes chaos once again underneath the waves [ch. xiv]. Essentially the process of creation as we saw it in *The Magician's Nephew* is, step by step, undone. Already the sky is black as at the beginning: there are no stars, for "Aslan had called them home" [p. 151]. Once the land has been drowned, our attention is turned to the dying sun (reminiscent of that weak luminary at the end of the world of Charn, in *The Magician's Nephew*) in whose rays "the whole waste of shoreless waters looked like blood." The vivid sensory images of Revelation have entered into Lewis's mind and are coming out at other places in the story—yet still as powerfully evocative parts of a whole picture, a Gestalt, that is in the apocalyptic tradition. There is a final Johannine touch as the giant Father Time throws "his horn into the sea" [cf. Revelation 18:21]. Time has ended; eternity is begun.

For the end of Narnia is the beginning of a new Paradise which turns out to be, in fact, the true Narnia—a notion very close indeed to the New Testament vision of a new heaven and new earth [2 Peter 3:13; Rev. 21:1]. But the image that dominates the last two chapters of Revelation is that of the city, the new Jerusalem, and Lewis prefers the garden. I find him much less Hebraic here, and owing more to Plato and Milton—and Wordsworth, for in Aslan's country a splendor has truly returned to the grass [p. 171]. The way the Narnians float effortlessly *up* a waterfall reminds me of Milton's concept that human bodies eventually could "turn all to spirit" and "winged ascend"—lines on which Lewis had particularly remarked in *A Preface to Paradise Lost* [p. 68]. But this, of course, is fully in keeping with those cryptic New Testament accounts of the resurrected body of Christ, and with

Christian belief in the mystery of bodily resurrection. So too in Aslan's country everyone has his physical being at its prime; age, pain, and stiffness are vanished. And this is only the beginning of new experiences. Over and over the motto is repeated, "Further up and further in." Lewis owes much here to the Christian Platonist views of the fourth century, which he says went into the making of the "Medieval Model": the view that "we are creatures of the margin."[22] As the Professor in *The Last Battle* sputters, "It's all in Plato" [p. 170]. That is the true "sunlit" country, to which Earth as we know it, and Narnia too, are mere "Shadow-Lands" [p. 183]. Earlier in the Chronicles of Narnia, Lewis's embodiment of similar ideas at some length in *The Silver Chair* shows how deeply Plato's myth of the cave affected his imagination. But as we've already seen in Lewis's emphasis on the body, he is too materially minded to go all the way with Plato. His Paradise is filled with delicious odors and "fruits such as no one has seen in our world." The first thought of the humans in the story is that fruit so tempting must be forbidden—but this is "the country where everything is allowed" [p. 137].

Lewis's church admonishes its adherents to think about the "last things," a phrase which includes, alongside the last judgement and the joys of heaven, death. This represents to us a common duality in the concept of time. The "time" of which we are abstractly aware is the whole of history, the world's time; but another "time" of which we are immediately aware is our own, individually, from birth to death. In one sense, within a scriptural context we know time as a reality that ends in apocalypse of the sort we have been speaking of; but in another sense, equally valid, we know time as a reality that is coextensive with our own life. This duality too is reflected in the Chronicles of Narnia. A familiar image of personal nightmare is evoked in *The Last Battle* when the stable door through which the heroes are thrown is described as "a grim door . . . more like a mouth" [p. 128]. As the newcomers move on to Aslan's country they meet the Phoenix, perennial symbol of resurrection, and they find the old Narnian heroes there to greet them. These, having died much earlier, have already come into their eternal Paradise. At the end of *The Silver Chair* we witness Caspian's resurrection and rejuvenation by a drop of Aslan's blood. Still earlier in the Chronicles, at the end of *The Voyage of the "Dawn Treader,"* comes (significantly, "when the third day dawned") a vision of Paradise in the Utter East, and one of the adventurers chooses to go on there. (Incidentally, the ease with which we find ourselves cross-referencing to other parts of the Chronicles, almost in the manner of a Bible expositor, is perhaps another result of Lewis's following Scripture as a generic model for his work.)

I have said that underlying the structure of the genre "scripture" is a concept of history as linear and directional. Something of this dynamic quality rubs off on the way the story is told. Lewis was able to do things in *The Last Battle* that he could not have done earlier, because it is the eschatological close of the work. In thinking about Creation, Fall, and Redemption in Narnia we had to pay attention to the many ways they differ from Earth's story as the Scriptures give it. What strikes us about the last things, and especially about Lewis's vision of heaven, is how little it differs. There is a reason. When the Children in *The Last Battle* get far enough in and high enough up, they discover that not Narnia alone but England too, in its ideal form, is a part of Aslan's country. All roads point toward the Center. The various worlds, real and imaginary, may be quite different at the beginning, but the end is one.

Eliane Tixier

Imagination Baptized,
or,
"Holiness" in the Chronicles of Narnia

IN his Preface to *Imagination and the Spirit*, Chad Walsh asked "whether esthetics can illuminate and perhaps rejuvenate our understanding of religion."[1] It seems to me that C. S. Lewis's Chronicles of Narnia could provide an answer to this question. Indeed, they appeal to our imaginations and our hearts—through a precise mode of expression which, after Lewis, I shall call *Holiness*—and rejuvenate our understanding of religion, or, I should rather say, bring us nearer to the mystery of God, and to a spiritual world we might otherwise have been tempted to reject as outdated and uninteresting.

When describing the genesis of his Narnian stories, Lewis said: "It all began with a picture."[2] In the light of some of his other writings, we could add: it all began with George MacDonald's *Phantastes*—with the baptism of Lewis's imagination one October night at Bookham. Indeed the special quality which Lewis acknowledged, and was happy to find, in *Phantastes*, seems to me to be the very quality which, years later, he himself offered to his readers in the Chronicles of Narnia. This special quality he called *goodness* in his anthology of MacDonald's works[3] in 1946, and *Holiness* in *Surprised by Joy* [p. 179] in 1954. One might be surprised to find these terms applied to a work of art, for they do not belong, properly speaking, to the vocabulary of literary criticism. Furthermore, Lewis never fully explained what he meant by the term *Holiness* when he used it to characterize George MacDonald's work. Perhaps the best way to understand the significance he attached to it is to recall how, through *Phantastes*, Lewis himself came to have, and finally to name, this imaginative experience.

136

As anyone who is even slightly familiar with Lewis will know, an important aspect of his personality was the intense feeling of longing which he felt time and again, more or less acutely, throughout his life. The episode of the black-currant bush, or of his reading of *Tegner's Drapa*, or his discovery of *The Twilight of the Gods*, all of which are recalled in *Surprised by Joy*, have become classical passages in Lewis's work, as familiar to readers as the skating or nutting episodes in Wordsworth's *Prelude*: they clearly illustrate the strong desire Lewis often felt for something outer and farther away, a far-off place or season, an unattainable world beyond our own. Very early, owing to the great number and variety of his readings in English and foreign literature, Lewis became aware that many romantic poets and writers had had the same experience, and had in their turn described their romantic aspirations in various terms, such as *sehnsucht*, homesickness, or nostalgia. Among these authors, one could name Wordsworth, Keats, and more particularly, William Morris. Lewis in fact counted himself among those "persistent admirers" of Morris he described in his essay "William Morris."[4] He once wrote to a friend that he "grew up on W. Morris and George Macdonald."[5]

In Morris's romances Lewis found the expression of feelings he had already sensed in himself. The "spur in the side" which made Ralph hasten from his father's palace on his quest for the Well at the World's End was a familiar one to Lewis, even if he gave it different names, like the "pang," or the "stab" of Joy. Morris's message to Lewis was one that he was most ready, even eager, to receive. In inciting Lewis to take his distance with the world, to "sail beyond the frontier of that earth and world" [*Selected Literary Essays*, p. 229], Morris was inviting him to take a first step towards the spiritual experience that was to come. He helped to make Lewis aware, not intellectually, but imaginatively—by the spell of his works—that this world is not all, that deep in our hearts is an unquenchable thirst for the water that gives immortality, eternal youth and happiness, eternal beauty and love, the treasures Ralph finds at the end of his quest. In part through Morris's influence, Lewis awakened—at least partially—from "the evil enchantment of worldliness,"[6] or what he described in one of his letters as "the mundane point of view" that makes you feel "your book and pipe and chair are enough for happiness" [letter to Greeves, 22 September 1931]. Morris invited him to listen to "the first, faint whisper of the wind from beyond the world" [letter to Greeves, 8 November 1931].

But it seemed that Morris's power ended there. He was able to

wake the reader from his drowsiness and "state the question" [Se-
lected Literary Essays, p. 230], but he could not help him further,
because he himself apparently did not know the answer. Although
Ralph reaches the Well, one is tempted to say that his quest is
not totally successful; admittedly, he finds the Well, but after being
"there," he turns back again to a life little different from the dreary
life he has left. After presenting us "in one vision the ravishing
sweetness and the heart-breaking melancholy of our experience"
[Selected Literary Essays, p. 231], Morris does not invite us to
"pitch our tents" in this long-sought place. The Well, once reached,
fades away from our minds and is forgotten, while Ralphs' journey
home is related to us and becomes the matter of the fourth book.
Morris, or his heroes, turned back to our world, and this return was
ever, to Lewis, a source of disenchantment. He felt as though he
had not been accepted into the dance, as though a door had been
shut in his face and the world he was left in was irretrievably dull:
"The whole glimpse withdrawn, the world turned commonplace
again" [Surprised by Joy, p. 16].

Morris was not the only writer who did not seek far enough. Lewis
on several occasions made allusions to the incompleteness of
Wordsworth's quest.[7] He spoke in the same vein of a lack of spiritual experience in Keats: "He knows about the hunting for 'it'
and longing and wondering: but he has, as yet, no real idea of what
it would be if you found it" [letter to Greeves, 8 November 1931].
Had Lewis met only such writers as these, he might have re-
mained forever dissatisfied; all his life he might have known the
uncomfortable "sense of desire and loss" which he described as
the sad sequel of the pangs of Joy [Surprised by Joy, p. 73].
Years later he became aware of this, and he wrote to Greeves that
Morris was "the most essentially pagan of all poets," adding:
"Of what this longing really pointed to, of the reason why beauty
made us homesick, of the reality behind, I thought he had no inkling" [31 (sic) June 1930]. By this time, Lewis himself had come to
"an inkling of the reality behind," and for this reason he could be
lucid about Morris and other romantics; what is more, he was able
to explain what our desires meant: a thirst to be in our "true country,"
to please God and be reunited with Him ["The Weight of Glory,"
p. 4].

The first time Lewis seems to have had a glimpse of a "reality
behind"—if not yet of a world which would be "our proper place,"
as he says in "The Weight of Glory" [p. 3]—was when he read
MacDonald's Phantastes. With MacDonald, he was made aware
of the "real symbolical import" of longing, and of the existence of

"something beyond pleasure and pain."[8] In some way this experience brought to a full expression feelings that works by other romantic writers had merely suggested. It took Lewis further into the mystery of life. Although this inner discovery was still only dimly perceived, too weak and hazy to touch his mind and reason, it was forcible enough to arouse his imagination, fill him with peace, and reconcile him with this world.

Indeed, *Phantastes* helped Lewis to cross an imaginative frontier: one might say that this book, as a work of art, existed at one time in Lewis's mind for what MacDonald called in his *Unspoken Sermons* "the show of things," and which he described thus: "Their show is the face of far deeper things than they. . . . It is through their *show*, not through their *analysis*, that we enter into their deepest truths. . . . Nature as well exists primarily for her face, her look, her appeals to the heart and the imagination, her simple service to human need" [*MacDonald Anthology*, p. 69—emphasis mine]. Lewis became receptive to deeper truths because of such a "quality," new to him—a "bright shadow" which shone through the book and which he was later to name "Holiness." At this point the name mattered little; the facts themselves (these impressions that came to him as "sheer qualities"[9] and not as reasonable deductions) were far more important.

With MacDonald, Lewis discovered that there were different types of longing, and that some of them, such as the wish to reach a long-looked-for place, or to grasp a long-coveted treasure, would never have a happy ending. Anodos and Cosmo in *Phantastes*, learn from experience that some treasures can be broken or snatched away at any time, like the musical crystal globe of the maiden in the wood, which exploded in her hands when Anodos held it too long. In the same story, Joy appears to be attainable at the end of another form of quest which could be called a quest for "goodness," and which is the true impulse that draws Anodos into the woods of Fairyland.

The *real* story in *Phantastes*, the *real* travels and adventures, have no other geography than that of the soul. The action takes place in what Anodos himself calls "the deeper fairy-land of the soul."[10] Joy is to be attained and kept within our own hearts, through an inner disposition that is hard to come by. It appears when our haunting shadow, the "demon shadow" [*Phantastes*, p. 86] that ties us to the ground and to reality, has ceased to follow us, when the wish to gather and to grasp has been abandoned, when "nobleness" has become incarnate, when we love enough to forget ourselves, to accept the death of any selfish wish, the death of our "shadow of darkness." Thus does Cosmo welcome death, "*good* Death," as Lewis calls it in his anthology of MacDonald's works [p. 21], death in the sense of self-denial and true love; he accepts the request of his Lady: "If you love me, set me free, even from yourself" [*Phantastes*, p. 113]. As a result of this inner disposition of detachment, the world is no longer that scene one wearies of and flees for a better place; it is now perceived with the wonderment of a child. Like the young girl after she has lost the globe she has clung to so tightly, one "does not care" any longer. The loss of the drive to possess and of the avidity for happiness enables one to sing freely, to bring forth the music hidden in one's soul.

There can be no disappointment, no disillusionment, at the end of a story by MacDonald, for unlike *The Well at the World's End*, his fairyland does not lie beyond the almost unattainable Great Mountains. Anodos's quest is not unique: whatever he has lived in his own soul can be experienced by the reader. The "bright shadow" Lewis had seen in *Phantastes* can brighten our own lives [*Surprised by Joy*, p. 181], the "Holiness" of this "dream" is able to shock us "more fully awake" than we are for most of our lives [*MacDonald Anthology*, p. 17]. It was in just this way that Lewis's imagination was baptized, and for this reason that he was able, consciously or not, to cast this bright shadow on his own Narnian Tales.

Lewis's discovery of "Holiness" in *Phantastes* was only a first stage in a long process of development. It had originally been a quality whose appeal was essentially to the imagination and whose originality was two-fold: it pointed to a new meaning for longing, which, instead of ending in disappointment and dullness, seemed to lead to "deeper mysteries." It also encouraged a liberation of the self, initiating, though in a very rudimentary way, what Lewis was to call a "centripetal movement": the sign of his decreasing subjectivism and the preparation for his welcoming one day the presence of Him whom he named, at the start, the "One" or the "Other." "Holiness," through *Phantastes*, was, as it were, opening a window that looked out on a mountain, whereas until that time, in the company of Morris and others, Lewis had been looking on a walled orchard. But just as awareness of the existence of a mountain makes one wish to climb it, Holiness once discovered, or, one might say, "tasted," enticed Lewis to go further still, to the logical conclusion of such a direction, to union with God, the "welcome into the heart of things," as he described it in "The Weight of Glory" [p. 11]. Holiness was a way of discovering what Bede Griffiths calls "the Golden String," "the grace . . . given to every soul," which helps us to "find our way out of the labyrinth of life."[11]

This second stage in Lewis's development was to take a long time. Almost fifteen years separate the baptism of imagination at Bookham and the "total surrender" in the Trinity Term of 1929 [*Surprised by Joy*, pp. 181, 228]. During these years, the experience of Holiness which Lewis had tasted so sharply with *Phantastes* mellowed, until finally what had been conceived in the imagination could become an act of life: "Enough had been thought, and said, and felt, and imagined," Lewis later wrote. "It was about time that something should be done" [*Surprised by Joy*, p. 225]. In what he called one of his first free acts, he knelt and prayed [*Surprised by Joy*, p. 228]. At the end of this period Lewis could give to "Holiness" its full meaning, and let this quality take him beyond longing to its very object, to the top of the mountain and to God:

> Hearing these old familiars . . . I knew that the enemy would take advantage of the vague longings and tendernesses to try & make one believe later on that *he* had the fulfilment which I really wanted: so I baulked him by letting the longings go even deeper and turning my mind to the One, the real object of all desire, which . . . is what we are *really* wanting in all wants. [Letter to Greeves, 1 June 1930]

By now, Holiness had fully become that inner quality which enables one to see the world anew, to see the beauty, and the divine imprint on it: that very quality which enables Psyche to see a castle where Orual sees but heather, or robes when Orual sees only rags [*Till We Have Faces*, pp. 125-26], and which makes us conscious, as Lewis phrased it in "The Weight of Glory," that "it is immortals whom we joke with, work with, marry, snub, and exploit" [p. 15].

The fact that this new insight into the world should have been initially given to Lewis, and now offered to us, not as the result of an effort of reason, but as the outcome of another mode of apprehension, the imaginative one, raises the question of the validity of this approach, and invites us to explain this confidence in imagination which Lewis's writings—and this essay—imply.

In the first place, Lewis, like many romantics, intuitively trusted the capacity of the imagination to be "a faculty of truth." The following formulation by his former student Bede Griffiths might have been written by Lewis himself: "I had discovered that there is a truth of experience, which is mediated through the imagination, and which often gives a deeper insight into reality than abstract thought."[12] Like Griffiths, Lewis believed that there had been a time when man could "only approach the divine mystery by means of images," and when the work of the artist was in fact "to represent or 'make present' the divine mystery in an image in such a way that the people may enter into communion with it" [*The Golden String*, p. 140]. In this view art, and therefore imagination, were clearly seen as a path to God and to true worship. Lewis held this belief to the end of his life. In one of his last works, *Letters to Malcolm*, he said again: "When the *purport* of [biblical] images . . . seems to conflict with the theological abstractions, trust the purport of the images every time. For our abstract thinking is itself a tissue of analogies. . . . The footprints of the Divine are more visible in that rich soil than across rocks or slag-heaps" [p. 52].

However, this belief of Lewis's was far from an abstract conviction; it had been preceded by experience. Lewis well knew that on the long winding road that had led him to Christ, one of the first steps, before he was even able to conceive any "reasonable" assent, had been the welcoming of a new quality which had come to him as a "visitation of Joy" appealing solely to his imagination. As the first calls had come to his imagination and sensibility through longing, so had the answer come along the same paths, with the imaginative experience of Holiness. It is his own story and experience he is describing in *The Pilgrim's Regress* when he has John hear these words near the Canyon: "For this end I made your senses and for this end your imagination, that you might see My face and live" [p. 171]. Lewis was first converted, "baptized," in his imagination, his sensibility, in his latent capacity for worship; the complementary faculty, the intellect, became involved and was "baptized" later on in Oxford.

This important role played by the imagination was not just a privilege of the early days, or of the first hints, in the time when the intellect was still spiritually dormant. Imagination again played its part when Lewis was hesitating before taking the last step, before "the absolute leap in the dark" [*Surprised by Joy*, p. 228]. It was imagination that came to his aid when the intellect was powerless to sweep away his last resistance:

Right in the centre of Christianity . . . you keep on getting something quite different and very mysterious, expressed in those phrases I have so often ridiculed ("propitiation"—"sacrifice"—"the blood of the Lamb") —expressions wh. I cd. only interpret in senses that seemed to me either silly or shocking. Now what Dyson and Tolkien showed me was this: that if I met the idea of sacrifice in a Pagan story I didn't mind it at all: again, that if I met the idea of a god sacrificing himself to himself . . . I liked it very much and was mysteriously moved by it: again, that the idea of the dying and reviving god (Balder, Adonis, Bacchus) similarly moved me provided I met it anywhere *except* in the Gospels. The reason was that in Pagan stories I was prepared to feel the myth as profound and suggestive of meanings beyond my grasp even tho' I could not say in cold prose "what it meant." Now the story of Christ is simply a true myth: a myth working on us in the same way as the others, but with this tremendous difference that it *really* happened. [Letter to Greeves, 18 October 1931]

Because of this conversation with his friends and other experiences, Lewis came to look upon imagination not as a poor *ancilla*, but as a reliable and important faculty, leading to a special and privileged sort of insight. We can the more easily appreciate the value he attached to myth, in which he saw "a real though unfocussed gleam of divine truth falling on human imagination" [*Miracles*, p. 139n]. It is for these reasons that he himself offered us in his works, and especially in his Narnian Chronicles, imaginative experiences that could touch us in the same manner as *Phantastes* had touched him, inviting us to taste true Joy in our real country.

Lewis had been a Christian for several years when he created the world of Narnia. There had been time for his spiritual life to deepen in proportion as his life of prayer and intimacy with God and with Scripture had grown. Perhaps we could say that Holiness had entered his life, not just as an imaginative experience, but in *fact*. As Walter Hooper said: "In Lewis the natural and the supernatural seemed to be one, to flow one into the other."[13] In 1954, the time had come for Holiness to emerge as the ripe and weighty fruit of Lewis's mystical experience. It was no longer a hint that he had received from another; it was now a quality of his own, overflowing from his soul and offered to us in the stories of Narnia.

Lewis had once written to Bede Griffiths: "It is often said that conversion alters only the direction, not the character of our minds" [unpublished letter, 8 January 1936]. The same might be said of Holiness, which, in one sense, is the apex of conversion. Neither an addition to nor an alteration in the character of the Chronicles of Narnia, Holiness appears simply as a new direction. It is not so much that we will find many religious themes properly speaking, but that the treatment of familiar themes will be different: it will bear the imprint of Holiness. As Holiness does not change the basic personality of a man, but merely his manner of living, so it does not change the basic content of his artistic work, but rather influences his manner of being, his way of telling a story.

LONGING

Longing was bound to be a recurrent theme in the Narnian tales, since it had dominated Lewis's life for so long. In general, in the Chronicles, it is a healthy longing that contains little of romantic

nostalgia, probably because it is either associated with memories
of past blessedness that inspire confidence, or involved with real
hopes which have a likely prospect of fulfillment. Before the end
of each tale, the "call" and "desire" implied in longing are perfectly satisfied. Sometimes the final answer comes unexpectedly as a
state of extreme happiness, as when Jill leaves behind her the school
playground where bullies have been pursuing her and discovers
Aslan's country, a never-conceived Garden of Eden, before her surprised, naive eyes [*The Silver Chair*, pp. 10-11]. In other instances,
Joy comes as the restoration of a long-lost happiness: when at last
Old Narnia triumphs in *Prince Caspian*, most of her creatures
welcome this denouement as a "Paradise Regained." Elsewhere,
happiness is a promise, a bliss at the very end of the journey
of life, as it is for Reepicheep, the chivalrous mouse in *The Voyage
of the "Dawn Treader."* His ardent hope and "quivering . . .
happiness" on reaching the very "end of the world" [pp. 212-13]
remind one of the promise of the Holy City in the Book of Revelation.

In all cases, whether it be the Garden of Eden, or Heaven reached
after "the Last Battle," longing always opens on a land of happiness, the land of Aslan, the land of God. The hope, the assurance
of such a final resolution actually prepares the way for Holiness.
For the certitude that God does not hide Himself, that He holds
out happiness to His creatures, gives to the tale a special direction
and marks it with a seal of Holiness.

But if in the Narnian tales all longing is satisfied, it still appears in a variety of forms, inspiring many different reactions in the
characters. A glance at some of these may help to illuminate Lewis's
conception of longing. First there is a form of humble longing that
is barely felt, so dim that it never reaches the level of clear consciousness, and still less knows its name. When its fulfillment
comes, it brings an answer to a never-asked question; at most it
may stir vague and pleasant memories. The cabby's polite and awk-
ward reply to Aslan's question is characteristic:

> "Do you know me?"
> "Well, no sir. . . . Leastways, not in an ordinary manner of speak-
> ing. Yet I feel somehow, if I may make so free, as 'ow we've met be-
> fore." [*The Magician's Nephew*, pp. 136-37]

In another kind of longing, the emotion may not have been analyzed or consciously felt, but light comes at the very moment of its
fulfillment, and with it comes the possibility of calling longing by
its name and of experiencing thankfulness for the gift received. Such

is the case of the Unicorn, who exclaims with relief at the end of
The Last Battle: "This is the land I have been looking for all my
life, though I never knew it till now" [p. 171]. Caspian makes a
similar discovery on drinking water from the Last Sea: "That's real
water, that," he says in amazement. "I'm not sure that it isn't going
to kill me. But it is the death I would have chosen—if I'd known
about it till now" [*The Voyage of the "Dawn Treader,"* p. 199].

Several kinds of conscious longing are to be found in the tales.
One of these is a longing that is sustained, even whetted, by
memory. Its fulfillment is long awaited and comes as the healing
of a wound: thus is Old Narnian life restored after Miraz's long
tyranny. Lucy's experience on the Island of the Voices is also a
beautiful illustration of this form of longing: in a Magician's book
she finds "the loveliest story [she has] ever read," and no sooner
has she finished it than she exclaims: "I wish I could have gone
on reading it for ten years. At least I'll read it over again" [*The
Voyage of the "Dawn Treader,"* p. 133]. In the same way, Lewis
had once "read in a rapture" Siegfried's story [*Surprised by Joy*,
p. 74] and yearned ever after to recapture the mood it inspired.
But for Lucy as for Lewis, "here part of the magic of the Book
came into play. You couldn't turn back." And so longing became
even more acute: "Ever since that day what Lucy means by a good
story is a story which reminds her of the forgotten story in the
Magician's Book." However, Lucy soon learns that her longing will
not be in vain:

> "Shall I ever be able to read that story again. . . ? Will you tell it
> to me, Aslan? . . ."
> "Indeed, yes, I will tell it to you for years and years." [*The Voyage
> of the "Dawn Treader,"* p. 136]

One is tempted to think that the story might be a kind of tale of
love between Aslan and Lucy, a story of the eternal alliance between the Lion and his creatures.

A last form of longing is embodied in Reepicheep's active, faithful, and jauntily confident quest. A profound desire to reach Aslan's
country determines his whole life, and the success of his quest is the
culmination of all that he has lived before. In spite of the passion
and faithfulness of Reepicheep's quest, however, we should not be
tempted to look upon it as superior to other expressions of longing.
It appears as one element in the general description, whose main
point is that there is not *one* accepted way of desiring Heaven or
one prevailing manner of feeling about it. Freedom is the only rule,
together with hope, for although the ways are innumerable, true

longing always leads to the same country. And although the greatest freedom exists, a guarantee is given that one *can* avoid erring if one wishes to. This is explained by the nature of longing as Lewis conceived it and as its humblest forms in the tales reveal it. The simple story of Shasta, the young boy brought up in Calormen and yearning for the North he knew nothing about, is very suggestive. When he says: "I've been longing to go to the north all my life," the horse replies, matter-of-factly: "Of course you have. . . . That's because of the blood that's in you. . . . You're true northern stock" [*The Horse and His Boy*, p. 12]. Thus, if longing can remain unconscious, though real, in Shasta's or in the cabby's heart, this is because it is more deeply rooted than could be suspected; it is inscribed in our flesh, it runs in our blood; longing is nothing less than a call for a home we cannot remember, the desire to return to the country we belong to by right of birth, where we are to be the King's sons and where, like Shasta—who in Archenland discovers he is actually Prince Cor—we are to be called by our true names. Through something so simple as a conversation between a horse and a boy in a fairy tale, Lewis can give us a strong feeling of confidence and hope. For not only is longing fulfilled, but it is in our nature to experience it and to go as far as it will take us.

VIGILANCE AND WAKEFULNESS

Longing for Heaven—this desire to be united with God in our true country—appears as an important concern in Narnia. There is an equally important, complementary preoccupation in a deep sense of the presence of God here and now, and of the necessity to wake and be vigilant, in order to avoid letting this presence pass unnoticed. The desire for God cannot be dissociated from intimacy with him; ardent longing must co-exist with an ability to recognize the "footprints of the Divine" in our world. These had been the two most important glimmers of light Lewis had received from *Phantastes* when he discovered that George MacDonald knew what longing pointed to and that in MacDonald's world, one "felt strangely vigilant" [*MacDonald Anthology*, p. 21].

Indeed, real waking and vigilance, a capacity to see beyond appearances, were important concerns with Lewis. On many occasions, in the Chronicles as well as in other works, he takes up this problem relating to spiritual life. The most striking examples are those in which, with a sad realism, he presents us with certain extremes of self-blinding and dullness. One of these is the Dwarfs' incapacity to discern a reality which is evident to most Narnians: the violets given to them by Lucy become "filthy stable-litter"

[*The Last Battle*, p. 145]; likewise, when they raise "golden goblets of rich red wine to their lips," they think they are "drinking dirty water out of a trough that a donkey's been at" [p. 147]. In the story of the beginnings of Narnia, we see Uncle Andrew, the quack magician, in his vain refusal to recognize something that is beyond him, disqualify himself from hearing Aslan's voice: "The longer and more beautifully the Lion sang, the harder Uncle Andrew tried to make himself believe that he could hear nothing but roaring" [*The Magician's Nephew*, p. 126], so that finally Aslan himself could be of no help to him: "If I spoke to him, he would hear only growlings and roarings" [p. 171]. If the reader does not feel as sorry for the magician or the Dwarfs as their unfortunate situation merits, it may be because these characters play disagreeable roles in the tales, and also because they have been observed at the very time of their refusal, so that their responsibility is apparent. Their story, however, awakens our sympathy as it reminds us of other scenes in Lewis's fiction, particularly of the painful dialogue between Orual and Psyche in *Till We Have Faces*:

> "Oh, have done with it, child. . . . There was no wine."
> "But I gave it to you. You drank it. . . ."
> "You gave me water, cupped in your hands." [p. 119]

Confronted with such situations, in life or in the tales, it seems that we can do nothing but remark sadly with Aslan: "Oh Adam's sons, how cleverly you defend yourselves against all that might do you good!" [*The Magician's Nephew*, p. 171].

For Lewis, however, this response is not sufficient. As a challenge to our dullness, to our self-blinding against what might dazzle us, he gives us his tales, in a gentle effort to prod us awake. The form of the fairy tale is particularly well suited to this end, in that it seems to provide conditions in which we can reconsider some essential questions.

First of all it presents us with some observations on human nature, and particularly on a weakness which often makes us incapable of conceiving things beyond our direct, immediate experience, or of taking account of them after we have experienced them. Thus Jill and Eustace, after they have been a moment in Underland, become uneasy: "The worst thing . . . was that you began to feel as if you had always lived on that ship . . . and to wonder whether sun and blue skies . . . had not been only a dream" [*The Silver Chair*, p. 128]. The same children, after they have escaped from this stuffy nightmarish world, almost forget about it, remarking: "Out here, in the cold, with the moon and the huge stars overhead

. . . , one couldn't quite believe in Underland" [p. 197]. If one can have such difficulty in remembering actual experience, how much more difficult it is even to conceive spiritual things. The very words of Orual clearly reveal this human failing and the anguish it may give rise to when she asks her tutor the Fox: "You don't think —not possibly—not as a mere hundredth chance—there might be things that are real though we can't see them?" [*Till We Have Faces*, p. 141].

A first remedy to this weakness, the first hint of a solution or a way out, is offered by a quality inherent in the form of the Chronicles. Indeed, as is widely understood, the fairy tale, by its very nature and because of the tacit agreement between author and reader (the latter accepting a "willing suspension of disbelief") invites us to cease taking things at their face value and to accept instead the idea of a world governed by other laws than our own. From the start we are receptive; this is why we merely smile at an aside like the following one from *The Lion, the Witch and the Wardrobe*: "Giants of any sort are now so rare in England and so few giants are good tempered that ten to one you have never seen a giant when his face is beaming. It's a sight well worth looking at" [p. 167]. Such an example would be no more than an amusing remark if, along with many others of its kind, it did not contribute to a general atmosphere in which we become imaginatively prepared to conceive things otherwise quite unfamiliar to us. It does not matter that we do not actually believe in giants or in fauns dancing on lawns, for our readiness to conceive these things while the tale lasts makes us capable of conceiving *other* things, nearer to truth and more lasting than the story we are reading, things which may have been stumbling blocks in our *real* world, where we tend to push aside what is not immediately evident or verifiable through our senses.

To this innate capacity of the tale itself to help us conceive the unfamiliar, Lewis added his own personal touch. For if the very nature of the tales serves to wake us a little, Lewis saw to it that we should not just wake with a start, blink sleepily, and go on with our naps. He further invited us to engage in a sort of spiritual exercise. Very often the reader of the Chronicles, in his own world accustomed to doubting the existence of fauns, of unicorns, or of gnomes, has the double surprise of encountering these creatures in the tales and of finding them, in their turn, express doubts about his own species and the world he lives in. Thus, among Mr. Tumnus's books, Lucy reads the following title: *Is Man a Myth?* [*The Lion, the Witch and the Wardrobe*, p. 12]. Thus also does Caspian marvel: "Do you mean to say . . . that you three come from a round world! . . . We have fairy-tales in which there are round worlds and I always loved them. I never believed there were any real ones. But I've always wished there were" [*The Voyage of the "Dawn Treader,"* p. 201; see also *Prince Caspian*, p. 66].

Not only does Caspian's wonderment communicate itself to us and cause us to see for a while our "round world" with new, admiring eyes, but the question he asks about our world, however fanciful, also has an important additional function. Episodes of this kind compel us, while we are under the spell of the tale, to forget our immutable certitudes and securities and to reconsider our beliefs from a different angle, even from an opposing one—that which is represented by the world on the other side of the wardrobe door. The inner movement which this sort of inverted outlook on our situation inspires appears as a form of "transposition"—not exactly in the sense Lewis gave to this term in his sermon "Transposition," when he mentioned a "Transposition from above" [*"The Weight of Glory" and Other Addresses*, p. 25], where the higher illuminates the lower in which it reproduces itself—but in the mode of an analogy, what I would call a transposition *from a different world*, which illuminates a situation *inside our world—our* situation—by reproducing it in an inverted mode. Thus the paradoxical presentation of a few facts in Narnia throws light on matters in our own world by making us consider all things in an inverted, *renewed* manner, and with a mind—in the etymological sense—converted.

This new outlook on the world—a form of Holiness closely woven into the very texture of the tale, since it is associated with its very mode of narration—soon bears fruit, and with the help of other analogies allows new discoveries and further insight. The firmness with which Caspian asserts his belief in the existence of the Great Lion comes from this new outlook: "If I hadn't believed in him before, I would now. Back there among the Humans the people who laughed at Aslan would have laughed at stories about talking beasts and Dwarfs. Sometimes I did wonder if there really was such a person as Aslan: but then sometimes I wondered if there were really people like you. Yet there you are" [*Prince Caspian*, p. 66].

Another element in the structure of the tales offering new understanding to the reader is the privileged Olympian position he is afforded, which enables him to become a witness to things, and gives him access to information about which the creatures in the tale are unaware. Thus, for example, we are able to verify that, in spite of appearances (what some would call "facts," real, "solid facts"), the Narnian creatures hiding in Aslan's Mound are not abandoned; for we are at the same time in the room, hearing their grumblings and rebellings, and behind the door with those who have

come to help. We do not need to be "told," we *see*, and may interpret these facts at whatever level we choose to, for Lewis leaves
his reader free to seize the hints or simply to enjoy the story.
It seems to me, however, that if we are willing to seize the "signs,"
we may be taken far and learn still more "wondrous" things. In
fact, we may find ourselves traveling in the opposite direction from
Uncle Andrew and, where he had heard roarings instead of music,
we may learn, like Lewis when he heard the wind roaring, not just
to hear "roars," but to "hear the wind," and finally to abandon *all*
distinctions and come to the moment when to hear the wind and
recognize its divine source is a *single* experience.

Up to this point, we have been concerned with Lewis's use of
the fairy tale form to encourage us to leave behind certain habits
of mind drawn from a prevailing mood of skepticism, and to open
ourselves to hear things that would otherwise have gone unheard.
There are times, however, when he moves still further—to the core
of the problem; for these successive discoveries are a preparation
for a greater one, for the "shock" of discovery that what we call
"life" is more often than not a dream in which, occasionally, a
few moments of more vivid consciousness may break in. These very
moments, which, Lewis would maintain, are actually glimmers of
real life, we might be tempted to call "dreams." This is the reason
why, in *Prince Caspian*, when Lucy witnesses the "country-dance"
of the trees, a prelude to Aslan's coming, Lewis makes it clear
that Lucy "was wide awake, wider than anyone usually is" [p.
135], suggesting that there exists a spiritual reality more real than
what we call real, although we may need to use fairyland to convey
an idea of what it is.

In fact, Lewis could have said with MacDonald that he believed
in "the wide-awake real, through all the stupefying, enervating,
distorting dream" [*MacDonald Anthology*, p. 65]. We see signs of
this belief in the new strength and youth which transform old
Professor Kirke on his return to Narnia, when he declares that he
feels "unstiffened" in comparison to the tiredness of old age he had
felt in this world. Lewis's conviction is that "at present we are on
the outside of the world, the wrong side of the door" ["The Weight
of Glory," p. 13], and that real waking, real strength and youth,
will come to us at the time when Great Joy will be ours. It seems
that all hints of Holiness—the call of longing or the call to vigilance
—have been directing us to this final assurance, which Lewis expressed by means of paradoxes. We hear the first of these from
Mr. Tumnus when he warns the children in Narnia: "The further
up and the further in you go, the bigger everything gets. The inside
is larger than the outside" [*The Last Battle*, p. 180]. At the same

time that we are invited to go "inside," to the center of things, we are given the certitude that there will be no unhappy surprises, no lassitude, and that the deeper we enter into the mystery of Real Narnia the deeper we shall find it to be. Joy will not dwindle or vanish but ever increase. At last, with renewed eyes, we shall see physical and spiritual things, soul and body, as they truly are and in their right relationship to each other. Lewis took up this point more explicitly towards the end of his life in *Letters to Malcolm*: "At present we tend to think of the soul as somehow 'inside' the body. But the glorified body of the resurrection as I conceive it—the sensuous life raised from its death—will be inside the soul" [p. 122].

The deepest reason for this is found in a second paradox, spoken by Aslan himself (who, as Lucy knows well, is the way to true Joy, more important even than Narnia: "It isn't Narnia, you know. . . . It's *you*," she exclaims on learning she will never visit Narnia again —*The Voyage of the "Dawn Treader,"* p. 215). When he wishes to help Lucy to better conceive who he is and to see that even with a deeper knowledge of him she will never fully comprehend the mystery of his divinity, he must use a paradox. In answer to her remark that she finds him bigger than the last time she saw him, he says: "That is because you are older, little one. . . . Every year you grow, you will find me bigger" [*Prince Caspian*, p. 136].

The last paradox appears as the logical outcome of the first two, and more immediately concerns us. It tells us how going through Shadowland is not, as the common expression goes, "meeting one's end," but on the contrary, heading towards a meeting with someone: the Son of the Emperor. Death is but the end of a dream and the beginning of waking, as Psyche sensed after having become the bride of her god: "If it was a dream, Sister, how do you think I came here? It's more likely everything that had happened to me before this was a dream" [*Till We Have Faces*, p. 112]. Death opens at last on fully awakened life and rejoicing: when the children meet him after the railway accident in *The Last Battle*, Aslan announces gently: "The holidays have begun. . . . This is the morning" [p. 183]. In these final pages of the Chronicles of Narnia, Aslan seems to be inviting us to have fun—"solemn fun," as Lewis called it in a letter to Sister Penelope only a few weeks before his own death [*Letters*, p. 307]; he seems to be welcoming everyone with that expansive joy Psyche felt when she greeted Orual: "Welcome, welcome, welcome. . . . Oh, how happy I am! . . . You have found my threshold cold and steep! You are breathless. But I'll refresh you" [*Till We Have Faces*, pp. 102, 104].

The theme of wakefulness—whether it be the wakefulness and

vigilance of consciousness or wakefulness as opposed to the dream of this mortal life—was bound to lead to the final alternative of our becoming, in Lewis's words, either "immortal horrors or everlasting splendours" ["The Weight of Glory," p. 15]. Faced with such a reality, all rational expression is weak and inadequate. The paradox, with its brevity, leaves room for the imagination to expand, achieves communication with few words, and allows understanding without a commitment to follow what has been understood.

JOY AND DANCE

The Narnian Chronicles would probably have been a little austere, had the call of Holiness in them merely appeared as a preparation for and a prelude to a better but remote life—the Real life beyond Shadowland. But in fact the reader soon discovers that the creatures in Narnia live not only with the hope of a promise to be fulfilled, but also with real joys and pleasures in their everyday lives; he sees that Narnia, like our own world, has its beauties and its delights, which are at one and the same time real experiences and prefigurations of more to come. Another form of Holiness to be found in the tales comes from Lewis's ability to make us see and recognize these privileged moments for what they are: "shafts of the glory" given us—if we wish to see them so—as little prophecies. Thus far Holiness has appeared in its active sense, inspiring a form of spiritual exercise, aiming at a clearer vision of the world, and, as it were, endeavoring to bring things into focus in the "fog which we call 'nature' or 'the real world'" [*Mere Christianity*, p. 168]. It has another, complementary aspect—a static receptiveness, a kind of contemplative quietness which acknowledges all experiences of beauty and joy in the present time as "messages," little patches of eternity in our lives, and, because of this, anticipates another world—coming close to the entering of it in rare, privileged moments.

One is struck by the number of examples of joy and extreme happiness in the Narnian Chronicles. Evanescent or lasting, coming over one child or a crowd, bringing tears of gratitude or causing ludicrous antics, joy is frequent and inspires various kinds of rejoicing, from play and games to dances and feasts. It seems that it is inherent in serene Narnian life; at least it was present at the very beginning, when Aslan chose among the animals those who were to become Talking Beasts, saying to them: "Laugh and fear not. . . . You need not always be grave" [*The Magician's Nephew*, pp. 118-19].

In the tales, the examples of joy are numerous, and seem like so many facets, so many expressions of a more fundamental Joy impossible to define, each in its own fullness also serving as a "pointer" to Real Joy, which will contain them all. This explains the great range of feelings of joy and the variety of their expression. When it comes as a victory over the suffering of bondage or of death, joy is light-hearted; it has the gladness and jollity of triumph, along with the wildness of sudden relief: thus the gnomes freed from the Witch's domination in Underland behave like boisterous children at recess, "leaping, turning cartwheels, standing on their heads . . . and letting off huge crackers" [*The Silver Chair*, pp. 179-80]. The same exuberance and almost tipsy gaiety of deliverance spreads over Narnia on Aslan's return after Miraz's evil reign. "It was not unlike Hunt the Slipper, but the slipper was never found" [*Prince Caspian*, p. 152]. Joy, in such circumstances, is ever associated with Aslan: either with Aslan's help, or with his very presence. In one of the tales, Aslan himself has a share in the game, and even seems to initiate it. His frolic of joy with Lucy and Susan after he has died for Edmund's sake and come to life again, the "happy laughing heap of fur and arms and legs" they form together, is the concrete sign of restored harmony [*The Lion, the Witch and the Wardrobe*, p. 160].

Joy, which often comes as an overflowing of life, is sometimes felt only by one privileged person: Lucy is one of these when, in *Prince Caspian*, she is able to see the trees moving in a dance and to join in it, taking hands "in a Great Chain with big dancers who stooped to reach her" [p. 135]. Most often, however, joy is meant for the many who come "leaping . . . and roaring and barking and neighing" [*Prince Caspian*, p. 198] and take part in the dance as best they can, like Trufflehunter the Badger, who "hopped and lumbered" [p. 78]. Those who do not join are those who are separated, cut off from the others, like Nikabrik the traitor Dwarf, who "stayed where he was, looking on in silence" at the dancers [p. 78].

When one remembers that the inventor of these dances and games was one "who never enjoyed any game and [could] dance no better than a centipede with wooden legs," as he said of himself in *Letters to Malcolm* [p. 92], one might wonder why Lewis chose to picture such festivities to evoke the Joy of recovered unity and harmony in Heaven. Lewis himself gave the answer to Malcolm, his fictitious correspondent: "I do *not* think that the life of Heaven bears any analogy to play or dance in respect of frivolity. I do think that while we are in this 'valley of tears,' . . . certain qualities that must belong to the celestial condition have no chance to get through, can project no images of themselves, except in activities which, for us here and now, are frivolous." Then, enumerating a few characteristics which may pertain to "the life of the blessed" as we imagine it, Lewis spoke in terms of paradoxes[14] of the "reconciliation of boundless freedom with order, . . . the most delicately adjusted, supple, intricate, and beautiful order." One could almost believe that Lewis conceived "the Great Snow Dance" of the fauns as a faithful illustration of this vision of life in Heaven; I think it deserves to be quoted for the wonderful correspondence between the terms "intricacy," "order," "suppleness," "freedom," and the figures of the dance:

> Trim little fauns, and dryads . . . were really doing a dance. . . .
> Circling round and round the dancers was a ring of Dwarfs. . . . As
> they circled round they were all diligently throwing snowballs. . . .
> They weren't throwing them *at* the dancers. . . . They were throwing
> them through the dance in such perfect time with the music and with
> such perfect aim that if all the dancers were in exactly the right places
> at exactly the right moments, no one would be hit. [*The Silver Chair*,
> pp. 192-93]

There is no frivolity in this dance. Its circumstances—"the first moonlit night when there is snow on the ground"—and the fact that all those present are in some way participating (except for Lucy, the only "outsider," who comes upon the dance by accident) even give it a certain solemnity. It is carried on with joy, and with such application and seriousness that we are reminded of Lewis's observation that "Joy is the serious business of Heaven" [*Letters to Malcolm*, p. 93]. One thinks of other circumstances of solemn and deep Joy in the tales, in which he makes the point that Joy and seriousness are not incompatible: "A happy place but very serious" [*The Magician's Nephew*, p. 158]: such was Digory's impression of Aslan's garden.

Thus, from the antics of the gnomes to the "adjusted" intricacies of the Snow Dance, from noisy "romps" to Joy mingled with gravity, Lewis endeavored to conjure a few possible images of bliss in Heaven. Whether they are "false as history" is not an important question in a fairy tale; what is more important is whether the faith and the art that conceived them succeed in touching us and in helping us to imagine and desire what we know so little of, to recognize in the small joys of our lives the promise of a greater Joy to come. If it is so, the images become "truth as prophecy" and Holiness lies at their core, for they are a help to our faith and they bring good news to those who wish to know.

GLORY AND BEAUTY

If Narnia contained anticipations of Heaven through its images of joy, it was also bound to present us with anticipations of beauty and of glory, which could at once stir up our desires and inspire our faith. Indeed, many images of beauty appear, of all kinds, from the homely beauty of Mrs. Badger sitting at her sewing-machine or being helped into her snow-boots—an image of simple affection, of the charity which is to be the normal currency of Heaven—to stranger, more impressive sights, such as the contrast between the green valley, the blue river, and the glaciers Digory passes on his way to Aslan's garden, a foretaste, an anticipation of greater lands and mysteries. Both of these forms of beauty—the familiar and the fantastic—had been unconscious helps to Lewis on his way to conversion. As he confessed to his friend Arthur Greeves afterward: "All the 'homeliness' (wh. was your chief lesson to me) was the introduction to the Christian virtue of charity or love. . . . On the other hand, all the 'strangeness' (wh. was my lesson to you) has turned out to be only the first step in far deeper mysteries" [unpublished letter, 1 October 1931].

These images of beauty belong to a category we may know from experience in our world, but sometimes Lewis went beyond all familiar contexts and painted other, purely imagined wonders. In his sermon "The Weight of Glory," he had echoed a biblical image when he said that a first indication of the presence of glory in the world is the fact that "God has given us the Morning Star already" [p. 12]. In the Chronicles he seems to play with this theme in several highly imaginative variations. We see the stars on their first rise when they have just been created, and when their "cold, tingling, silvery voices" [*The Magician's Nephew*, p. 99] join with Aslan's, an image of their submission to and harmony with their creator, of the harmony of the spheres. We also see them when their task of brightening Narnian nights is ended and when they fall in a "silver rain," personages with silver hair and silver spears, called home by Aslan at the end of the Narnian world [*The Last Battle*, pp. 150-51]. With these extraordinary images of beauty, a new quality appears, a new mode of Holiness. For here it is no longer a question of analogy; a new method is introduced: fantasy is given free rein. In places it is so highly developed that even the stars are personified—Narnian stars are never merely "the great flaming globes" they are in our world; "they are people" [*The Last Battle*, p. 151]. They are living characters and, like other living characters, they grow old. But what is wonderful is that they can sometimes be rejuvenated. In *The Voyage of the "Dawn Treader,"* the children are amazed to see birds coming at dawn to bring Ramandu "a fire-berry from the valleys in the Sun" and to learn that "each fire-berry takes away a little of [his] age" [p. 180].

There is great beauty in these scenes of fantasy, and perhaps they serve their most important purpose simply in being beautiful. At the same time, the fact that Lewis has used such a profusion and richness of images shows us the difficulty of conceiving life in Heaven in other than what seem extravagant and fanciful terms. The fantasy prefigures the mystery and beauty of another world even while making us aware that the most glorious of visions will remain pale compared to the reality of Heaven, in the same way that the silver and gold of our mines are "dead" compared to the "bunches of rubies that you can eat," or the "cup full of diamond-juice" you can drink, in the Land of Bism [*The Silver Chair*, p. 182].

Thus the more familiar forms of beauty—involving snow-boots and glaciers—can be experienced as little foretastes, "anticipations," which, by analogy, give us an idea of the beauty of Heaven; the more fantastic, while also firing our imaginations, announce to us at the same time that no imagining, no poetry, will ever give us a truly satisfactory idea of it. The imparting of this new truth through the beauty and exuberance of fantasy is the second mode in which beauty in Lewis takes on Holiness.

If Lewis's images of Heaven can vary so widely, from humble scenes to impressive ones, this is because to him, what will determine our reactions is not so much what the images, in their simplicity or splendor, can do for us, as the attitudes we bring to them—how much we are willing to think in terms of the relationship of Heaven and earth. Our capacity to conceive Heaven thus depends less on the images we are given of it in fantasy or on the appearance of the earthly things we see, than on our ability to adequately interpret and respond to these things, and, through them, pass to the Source of all things. Lewis described this attitude of mind as running "back up the sunbeam to the sun" [*Letters to Malcolm*, p. 90]: from the beauty displayed before our eyes—the beauty of the brook or the "cushiony moss," the beauty of the place "where we are"—to its Cause. Reepicheep's last days in the Narnian world (in *The Voyage of the "Dawn Treader"*) provide a concrete image of this passage—this "running back up"—from the simple things, which are signs of Holiness. No sooner has he fallen, by accident, into the Last Sea and discovered the water to be sweet, than he remembers a prophecy in which sweet water is to be the sign that he is soon to encounter Aslan:

> "Where the waves grow sweet,
> Doubt not, Reepicheep,
> There is the utter East."
>
> [p. 198]

Immediately he understands this sign, which, for him, becomes the way to Aslan—so much so, in fact, that the water itself becomes the means by which he reaches Aslan. We see him rush "up the wave's side" [p. 213] in his little coracle and literally climb the water, from the sea, which had been the sign, up to the Source, up to Aslan's country. Because he knows how to read the signs, he goes beyond the contemplation of beauty to its giver; he is now ready to meet a Person, and to worship.

A similar image appears in another tale, when the animals, in their long, happy race "further in" to Aslan's country, appear to be "climbing up light itself" [*The Last Battle*, p. 174]. It seems that *here* is the normal end and that it is no good running ever to the core, being moved here and there by anticipations and prophecies, if one does not, at last, climb up to the Source, to the Light of all things, climb up light itself to a person, Aslan in the tale, Someone who has "another name" [*The Voyage of the "Dawn Treader,"* p. 216] in our world. In fact, the normal, final consequence of anticipations of Joy, of beauty, of glory in the tales, besides waking our desires and encouraging our faith, is to enable us to see, in everything beautiful, the giver of all things, to hear the divine presence in the roaring wind or to see it in the "cushiony moss" by a brook. Indeed, when any moss, any brook, is the sign of glory, the whole world will be a "sign" and an "anticipation" and, in faith, we shall be able to live and to endure "as seeing him that is invisible" [Hebrews 11:17]; every pleasure will become a "tiny theophany" and (even if only "adoration in infinitesimals") "a channel of adoration" [*Letters to Malcolm*, pp. 89-91].

This route to Holiness which we have discovered winding through the adventures of Narnia is not a compulsory way. It is not the only way to travel through Lewis's imaginary land. Although Holiness is present in the tales—as present as it was in *Phantastes* to Lewis's eyes, though not to everyone's—one may prefer not to see it, or to call it by another name. This is the advantage of a story in fairy-tale form: it respects the liberty of all, and gives according to everyone's desires; and, if one desires much, one is given much.

If this quality of Holiness is recognized in the tales, certain questions often raised concerning Narnia lose their importance: for instance, the question whether or not it is a moral, didactic work. In fact, one can find numerous episodes dealing with what I would more readily call practical wisdom than moral teaching, such as Lucy's discovery in the Isle of the Dufflepuds that it is wiser not to eavesdrop. But it seems that such questions are of little importance when compared with Lewis's wider purpose: he is inviting us not just to "be good" but to aim for Holiness. He does not need to raise barriers and interdictions, to give good advice. Instead, he offers hints of promise and, by comparison, other, "moral" questions lose their interest; they just become "dull, cold, abstract, and artificial."[15]

In the same manner, various episodes in Narnia lend themselves to a comparison with the Gospels: is Pole a new Samaritan when she wants to drink from the river near Aslan [*The Silver Chair*, p. 17]? And is Aslan's breath, which pushes her into Narnia, the breath of the Holy Spirit? One is reminded of these things; but that is probably enough, for Lewis did not aim at any *systematic* teaching. He did not create Narnia with any *definite* moral or religious purpose, but with the attitude of someone who believed that we now see "the flat outline" of a world which "elsewhere veritably is in all the round of its unimaginable dimensions,"[16] who could not help thinking and meditating and dreaming on what it might be like, and who, through his tales, invites us to peek in and have a glimpse of what he saw.

John D. Cox

Epistemological Release in *The Silver Chair*

I readily believe that there are more invisible than visible Natures in the universe. . . . The human mind has always sought the knowledge of these things, but never attained it. Meanwhile I do not deny that it is helpful sometimes to contemplate in the mind, as on a tablet, the image of a greater and better world, lest the intellect, habituated to the petty things of daily life, narrow itself and sink wholly into trivial thoughts. But at the same time we must be watchful for the truth and keep a sense of proportion, so that we may distinguish the certain from the uncertain, day from night.

—Thomas Burnet (used by Coleridge as his
epigraph to *The Rime of the Ancient Mariner*)

If the widely various sources and analogues of the Chronicles of Narnia are a tribute to Lewis's encyclopedic reading, they more importantly reflect the synthesizing power of his imagination. Everyone remembers Professor Kirk's scholarly observation that "It's all in Plato" at the end of *The Last Battle*; yet it's not all in Plato, for like most scholarly theories, this one, however insightful, can only claim partial truth. A beginning list of sources for *The Last Battle* would include the biblical Apocalypse, Malory's *Morte D'Arthur*, Wagner's *Ring*, the *Enneads* of Plotinus, George MacDonald's sermons, ancient Roman religion, and probably Aesop's *Fables*. The most remarkable aspect of this scholarly abundance is that we are scarcely aware of it in the Chronicles, surely a tribute to Lewis's respect for generic decorum: these are stories for children. Yet the riches are real, and a consciousness of the dimension they add to their humble setting can only increase our appreciation of Lewis's accomplishment. In few of the Chronicles does he arrange his riches as brilliantly as in *The Silver Chair*, where the most important images

159

complement a structural pattern and self-reflective critical commentary that consistently deal with the problem of knowledge.[1]

The problem is addressed most directly in the central confrontation between Prince Rilian's rescuers and his demonic enchantress, the Queen of Underland. Attempting to reimpose her control over the prince, the witch initiates a process of magical brainwashing designed to eradicate her victims' knowledge of the world beyond her subterranean palace. With remorseless logic she successively reduces their memories of reality to fantasy: Narnia, England, the sun, Aslan, each one is represented as a wish-fulfilling daydream based on the perception of reality in Underland. The prince and his rescuers are forced to reduce their knowledge to what the witch verifies. "There never was any world but mine," says the witch. "There never was any world but yours," her victims helplessly respond [p. 154]. The witch's attempt ultimately fails, of course, and the details of its failure will concern us in due time. First, however, in order to deal more broadly with the issues this episode raises, three central images from *The Silver Chair* demand attention, all of them illustrating how consistently Lewis's sources affected his imaginative treatment of how reality is known.

The first image is Prince Rilian himself, the lost heir whose restoration is the work's subject. When Eustace, Jill, and Puddleglum find the prince, he is an instant source of corrosive doubt, a destroyer of certain knowledge. Though relieving their oppressive uncertainty about the mysterious Underland with his "clear, ringing, perfectly human voice," he is not wholly reassuring: "There was something about his face that didn't seem quite right" [p. 131]. Though the travellers know they have been maliciously misguided by the lady in the green kirtle, the prince puzzlingly asserts that she "is a nosegay of all virtues" [p. 132]. Worse still, the prince easily undermines the travellers' naive confidence in the sign "UNDER ME," by which they had entered the Underland. They had taken the sign as having Aslan's authority, but on the authority of his lady, the prince offers a more persuasive exegesis, complete with an explanation of the sign's original literary context and historical circumstances. His theory severely shakes the confidence of Eustace and Jill, "for it seemed to them very likely that the words had nothing to do with their quest at all, and that they had been taken in by a mere accident" [p. 134]. Given all this in the first few minutes of acquaintance with the prince, we can see that the narrator's comparison of Rilian to Hamlet suggests more than the trappings and the suits of a Renaissance prince [p. 131]. "The world of *Hamlet* is a world where one has lost one's way," Lewis comments in his British Academy Lecture on Shakespeare's play.[2] His point is that Hamlet's world is one where doubt and uncertainty prevail, the same world where the travellers find Prince Rilian. Lewis's remark in his lecture that "the Prince also has no doubt lost his [way]" might apply equally to Hamlet and Prince Rilian. In short, the allusion to Hamlet is not gratuitous: imaginatively it is a perfect detail for reflecting the work's central theme, the problem of knowledge.

A second image is more complex, but equally appropriate. This one is the prince's captor, the femme fatale in poisonous green who is repeatedly identified as Queen of the Deep Realm or Queen of the Underland. Though elucidation of her mythical and folkloric origins would no doubt tax the erudition of Sir James Frazer, we can identify the literary contexts where Lewis met her. George MacDonald's Lilith, for instance, also changes into a snake and goes about seeking males whom she may devour. Lewis's Emerald Witch is identified as "the same kind as that White Witch who had brought the Great Winter" [p. 200], and the White Witch is elsewhere identified as a descendant of "Adam's first wife, her they called Lilith" [*The Lion, the Witch and the Wardrobe*, p. 77]. More closely linking a lamia to knowledge in *The Silver Chair* is Spenser's monster Error, half woman and half serpent, who battles the Red Crosse Knight. Rilian's fight with his enchantress, immortalized in Pauline Baynes's drawing, is clearly modelled on Spenser's account:

> Much daunted with that dint, her sence was dazd,
>   Yet kindling rage, her selfe she gathered round,
>   And all attonce her beastly body raizd
>   With doubled forces high aboue the ground:
>   Tho wrapping vp her wrethed sterne arownd,
>   Lept fierce vpon his shield, and her huge traine
>   All suddenly about his body wound,
>   That hand or foot to stirre he stroue in vaine:
> God helpe the man so wrapt in *Errours* endlesse traine.
>
> His Lady sad to see his sore constraint,
>   Cride out, Now now Sir knight, shew what ye bee,
>   Add faith vnto your force, and be not faint:
>   Strangle her, else she sure will strangle thee.
>   That when he heard, in great perplexitie,
>   His gall did grate for griefe and high disdaine,
>   And knitting all his force got one hand free,
>   Wherewith he grypt her gorge with so great paine,
> That soone to loose her wicked bands did her constraine.[3]

God help the man so wrapped, indeed! But as Red Crosse had done before him, Rilian frees himself from Error's train, and thus restoring his better knowledge, he goes on to restore a kingdom.

The third and most important image associated with knowledge in *The Silver Chair*—and perhaps the most remarkably erudite—is the book's central image: the silver chair itself. What makes it erudite is its apparent origin in the Eleusinian mysteries. Admittedly the search for esoteric origins may itself become another kind of silver chair: an academic seat of ignorance. Fortunately, however, we can resist the enchantment of occult speculation about numerology, dark gods, and anagrams in the penultimate Narnian Chronicle, for the silver chair's relation to knowledge is not that sort, however obscure its ultimate origin may be. On the contrary, the most important literary analogue of the silver chair can be identified in a well-known context that once again points directly to the problem of reductive knowledge. The context is again *The Faerie Queene*, this time the Legend of Temperance, whose champion, Sir Guyon, encounters a "siluer seat" during his sojourn in the Cave of Mammon.[4]

Like Lewis's Underland, Spenser's Cave of Mammon is both a subterranean location and a spiritual ordeal. Guyon's ordeal resembles Christ's temptation in the wilderness: both last three days and both involve the temptation to trust created goods—especially power and wealth—as if they had a value of their own. Mammon asserts his self-sufficiency in godlike terms, and blasphemously parodies religious language in describing the ultimate value of material wealth:

> Loe here the worldes blis, loe here the end,
> To which all men do ayme, rich to be made:
> Such grace now to be happy, is before thee laid.
> [II.vii.32]

Guyon resists the temptation by answering that he has "Another happinesse, another end" [II.vii.33], though they are less tangible than Mammon's offerings. In short, Guyon refuses to accept Mammon's reductive view of the material world as an end in itself. He refuses again when Mammon shows him a garden that seems to be as perfect as Eden, with a tree bearing golden apples, though it is really a demonic perversion of the earthly paradise, a garden of death rather than life: "The *Gardin of Proserpina* this hight; / And in the midst thereof a siluer seat" [II.vii.53].[5] Just as Eve had tempted Adam to enjoy the tree of knowledge, Mammon tempts Guyon to enjoy what he sees: "Why takest not of that same fruit of gold, / Ne sittest downe on that same siluer stoole" [II.vii. 63]. For Guyon to sit down would be to accept reality on Mammon's reductive terms, a literally fatal move because an ugly fiend walks just behind the knight, "Threatning with greedy gripe to do him dye," if he so much as yields to Mammon in his mind [II.vii. 27]. To sit in the silver seat, in other words, is to imitate Adam who accepted the world on the serpent's reductive terms: by affirming the supremacy of a fellow creature, Adam implicitly denied his own source of life, a move effectively surrendering life to death, knowledge to ignorance.

Numerous parallels suggest that Lewis's silver chair functions like Spenser's. Proserpina is queen of the underworld, wife of Pluto lord of the dead. Her association with death, hell, and a silver seat clearly makes Proserpina the archetype of Lewis's Queen of Underland. In choosing the ruler of the Deep Realm as his ambiguous paramour/stepmother, Rilian chooses death and darkness over life and light, for the Emerald Witch had killed his real mother, the star's daughter, who had ushered in the last adventure of light and enlightenment in *The Voyage of the "Dawn Treader."* The eradication of knowledge is portrayed in the prince's ordeal of being bound in the silver chair while it saps his sanity. His fierce vengeance on the engine of sorcery is thus a vengeance on the loss of his better knowledge, a loss that would eventually have issued in the destruction of the true prince of Narnia. For without the knowledge of his identity, the prince would be a zombie, a walking emblem of spiritual death, like the knight in black armor whom the travellers meet on the ruined bridge, and whose identity Puddleglum perceptively guesses: " 'How about a skeleton?' asked the Marshwiggle with ghastly cheerfulness. 'Or perhaps,' it added as an afterthought, 'nothing at all' " [p. 78].

In summary, the consistent significance of Lewis's sources seems to suggest that *The Silver Chair* centers in a fictional representation of epistemological problems. The Hamlet-like prince who has lost his own identity, the lamia who has robbed him of it, the silver seat of oblivion, all derive from imaginative contexts that threaten delusion and disorientation. Even the seemingly superfluous and merely amusing incident of the stupid giants playing cockshies has a significant forebear. Just as Jill thinks the giants' heads are piles of rock, so Dante, approaching the ninth circle of hell, sees the heads and shoulders of giants protruding from the gulf below and mistakes them for city towers; like Lewis's travellers, Dante is overcome with fear as the monsters bellow nonsense; and Dante too is ultimately impressed by the giants' stupidity, recognizing that the inevitable concomitant of evil is the irreversible decay of true knowledge [*Inferno* XXXI.28-145]. If Lewis composed in pictures, he must have read in them as well, experiencing an atmosphere as much as he understood an idea. In Red Crosse's struggle with Error the strangling panic of the knight and the rib-cracking pressure of the monster must have been as memorable as Spenser's doctrinal point. Or perhaps one should say (as Lewis probably would) that Spenser's point cannot be fully understood unless the debilitating mental suffocation of destructive uncertainty is imaginatively experienced in Red Crosse's battle.

If the sources of *The Silver Chair* seem to yield a consistent pattern, the same pattern might well be sought in other aspects of the work. We have already noticed how directly the problem of reductive knowledge is addressed in the central confrontation between the witch-queen of Underland and her Overworldly visitors. Nor is this the first episode dealing with the same problem: the mental conflict over comparative realities has been a constant issue from the beginning of the work. Indeed the witch's argument for a definitive reality in Underland derives much of its force from familiarity: whether they recognize it or not, the children have met it before. In short, the epistemological issues suggested by Lewis's sources in *The Silver Chair* are also a feature of the work's structure.

In the oldest terms of formal analysis—those of Aristotle—Lewis's structure is untidy. Though a passable comic action might be made of the prince's story (with a classic "recognition" and a "sudden turn" occurring together when Rilian is released by his rescuers), the opening and closing episodes in England are superfluous by Aristotelian standards, and so are the intermediary visits to Aslan's Land. If our concern is the restoration of the prince, the story should end with the "solemn, triumphal music" that signals Rilian's reunion with his father [p. 209]. But the story goes on anticlimactically: the music becomes funerary as we learn of King Caspian's death; the children return to Aslan's Land; Caspian is unexpectedly resurrected; and the children finally return to England. Since this loose-ended structure seems inept by the standards of Aristotle's unified action, we are compelled to account for Lewis's plot in other terms.

Appropriate terms can again be found in the issue raised by the Emerald Witch: the relative knowledge of comparative realities. For no fewer than five distinct worlds are encountered in the course of the narrative, and the order of our encounter with them is significant. The first, of course, is our own everyday reality, a British world Lewis designed to be familiar to his young readers in the 1950s. From England we go directly to Aslan's Land, a transition unique to *The Silver Chair* among all the Narnian Chronicles. This unusual feature of the work is complemented at the end by the return to Aslan's Land before the final return to England. The precise symmetry thus established characterizes the whole work, for the third world we encounter is Narnia—or more correctly, the Narnian world at large—and from this world we return to Aslan's Land again at the end. The fourth world is Underland, and the fifth is Bism, the Really Deep Land that stands structurally at the center of all the worlds, for after seeing it we return again to Underland and thence to Narnia, reversing the order in which worlds were encountered in the first half of the work. Structural symmetry thus demands the return to Aslan's Land and England that looks superfluous by Aristotelian standards. An essential question to ask, therefore, is whether the symmetry itself serves a purpose.

A plausible explanation is that the worlds are like the layers of skin in an onion, with a decreasing awareness of wider (or "outer") realities in each successive world, or layer, we encounter. Though this explanation is inadequate for all the worlds, it does apply to three of them in a way that deserves attention. For the relationship of Underland to Narnia is a copy, as it were, of the relationship between Narnia and Aslan's Land. Proceeding from Aslan's Land "inward," we successively encounter diminished realities that tend to make definitive claims for themselves, and thus threaten the knowledge of worlds "beyond" them.

The travellers know, for instance, that the witch is wrong when she asserts that there never was any world but hers. Since their knowledge is based on the experience and memory of other worlds, the witch's attempt to eradicate their knowledge depends on her success in confusing their memory. This she attempts to do by magical incense and specious reasoning. Similarly, the air of Narnia confuses the mind about the reality of Aslan's Land. "Remember the Signs," Aslan tells Jill. "Here on the mountain, the air is clear and your mind is clear; as you drop down into Narnia, the air will thicken. Take great care that it does not confuse your mind. . . . Remember the Signs and believe the Signs. Nothing else matters" [p. 21]. While the witch uses incense to cause confusion, however, the "thick air" Aslan refers to is nothing so obviously sinister: more often it is the simple desire for reasonable relief and comfort, a much subtler kind of confusion than the witch's. " 'I say, Scrubb,' " says Jill, now bathed and "splendidly dressed" soon after her arrival in Narnia, " 'isn't it all simply too exciting and scrumptious for words.' She had forgotten all about the Signs and the lost prince for the moment" [p. 37]. Her memory is confused by the innocent delight of adventure lined with comfort.

The parallel between Narnia and Underland is also evident in the threat each world poses to volition as well as memory. The witch finally fails in Underland because she cannot dominate the freedom of her victims' will. Though their memory and reason may be confused, she cannot persuade them to act as she wants them to while they determine to act as if she were wrong and they were right. In Puddleglum's words: "I'm on Aslan's side even if there isn't any Aslan to lead it. I'm going to live as like a Narnian as I can even if there isn't any Narnia" [p. 159]. Though Puddleglum's brave determination is seconded at once by Eustace and Jill, the children have already been responsible for earlier misadventures by failing to show a similar willing resolution in Overworld. When the witch tempts them to go to Harfang, for instance, their failure to resist her is due as much to their legitimate wish for protection and comfort as to her malice: "Whatever the Lady had intended by telling them about Harfang, the actual effect on the children was a bad one. They could think about nothing but beds and baths and hot meals and how lovely it would be to get indoors. . . . And Jill gave up her habit of repeating the Signs" [p. 79]. In short, whether the threat comes in Narnia or in Underland, preservation depends on an act of will, a determination to persevere in light of what one knows about another world, in spite of adverse appearances in the world where one finds oneself. A similar act of will preserves Spenser's Guyon: despite three sleepless days under the ground, the knight refuses to accept Mammon's temptation to relax and sit in the silver chair. For to relax and sit would deny his knowledge of "another happinesse, another end," and the denial of that knowledge is spiritual death.

Keeping in mind the special relationship between the onion-layer worlds (Aslan's Land, Narnia, Underland), we can better account for the structural symmetry we noticed earlier. The return to Aslan's Land at the end is a way of affirming that it is a definitive or "larger" reality than the two it "encloses." What we know of Narnia in the end is darkened with ambiguity: the "healing of harms," as the last chapter has it, is partial at best. The prince is restored, the witch's plot is foiled, but King Caspian, the old friend whom we have known since he was a boy in *Prince Caspian*, is dead, and the music is playing "a tune to break your heart" [p. 210]. From the perspective of Aslan's Land, however, the elegiac reality of Narnia is analogous to the snowstorm in the ruined city or the innocent delights of Cair Paravel: their tempting claim to finality is false. Harms are finally healed in Aslan's Land, not in Narnia, where every restoration of the land is poorer than the restoration before it, and none is free from sorrow. The adven-

tures of *The Silver Chair* begin in Aslan's Land in order to provide
an undiminished perspective on the worlds to follow. Nor are we
left with reductive knowledge in the end, but with the full perspective restored.

We noticed earlier that the onion-skin analogy is inadequate to
account for the relationship between all the worlds in *The Silver
Chair*, and it is time now to consider the two worlds not encom-
passed in the analogy: Bism and Earth. Bism is a world "inside"
Underland in the same sense that Underland is "inside" Narnia.
Yet contrary to expectation Bism is not a diminished reality, but a
place of freedom and delight, like Narnia. Except for intense heat,
all our associations with Bism are unambiguously positive: the "rich,
sharp, exciting" smell of the place, its extraordinary brightness
and color, the lure of fantastic creatures—witty and eloquent sala-
manders who speak from the river of fire. Moreover, the gnomes
who are native to Bism regard Underland as a place of horror and
gloom, a place that has made them forget their desired homeland:
"We didn't know who we were or where we belonged. We couldn't
do anything, or think anything, except what [the witch] put into
our heads" [p. 177]. This reaction to Underland is precisely the
reaction of the prince and his rescuers from Narnia: paradoxically
one can recognize a world of diminished knowledge both from
"outside" it and from "inside" it.

The paradox seems a deliberate attempt to qualify the spatial
metaphor that Lewis has developed by a continual downward progression from Aslan's Land to Narnia to Underland. Indeed Lewis
invites laughter at his own metaphor (representing full knowledge
as "upwardness") when Golg exclaims about the prince's preference
for Narnia: "I know you Overlanders live there. . . . But I thought
it was because you couldn't find your way down inside. You can't
really *like* it—crawling about like flies on the top of the world!"
[p. 179]. The spatial metaphor is useful, as we have seen, in
comparing realities and one's knowledge of them. But the assumption that reality is literally spatial is not an assumption Lewis would
have wished to encourage because it has an obvious affinity with
materialism—another kind of reductive epistemology. No spatial concept can survive a land like Bism whose inside is larger than its
outside, a phenomenon we meet again in the apocalyptic stable of
The Last Battle.

If Bism is a large world at the center of a small one, the other
world that does not fit the onion-skin analogy is the reverse: a
small world that encloses a large one. This small world is Earth,
seemingly enveloping the other worlds because it is the place where
we begin and end. Though it appears to be "larger" than Aslan's

Land, however, Earth has all the characteristics that go with a diminished reality—a world of reductive knowledge. The conversation between Jill and Eustace in the garden of Experiment House is our first introduction to the confusion that belongs to such a world [pp. 4-5]. Eustace is plainly reluctant to talk about his memories of the "Dawn Treader," recognizing that they are likely to seem ridiculous to Jill. On her part she is afraid of being made ridiculous if she believes him and he suddenly laughs at her gullibility. Their problem is not merely mistrust: it also includes uncertainty. In a world like Experiment House, where reality is dominated by selfishness and cunning, "the sorts of things you have in fairy tales" (as Eustace puts it) are not very convincing: their authority withers before the absolute demands of power and fear. Such demands make the air of Earth as thick as the air of Underland. When the door in the garden wall opens unexpectedly at Eustace's touch, the moment offers more than physical escape: it also offers release from the epistemological bondage of Earth, a release that is echoed in the freeing of Rilian, the opening of Bism, and the children's meeting with the resurrected Caspian.

The escape of Eustace and Jill from Earth to Aslan's Land suggests another release in *The Silver Chair*: the reader's.[6] Tolkien argued that one of the functions of fairy stories is escape, a view Lewis echoed, with some modifications, in his essay "On Three Ways of Writing for Children."[7] The charge that escape is infantile regression because fairy stories are childish is a charge that Lewis's narrator answers obliquely in *The Silver Chair* itself: "Even in this world, of course, it is the stupidest children who are the most childish and the stupidest grown-ups who are most grown-up" [p. 212]. Eustace's comparison of his earlier Narnian experience to a fairy tale works on more than one level, if Lewis and Tolkien are right. In one sense his remark is a truism, since *The Voyage of the "Dawn Treader"* obviously *is* a fairy tale. On another level, however, he is saying a good deal more: he is claiming to have escaped—"right out of the world," as he puts it—and where he went, the reader followed. According to Tolkien, the fantasist "proves a successful 'sub-creator.' He makes a Secondary World which your mind can enter." To enter it is to realize that one has been in prison, and "why should a man be scorned, if, finding himself in prison, he tries to get out and go home?"[8]

IV: TILL WE HAVE FACES

Clyde S. Kilby

Till We Have Faces: An Interpretation

LEWIS believed *Till We Have Faces* to be his best book. Although it also may be his most difficult book, it amply repays a reader's effort. It is the account of Glome, a pagan city of long ago where a nature goddess called Ungit is worshipped with blood sacrifices, but where, because of the teaching of a Greek slave purchased by the king, such sacrifices are in process of ceasing in favor of a clean Greek goddess. Against such a background Lewis tells the story of two daughters of the king of Glome, one called (in Christian terms) from childhood to follow the true God, the other, though equally called, to spend forty miserable years resisting before she finally discovers her foolhardiness and also turns to God.

It is a story of true love and false love, of the selfless but also of the selfish parading as selfless. The story is addressed to the Greeks, but then the reader learns that perhaps he is at least partially a Greek, i.e., a believer in nothing more than reason and the laws of nature to explain all events in the universe. It is also a story setting forth Lewis's belief that even pagan blood is thicker than rationalistic water.

I have read it at least a half-dozen times, but the present reading suggests a wholly new story. Perhaps the most noteworthy new view is that of the number of witnesses from the gods to Orual.

In the first place, Orual is clearly aware that the blood of the gods is in her family. She begins with this "connection" with them, suggesting at once the Light "which lighteth every man that cometh into the world." The lengthy teaching of the Fox that the gods are

Reprinted by permission from *Orcrist*, No. 6 (Winter 1971-72). Copyright © 1972 by *Orcrist*.

lovely poetic inventions never quite wipes out a deep sense of their reality in Orual. When the Fox's death at the hands of her father seems imminent, she asks him, "Do you really in your heart believe nothing of what is said about the gods?" and she notices his trembling as his feelings overcome his Stoic philosophy [pp. 17-18]. So even apart from Psyche, Orual experiences a general witness.

But it is chiefly through Psyche that the epiphanies take place. Orual loved (or thought she loved) Psyche, and Psyche's beauty and goodness were constant witnesses to her. Psyche was the first Christian in her tribe, and a glorious one at that, but Orual failed to look beyond her toward the god of the mountain, the brightest spot in Psyche's life [p. 76]. The at times overpowering, yet suppressed, supernatural force on Orual's existence keeps manifesting itself. When Psyche, in the palace prison and facing death, ironically repeats the Fox's fair-time philosophy about accepting misfortune, Orual says that it then "seemed to me so light, so far away from our sorrow. I felt we ought not to be talking that way, not now." Then she adds, "What I thought it would be better to talk of, I did not know" [pp. 68-69].

Then comes a series of overwhelming witnesses. The first is that rain, the need for which was the cause of Psyche's sacrifice, actually followed that sacrifice. The fields were wet, the river refilled with water, the birds returned, and the people of Glome were happy in the belief that the gods had accepted their sacrifice and been placated.

Next comes Orual's finding of Psyche "alive" and looking healthier and happier than ever. Though Orual does not believe either in Psyche's palace or her loving husband, she sees before her an incontrovertible fact—her glorious sister full of life and warmth of welcome. And then, after their violent parting, Orual goes down at twilight to drink from the stream and momentarily, but truly, sees the palace. In her own words there it stood "solid and motionless, wall within wall, pillar and arch and architrave, acres of it, a labyrinthine beauty . . . like no other house ever seen in our land or age. Pinnacles and buttresses leaped up . . . unbelievably tall and slender, pointed and prickly as if stone were shooting out into branch and flower" [p. 132]. Orual later stated her doubts about seeing the palace, but reading this account of its bulk and details one knows how she was fooling herself.

Another strong witness occurred on the second trip when Orual had won the victory over Psyche by commanding her to test her unseen husband and pledging her own suicide unless it was done. Yet promptly Orual was beset with the fear that she might have been wrong and that "a real god" is involved. She was terribly tempted to run back and stop what she had put into motion, but, she says, "I governed it" [p. 169]. What a difference had she succumbed.

For the Christian one of the great scenes of the book is what follows Psyche's forced testing of her husband. Lewis always wishes to say that "Aslan is not a tame lion," i.e., that there is another side to God than His love, and both aspects are clearly seen here. There is a great flash and thunder and lightning and a vast flood. Then comes the voice which "even in its implacable sternness" was "golden." Her response, Orual says, is "the salute that mortal flesh gives to immortal things" [p. 171]. For a moment Orual experienced a theophany, the very face of God, and she said it was mainly the beauty, not the terror, that mastered her.

But now a new stage of both Psyche's and Orual's lives must begin, an Oedipean wandering, particularly a wandering of the soul, day after day and year after year. The beginning of it is marked by "the passionless and measureless rejection" with which the face of God looked on Orual. A voice "unmoved and sweet; like a bird singing on the branch above a hanged man" said that Psyche was going out into exile and suffering, and then added, enigmatically, that Orual "also shall be Psyche" [pp. 173-74].

Having undergone and successfully resisted the witness, Orual now begins to suffer the consequences. Yet one of those consequences is that God did not forsake her. The road back was a long, miserable road, and in many ways strikingly like the road taken by C. S. Lewis himself.

The story suggests two extreme sorts of response to God. One is that of Psyche herself. From earliest childhood her longing had been toward the mountain. Intuitively she believed she belonged there; she seemed natively to love and to possess religious virtues. She was born into a pagan home and a pagan city, yet she had a natural beauty of both body and soul. (All of us know of some pagan family today who produces a Psyche.) The other extreme type is represented by Orual, an instance of a person to whom God seemingly says, "I will have you, whether or no." St. Paul was such a man, and C. S. Lewis was another. At sixteen, Lewis wrote his boyhood friend Arthur Greeves of how God liked to get hold of some first-rate person and torture him with "cruelty after cruelty without any escape." He had nothing but contempt for "all the . . . tomfoolery about virgin birth, magic healings, apparitions, and so forth."[1] After her experience beyond the mountain, Orual now realizes that the gods exist and, taking the anthropomorphic view, concludes that the gods hate her and intend to be revenged on her. She has heard that the gods sometimes turn men into beasts, so she puts her hand up to see if she can feel cat's fur or hog's tusks beginning to grow on her face [p. 175]. But her wounds are of another sort, the kind that most men are acquainted with.

For one thing, she says she went over the religious view of things "many thousand times" [p. 72]. Yet, forgetting the pathos of the face and the voice she experienced in the storm, she retains her hatred of the gods. Sometimes she pities herself [p. 209]. Other times she becomes very hard. She wishes for the death of her father [p. 202]. She hardens herself. She decides to destroy the Orual of the past by plunging into her duties as the new queen and for a while she is successful. She kills a man in a duel. Meantime she concludes to hide her ugly face under a lifetime veil. Have we not seen people wearing this sort of veil; indeed. have we not ourselves worn such a veil? Orual's experience proves it cannot hide her from God but only, in part, from the people around her.

She comes to wonder who "sends us this senseless repetition of days and nights and seasons and years" and feels it is "like hearing a stupid boy whistle the same tune over and over, till you wonder how he can bear it himself" [p. 236]. What a contrast this is with the Green Lady in *Perelandra*, who accepts at God's hand each day as a precious new gift, the best day of all. Orual gains just one brief period of happiness, about the time when she knows she is in love with Bardia and when she for a little appears to succeed in killing the old Orual [p. 222].

Interestingly, once Orual falls down seriously before the gods and prays to them [p. 150]. Yet there is no response from the gods. She confesses, however, that she came "without a sacrifice" and requiring of the gods a sign. With what a stroke of genius does Lewis handle this experience of Orual's. There *was* a sign, not a new sign but a repetition of one of the clearest signs Orual had experienced of the gods. Had she not been warmly conscious that the dread drought ceased and the birds returned after Psyche's sacrifice on the mountain? She says that all the time she lay on the floor asking the gods for a sign there was rain on the roof. Rain, often a symbol in the Bible of God's presence and care, was for Orual also a sign. We can imagine what results might have ensued if her very abject confession before the gods had had no strings attached. Even with the strings the sign was there all the time and actually heard by her, yet without any spiritual recognition. She was not yet able to get her eyes opened to an unbargaining God.

What was the underlying problem of Orual? It was something that I think Lewis understood almost as well as any person in history—understood and desperately feared. It was the insidiousness with which self crawls into every single crevice of one's being. In this respect Orual was a replica of pagan and Christian alike.

Orual was in most respects an excellent and admirable person. She was reasonable, enthusiastic, brave, friendly, progressive, and a lover of justice. She was an excellent queen, efficient and just. She would have made a good neighbor. She vigorously took Psyche's part when she thought her sister unjustly sacrificed by the people of Glome. She hated her father's rages and was desperately ashamed of his cowardice when the lots were drawn for the sacrificial victim for the city of Glome.

Orual's great defect was selfishness and selfishness masquerading under the perfectly serious mantle of love. Orual is Maia. In Hindu religion Maia means "illusion." Maia is also "nature" or what Christians would call "the natural man." Almost from the moment of Psyche's birth, Orual loved her deeply and as Psyche grew up she and Orual and the Fox spent deliriously happy days together. After Psyche's sacrifice on the mountain, the world for Orual was like a "dead desert" [p. 89]. The trouble arose the moment it appeared that Psyche was to be lost to another [p. 104]. The Fox himself had to tell Orual on one occasion that she hates, rather than loves, her sister. "There's one part love in your heart, and five parts anger, and seven parts pride," he tells her [p. 148]. Orual's agitated attitude that Psyche must not be sacrificed is in some respects like that of the disciples who told Christ that He must not go to the Cross.

Through the long years of Orual's successful queenship, there was little cessation of the calling. She was constantly reminded, much as she tried to avoid them, of little memories of the happy days of childhood. The rain on the roof always spoke to her. But the beginning of her real enlightenment to her evil self-defensive attitude appeared when Orual visited the little temple in the woods and, full of astonishment, heard her own story retold as a myth. She was nonplussed about the priest's account of how the Orual of the myth really saw the palace, as she had carefully hidden that part of her experience from everybody. The only conclusion she could draw was that the gods themselves had somehow implanted that fact in the myth [p. 243]. But the thing which really incensed her was the claim of the myth that she hated Psyche [p. 244]. She had not taken the earlier hints of this seriously, and now she promptly decided, in her insulted state of mind, to write down her case against the gods. She felt that since the terrible story that she hated her sister had gone abroad while she was yet alive, she must correct it by assuring the world of the truth, that is, of her great love for Psyche. It was the door which opened up for Orual all the "terrors, humiliations, struggles, and anguish" [p. 247] of her life and she wanted the real facts to be known.

On this note the first book concludes.

The second opens with the remark, "I must unroll my book again." A whole new element had loomed up. The thing which caused the second account was the writing down of her case against the gods [p. 253].

Orual now began to sort out the threads of the tangle in her mind—to review the whole of her life with a different viewpoint. Sometimes the sorting took place in her dreams and once she found herself "separating motive from motive and both from pretext" [p. 256]. It was like a vast pile of different kinds of seeds which needed to be separated but could not be. Then the first great blow to Orual's pride came in the form of a real event. Bardia died and Orual went to comfort his widow and made the horrendous discovery that her love-hate of Bardia had destroyed him. Ansit told her, "Your queenship drank up his blood year by year and ate out his life." When Orual remonstrated and asked why Ansit never told her this, Ansit replied that he was a soldier and she must not "make him so mine that he was no longer his" [p. 264]. Note the double meaning here of 1) Orual's selfishness and 2) the way of God, who wants each person to be a free agent living the particular and peculiar life He has bestowed on him or her, rather than an automaton. (Psyche also loved Bardia but, like Ansit, she never thought of "devouring" him.) Orual now for the first time realizes that she is a destroyer of freedom in people's lives, that, like the legend of the Shadowbrute, the loving and devouring are all one.

"And now," says Orual, "those divine Surgeons [Lewis capitalizes the word] had me tied down and were at work." She had to confess to herself that in reality she hated Bardia. "A love like that," she said, "can grow to be nine-tenths hatred and still call itself love" [p. 266]. But to be able to see and say such a thing as that meant that now Orual was clearly on the right way. She was in position to get a new and correct view of the way things really are. Mainly she simply came to the end of herself. Thereafter she was "drenched with seeings." In his autobiography, Lewis tells how his "Adversary [God] began to make His final moves" [Surprised by Joy, p. 216]. Later he adds, "Amiable agnostics will talk cheerfully about 'man's search for God.' To me, as I then was, they might as well have talked about the mouse's search for the cat" [Surprised by Joy, p. 227].

One thing which Orual discovered is that people really are helped and made happy by the ancient and bloody Ungit, not the clean and pretty one set up by Arnom. Then she experiences the vision of her descent down through one Pillar Room after another until finally she comes all the way down to "living rock" [p. 275], where she must stand and see herself as she really is. She knows now that she has indeed been Ungit, "that all-devouring womb-like, yet barren, thing" [p. 276]. Under the burden of these things, she decides to kill herself, but at the moment of flinging herself into the River Shennit, a god speaks to her. Even in her desperate intent to commit suicide, she is on the way to God. The rebel in her is now gone and she finds herself a "cold, small, helpless thing" [p. 277], a necessary condition to any real progress. "Die before you die. There is no chance after," says the god [p. 279]. Psyche had long before told Orual, "If I am to go to the god, of course it must be through death" [p. 72], and I think it is not wholly out of place here to believe, looking back, that Psyche meant death to self.

But still Orual has a way to go. Her next step is self-reformation based on the Fox's philosophy. She fails. Fate, she believes, is against her. It is at this point that she has the vision of the rams of the gods whose "gladness" injures her. God will have no mere reformation. There is a way to successfully get the golden fleece —a way made apparent when Orual sees another woman able to pro-cure it, to procure it from "the thorns" and thus win it without any effort [p. 284].

Thus Orual failed the first two tasks, the separating and the getting. Now she has the vision of walking over burning sands to get a bowl full of the water of death. Again she fails. An eagle dis-covers Orual on the sands, picks her up, and carries her into the Deadlands to be placed on trial [p. 287]. In this judgement hall, before her father, the Fox, Batta, and others, Orual is ordered to read her lifelong complaint against the gods, but it works out very differently from what she expects. Her last great stronghold is de-stroyed—the conviction that she had always loved Psyche. As she reads her complaint she discovers that she really preferred Psyche dead to Psyche made immortal. "She was mine. *Mine*," the com-plaint said. The gods, she charged, are "a tree in whose shadow we can't thrive. We want to be our own. I was my own and Psyche was mine and no one else had any right to her. . . . You stole her to make her happy." She continues to read her complaint over and over (Have we not all known someone exactly like this?) until finally the judge stops her. He asks, "Are you answered?" and she says, "Yes" [pp. 291-93].

All along the two sisters were alike and different. Both pay the

price of failure to recognize the divine calling, Psyche for disobeying her husband and Orual for her spiritual blindness. But Psyche,
we know, is married to Love, that Love which Orual has steadily
rejected. And thus Psyche is helped in the tasks in which Orual so
abjectly fails. "We toiled together over those burning sands, she
with her *empty* bowl, I with the book *full* of my poison" [p. 300].
My italicized words show the difference—Psyche now emptied and
eager for her husband, but Orual with her full bowl of complaints
that shut out Love.

Then we have that great page in the novel on which Orual confesses, "The complaint was the answer. . . . I saw well why the
gods do not speak to us openly, nor let us answer. Till that word
can be dug out of us, why should they hear the babble that we
think we mean? How can they meet us face to face till we have
faces?" [p. 294]. Feeling that the gods have stolen her sister from
her, Orual spends almost a lifetime putting down her case against
them. Towards the end of her life she discovers, through a series
of dreams and visions, how shoddy her case actually was.

But now, as in any good courtroom, the defendants must answer
the plaintiff. The gods have been called into court. Orual fearfully
asks the Fox what is likely to happen to her. In reply the Fox says,
"Whatever else you get, you will not get justice." "Are the gods not
just?", Orual asks. "Oh no, child," is the answer. "What would become of us if they were?" [p. 297].

In the last beautiful and powerful portion of the story Orual finds
not the justice but the love of the gods. By means of living pictures
Orual learns of another attitude and another response toward the
gods, mostly through seeing Psyche's means of sorting the seeds,
acquiring the golden fleece, and filling the bowl with the water of
death. When she asks how she could do such things and be happy,
the answer is, "Another bore nearly all the anguish" [p. 300].
There seem to be at least two meanings here. One is that Love
bore the anguish. Another is that in suffering Orual discovered the
anguish of God over one lost to Him, as Psyche seemed to be lost
to Orual. God is jealous for what is truly His own. Orual learns
that the cry of foolish men for heavenly justice is not at all a cry
for justice, but a mere muttering and whining [p. 301].

Orual's "seeings" have now brought her almost full circle. Having
discovered the nature of Love Himself, she is prepared for the last
great vision of Psyche going into the deadlands to bring back the
casket of beauty from "death herself" [p. 301]. This trip illustrates
the manysidedness of myth as Lewis sees it. It has at least three
important aspects. It is the token of Psyche's unswerving obedience
to her husband. In Apuleius, Psyche, on the brink of success in her

trip to and from Hades, failed because at the last moment her curiosity and the wish to have a little of the beauty in the casket for herself overcame her. Not so with Lewis's Psyche. Here she refuses to listen to the voices crying to her to take care and to return to safety and goes straightforward to the completion of her task. Orual herself was one who cried, "Come back. Come back" [p. 304], and now Orual discovers her own terrible mistake in the two visits she had paid to Psyche long before. But there is a third and significant overtone of another "descent into hell" in which, by obedience to the point of bloody hands, feet, and side, an ineffable beauty was brought back to men. Like Orual, the reader at this point in the story is himself "drenched with seeings," and is as overjoyed as Orual herself at the glorious appearing of Love Himself to replace her lifetime ugliness with a heavenly beauty.

Such, I think, is the main interpretation of this Christian myth. The place of the Fox in the story is clearer than anything else, I think. For him nature and reason are "the Whole," with allowances also for "custom" [pp. 85, 87]. The gods are in nature. The Fox believes in the gods after the fashion of an "enlightened" man. They may be good for ignorant people, but, after all, he comes into Glome as an "expert" from abroad, as the man with the last word in philosophy and ethics. Finally he has to confess that his philosophy was as clear, but also as thin, as water. There is also the telling fact in his rationalism that it breaks down frequently when his heart is moved. The Fox seems to be Lewis's old tutor, the Great Knock, a logician and an atheist who nevertheless on Sundays put on a nicer suit than usual to go out and do his gardening. One must not miss the significant postscript to the book which says that the whole account was intended for the Greeks to read, that is, the people today who are like the Fox.

I think the place of Ungit in the story is also very clear, at least in its main theme. Ungit's house is said to resemble "the egg from which the whole world was hatched" [p. 94]. This is obviously another allusion to Lewis's belief concerning the meaning of myth. Here it primarily means that pagan myths are often involved with blood sacrifices and this Lewis explains is owing to an initial revelation to all nations of the essential nucleus of a theme which was made finally and fully clear in the Incarnation and Crucifixion of Jesus Christ. In the sweet-smelling little temple which Orual found in the forest it was not blood that was sacrificed but flowers and fruit, if indeed there was any sacrifice at all. The difference between Ungit and the woodland temple was the difference between the sacrifices of Cain and Abel. Even in Glome, pagan as it was, the blood in some mysterious way "worked."

Bardia seems to be given us not only to show another instance of Orual's devouring but also to show the sort of man who might be found walking down almost any street or even sitting in a church. He is a Stoic, a man who "does his duty" [p. 90], but, though a "god-fearing man" [p. 99], really manages to leave the gods alone. He readily remembers the saying in Glome that "beyond the Tree, it's all gods' country" [p. 100], but it is a saying, not a reality, to him. That belief is part of the mythology of Glome and illustrates Lewis's conception of how myth becomes encrusted with "filth," for Bardia and all the people of Glome had quite literally "brutalized" "the gods' country" by substituting a Shadowbrute for what Psyche and finally Orual knew to be the land of Love Himself. (If we do not accept God, we tend to brutalize him.) Bardia is a prudent, courteous, hard-working, duty-fulfilling man [p. 69] who gives the gods their due and otherwise steers clear of them.

Redival, by the way, is apparently the selfish, lustful worldling more concerned about "getting and spending" and a good time than anything else. Ungit means nothing to her. The interesting thing is that the resentful and hateful Orual, the rebel who vigorously makes her case against the gods, is the one who comes through, not Redival.

A troublesome element in the story is the "transformations" which keep appearing. The people of Glome say that as healer Psyche is Ungit and they worship her [p. 32]. Orual tells Psyche that she has always been the only father and mother and kin—"and all the King too"—that Psyche has ever had [p. 158]. "You also shall be Psyche," says the god to Orual [p. 174]. I think that one way at least in which Orual became Psyche was the long years in which Orual suffered the memory and the pain of her injury to Psyche. Without going into detail, we can perhaps best explain this element in the story by reference to the teachings of Charles Williams, Lewis's close friend, on co-inherence and substitution. Behind this conception is the idea that the world is inevitably a unity and therefore that men, made in the image of God, are capable of knowing and indeed undergoing the joys and sorrows of another. The most striking illustration of it in Lewis is the fact that for a period he took the pain from his wife's cancerous thigh and suffered while at the same time she was relieved of her pain.[2] The great co-inherence is suggested by a poem of Lewis's, two lines of which run, "Nearly they stood who fall" and "Nearly they fell who stand."[3] How close Orual came to "standing" that time when she was all but overpowered with the idea of rushing back to Psyche and cancelling the promise of Psyche to "test" her husband.

My present reading of the story has suggested to me all over again something of its almost unlimited mythic quality. There seems to be hardly a page—sometimes hardly a sentence—which has not its overtone about which one must ask, "Is there something else here?" For instance, the unseen lover of Psyche suggests more or less the whole relationship between the Christian and Christ. Though unseen, He is our great love and worthy of the test to "forsake all others." Even the sexual relation, as Bible students well know, is one of the important metaphors of the New Testament. Also, this whole palace picture often suggests the glories of heaven as seen in the book of Revelation and the final goal of the Christian, to be the bride of the Lamb, as Psyche herself suggests the perfection of the Church, "without spot or wrinkle."

One characteristic of a great book, said Mortimer J. Adler, is that it will not let you down if you try to read it well. By this standard I think that *Till We Have Faces* is surely a great book.

Steve J. Van Der Weele

From Mt. Olympus to Glome:
C. S. Lewis's Dislocation of Apuleius's
"Cupid and Psyche" in *Till We Have Faces*

WHEN Polonius, reading the license which the visiting players have brought with them to the Danish court, classifies actors as "either for tragedy, comedy, history, pastoral, pastoral-comical, historical-pastoral, tragical-historical, tragical-comical-historical-pastoral-tragical," he offers a useful strategy for classifying what is generally recognized as among C. S Lewis's most profound works, *Till We Have Faces*. For he has chosen to impart the wisdom of a near-lifetime in the form of a romance-myth-allegory-autobiography-confession. In a brief preface to the novel he stated,

> This re-interpretation of an old story has lived in the author's mind, thickening and hardening with the years, ever since he was an undergraduate. That way, he could be said to have worked at it most of his life. Recently, what seemed to be the right form presented itself and themes suddenly interlocked: the straight tale of barbarism, the mind of an ugly woman, dark idolatry and pale enlightenment at war with each other and with vision, and the havoc which a vocation or even a faith, works on human life.[1]

Lewis, of course, derived his knowledge of the story from Apuleius, a late Latin writer of the second century, author of *Metamorphoses*; he suggests Robert Graves's translation as a suitable one for the reader interested in the original version.[2] In his retelling, Lewis carries out a strong belief of his, namely, that the treatment of any subject by a Christian writer should be superior to the treatment of that subject by a non-Christian writer. What he has done is not only to amplify Apuleius's story of Cupid and Psyche, making explicit what is implicit, but also to impose levels of meaning far beyond the scope and purview of this raconteur. I should like in this paper to set forth the nature of his adaptations—dislocations, as I indicate in my title, is a better way of putting it—and to assess the significance of that achievement.

Lewis, of course, was not the first to be haunted by the power of this tale. It has often been told and retold in literature and has been treated frequently in art. There is an archetypal quality about the story, and it has generated many meanings. Francis Bacon, for example, in his too little known *Wisdom of the Ancients*, attempted to ferret out the allegorical significance of at least the figures of Cupid and Venus.[3] It engaged the poetic energies of John Keats, William Morris, and Robert Bridges. Walter Pater sensed the peculiar excellence of this story, calling it "a true gem amid mockeries . . . full of brilliant, life-like situations, . . . abounding in lovely visible imagery . . . full also of a gentle idealism. . . . With a concentration of all his finer literary gifts, Apuleius had gathered into it the floating star-matter of many a delightful old story."[4] Bullfinch retells it at some length in his *Mythology*, and it even gets included in Magill's *Masterplots*.

Lewis retains, at least superficially, many of the ingredients of Apuleius's account. He appropriates the crucial elements of the wrath of Venus, the envy of the sisters, Psyche's sacrifice, the impossible tasks which Venus assigns her. It is the story of two sisters who fall out with a third sister, Psyche, because she is so beautiful that the gods single her out for special attention. As a punishment for the neglect which she suffers as a consequence of Psyche's beauty, Venus orders Cupid to punish this upstart. Cupid, wholly contrary to his mother's intent and command, himself falls in love with Psyche. The sisters set out to destroy her but are themselves destroyed. Thereupon Jupiter calls an assembly of the gods (a penalty of 10,000 drachmas for nonappearance) and has Cupid marry Psyche in order to establish for humanity that greater stability which monogamy brings over promiscuity.

It is well at the outset, however, that we remind ourselves that Lewis felt no particular obligation to retain fidelity to Apuleius. When he called his novel "A Myth Retold" he was not attempting yet one other version or translation of this tale. He says,

> Nothing was further from my aim than to recapture the peculiar quality of the *Metamorphoses*—that strange compound of picaresque novel, horror comic, mystagogue's tract, pornography, and stylistic experiment. [p. 313]

He regards Apuleius, he tells us, as a "source," an "influence," not a model.

We must nevertheless begin with some notice of what Lewis found useful to his purpose, remembering all the while, though, that there is hardly a detail which he retained which does not get baptized, does not undergo some radical "sea change" in his telling. Readers of Lewis's novel will recognize such Apuleian motifs as the following:

The extraordinary beauty of Psyche, which leads to people's identifying her with the gods

The resulting neglect of the orthodox deities

The summons to the king to sacrifice Psyche for the well-being of the country

The sacrifice-marriage episode

The freeing of Psyche by her lover through the instrumentality of the West Wind

Psyche's life with the god, whom, however, she is commanded not to see

Cupid's warning of the evil and treachery of Psyche's sisters

The sisters' visits (only one in Lewis's version) and determination, from a variety of causes, to break up the marriage

Psyche's plea to see her sisters and Cupid's reluctant consent to this request

Psyche's fantasizing to her sisters about her life with her husband

The promise of Psyche to light the lamp by which she will see Cupid's face, and the ensuing disasters when the drop of hot oil falls on his body and awakens him

Cupid's divorcing of Psyche

The nearly-impossible tasks which Venus imposes on Psyche, but which she manages with supernatural help

The ultimate bestowal of immortality on Psyche

But Lewis also omits some details of Apuleius's telling:

The whole mythological setting, the pageant of Olympian deities, including such allegorical characters as Anger, Grief, and Sobriety (It is an important point of this paper that, throughout, Lewis substitutes reconstructed history for classical mythology.)

The temptation of Psyche to look in the box for beauty, the motif which, in Apuleius's telling, puts her to sleep until Cupid finds her

Psyche's naivete about the facts of life, including the source of her pregnancy, and Venus's taunt that the child will be immortal if Psyche keeps the secret, but mortal if she reveals it

The crude jealousy of the sisters, who resent their husbands and feel humiliated by them

The long process needed for Cupid's recovery from the burn

The curses on the land in the wake of Psyche's lighting the lamp

The birth of the child, who is called Pleasure

What Lewis adds, of course, is what makes the retelling peculiarly his. Far beyond what any listing can indicate, Lewis alters details and amplifies hints to construct a truly great work—authentic, wise, and penetrating. He saw in the Apuleius version potentialities which gave him an opportunity to exhibit what he had by this time come to think of reality, "the real universe, the divine, magical, terrifying and ecstatic reality in which we all live."[5] I submit two examples as particularly instructive of Lewis's procedures.

The two kings—Apuleius's and Lewis's—could not be more different. Apuleius's king acts out of piety; he fears that his daughter and his country may have committed blasphemy. Lewis's is self-centered, irreverent, autocratic, and arbitrary. He is also insensitive. For example, in his euphoria after learning that the priests' lot has passed him by, he has little sympathy to squander on his own daughter Psyche, who has been designated as the sacrifice.

The second example is a reminder of Lewis's alterations of the sisters. In Apuleius, the two sisters are bound together in perfidy against their innocent sister and meet death because of their wickedness. None of the sisters dies in Lewis's version (except, of course, that Orual's death ends the story). Lewis sets Orual at odds with both sisters and has her perpetrate on Redival in mild form the harm that she later works on Psyche.

Thus, Lewis establishes a far more complex relationship among the sisters than appears in the original version. The characterization and narrative are far more profound, more vivid, and wider-ranging than in Apuleius.

These are only two obvious examples among many which can be used to indicate how Lewis, with his "baptized imagination," reshaped the story to achieve his own purposes. But it will be more useful at this point to examine the larger patterns of alteration which he employed. I find these four to be especially crucial:

1) The historical reconstruction of life in the city-state of Glome, the everyday life of the people in this place at that

time, the narrative which provides the matrix for the episode of Cupid and Psyche

2) The strategy of having the story told from the point of view of Orual

3) The episode of Orual's glimpse of the castle and her subsequent enlightenment

4) The exhibition of the anatomy of love—the careful probing of its diseased as opposed to its healthy state, the detection of its atrophied tissues, its malignant and toxic cells

This latter motif, of course, relates the novel to Lewis's many treatments of the subject of love.

One is well advised to take seriously Lewis's statement about the first of these—his substitution of the history of Glome for Apuleius's mythology. He calls it "a work of (supposed) historical imagination. A guess of what it might have been like in a little barbarous state on the borders of the Hellenistic world of Greek culture, just beginning to affect it" [*Letters*, p. 273]. But experienced readers of Lewis, aware of his contempt for the modern smugness about the supposed superiority of all things contemporary over things past (everything that is not eternal, he reminds us, is out of date, all times are equidistant from eternity), will not be lured into thinking that he is merely exercising an antiquarian interest, or that his concern is limited to anthropology. The framework of his tale, as set forth in the beginning and the conclusion, consists of an indictment against the gods (a theme, incidentally, nowhere to be found in Apuleius). But that motif lies dormant for many chapters as he supplies from his knowledge of history and his lively imagination details and atmosphere that Apuleius had no need to include. Thus, the story of Part I has an integrity of its own. Television productions have been made with far less substance.

Lewis's decision to demythologize Apuleius in favor of history gives him the freedom to achieve a major expansion of Apuleius's world and becomes the means by which he conveys the wisdom and insight of the work. He gives that world "a local habitation and a name," and thus furnishes a historical context which supplies the basis for action and judgement. The story of the jealousy of the two sisters is told in a setting of the political and religious life of Glome. One derives unforgettable impressions of the barbaric setting, of life in a feudal arrangement in a world quite distant from the more civilized areas of Greece, of people dealing with the elementary realities of living in a society which takes the gods seriously. It must have occurred to many of the poor that enough livestock was being slaughtered as an offering to the deities to feed the populace during its times of famine. Politically, the kingdom has to cope with pestilence, drought, war, wild animals desperately seeking food, and the problem of succession. Philosophically, the issues center in the Fox, the educated Greek slave, the religious demythologizer. Representing Hellenic Greece, he imports into the half-barbaric state of Glome doubt and skepticism about the gods, proposing a naturalistic explanation for everything the priests interpret religiously. It is the Fox who tries to demolish the logic which links the touch of a hand to the healing of disease, drought to the lack of male sons, rain and fertility to the sacrifice of the Accursed, the proper selection of wood used for the royal bed to male heirs. And it is, incidentally, part of the wisdom of the book to show that both Greek rationalism and barbarian religious intuitions are both superseded by transcendental, supernatural love.

Orual, from whose point of view the story is told, accentuates the historical character of the novel by reciting at the end of Part I some of her achievements as queen. She develops the silver mines to make them productive, begins a library, revises the laws, improves the water supply, commissions a history of Glome. Peace reigns, and Glome can almost rule itself. There is nothing more for her to do. Still, a sense of failure haunts her. Success is not enough. *Vanitas, vanitatis*; nothing matters, really. By ending with this depiction of a spiritual vacuum, Lewis keeps the narrative open and prepares us for the second part, the section which portrays her ultimate enlightenment. In all this, Lewis has explained the myth by placing it within a larger story, one which he would like to have us regard as fairly authentic history.

A second crucial component of Lewis's strategy is his decision to tell the story from the point of view of Orual. This is a major reorientation, a radical departure from Apuleius. By careful design, the full significance of this strategy is seen only in retrospect. His interest, he tells us in his note, is in Orual rather than Psyche, the key figure in other versions. Orual's very act of narrating turns out to be as important an event as any of the episodes which she relates. For this process leads to her own awakening. Her conclusion to Part I ends with this rather existential conclusion:

> I say, therefore, that there is no creature (toad, scorpion, or serpent) so noxious to man as the gods. Let them answer my charge if they can. It may well be that, instead of answering, they'll strike me mad or leprous or turn me into beast, bird, or tree. But will not all the world then know (and the gods will know it knows) that this is because they have no answer? [pp. 249-50]

But to her amazement and chagrin, she discovers that she needed instead to rewrite her story, though there is really no time to do so except for a postscript. She now says, in the opening to Part II:

> What began the change was the very writing itself. Let no one lightly set about such a work. Memory, once waked, will play the tyrant. . . . The past which I wrote down was not the past that I thought I had (all these years) been remembering. . . . The change which the writing wrought in me . . . was only a beginning—only to prepare me for the gods' surgery. They used my own pen to probe my wound. [pp. 253-54]

Little more needs to be said here about this shift in the Apuleius tale. A discussion of the remaining two points will further indicate the significance of Lewis's use of Orual's point of view.

The third alteration of Apuleius is the one which to Lewis, as he informs us, is the most crucial, "making Psyche's palace invisible to normal, mortal eyes—if," he adds, " 'making' is not the wrong word for something which forced itself upon me, almost at my first reading of the story, as the way the thing must have been." (Note, incidentally, how that last phrase indicates once again how firmly Lewis believed in the generative power of myth.) He continues, "This change of course brings with it a more ambivalent motive and a different character for my heroine and finally modifies the whole quality of the tale" [p. 313].

This hint, indeed, gets us close to the heart of the novel. It has to do, actually, with spiritual perception and blindness. Does or does not Orual see Psyche's palace? "Nothing at all, yet all that is I see," says Gertrude when Hamlet asks her, in exasperation, whether she cannot see what he sees all too plainly, the ghost coming to whet his almost-blunted purpose. This spiritual blindness is akin to that of Orual upon the vision she experiences of Psyche's castle, her refusal to disclose to anyone that she had seen the vision, and her refusal to act appropriately—crossing the river and asking Psyche's forgiveness. For this perversity she pays dearly. She forfeits the serenity and newness of spirit that she achieves only at the end of her life. She comes to understand that it was her spiritual idiocy which has kept her from hearing the voice of the gods all these years: "How can they meet us face to face till we have faces?" [p. 294]. Only in her extremity does she face up to this fleeting trace of reality, using it as a base from which to deduce the full truth about herself by sloughing off her complex of evasions and rationalizations and owning up to the destructive quality of her love for Psyche which had kept her from attaining peace with herself and her sister. What occurs is nothing less than the appropriation—to use biblical language—of a clean heart and a new spirit.

Although her rehabilitation occurs in Part II, Lewis drops several

clues already in Part I. Early in the novel, as Orual waits on the
porch for Psyche, the scene alters with the movement of the sun.
She writes: "I watched the shadows of the pillars slowly changing
their position and it was then I first saw how the things we have
known ever since we were weaned can look new and strange, like
enemies" [p. 38]. It is against this comment about perception
that Lewis traces the growing animosity of Orual towards Psyche,
the growing sense of alienation when Psyche becomes less depen-
dent on her. Though at first Orual is able to say, quite sincerely,
"I would have died for her" [p. 71], she becomes resentful and
bitter. She feels betrayed, especially as Psyche explains her longing for the marriage-sacrifice. And now she is compelled to say,

> Since I write this book against the gods, it is just that I should put into it
> whatever can be said against myself. So let me set this down: as
> [Psyche] spoke I felt, amid all my love, a bitterness. Though the
> things she was saying gave her (that was plain enough) courage and
> comfort, I grudged her that courage and comfort. It was as if someone
> or something else had come in between us. If this grudging is the sin
> for which the gods hate me, it is one I have committed. [pp. 74-75]

It adds to the power of the novel that Orual's attitude towards
her sister and the motives for her deeds are superior to those
Apuleius assigns in his tale. In fact, she emerges as an island of
sanity and wisdom in a rough-and-tumble, promiscuous court.
Lewis has the novel end with a tribute to her from the priest, who
calls her "the most wise, just, valiant, fortunate and merciful of
all the princes known in our parts of the world" [pp. 308-09].
She is much more attractive than the sensuous, superficial, hedo-
nistic Redival. She vows that no monster is going to destroy Psyche,
her beloved sister, and feels strongly the obligation to remove her
from the palace. Psyche must not be allowed to carry a beggar's
brat in her body. Nor must she let her sister be the sport of a demon.
But her love gradually becomes more possessive, less concerned
for Psyche than for herself, and she admits that it gets to consist
of "one part love . . . , and five parts anger, and seven parts
pride" [p. 148].

In the crucial scene, a discontinuity develops between Orual and
Psyche. She feels remote from Psyche, whose robes appear like
rags, who feeds her what she experiences as water, not ambrosial
nectar. Psyche pleads with her, begging her to acknowledge the
reality of the situation. Then comes the brief view of the palace:

> There stood the palace, grey—as all things were grey in that hour and
> place—but solid and motionless, wall within wall, pillar and arch and
> architrave, acres of it, a labyrinthine beauty. [p. 132]

But though there may be some legitimate doubt about the reality of the vision, the truth of the matter is that she doesn't want to see it, and the castle vanishes. She chooses to deny its reality. And at this point she employs—in a scene, once again, which goes far beyond Apuleius, whose sisters were only jealous of the good luck which had befallen their sister—a form of blackmail by slashing herself to extract the promise from her sister Psyche that she will gaze at her husband by lamplight to see what manner of creature she had married. Orual becomes a temptress, a spiritual enemy of Psyche.

Once the transformation begins, events happen quickly. They must, for Orual is nearing the end of her life. She desperately seeks to extricate herself from the marmalade of her deceptions. "It was a labour of sifting and sorting, separating motive from motive and both from pretext" [p. 256]. One of the most shattering episodes in this process is her encounter with Bardia's widow. Here she comes to understand that all the while she was taking this faithful servant for granted, she was at the same time subtly jealous about his family attachments, tyrannizing him by exploiting his sense of duty and loyalty. His widow supplies the statistics: "Five wars, thirty-one battles, nineteen embassies, taking thought for this and thought for that. . . . The mines are not the only place where a man can be worked to death. . . . You have been a fortunate queen; no prince ever had more loving servants" [pp. 260-61].

Orual reels under the widow's "You're full fed. Gorged with other men's lives, women's too: Bardia's, mine, the Fox's, your sister's—both your sisters' " [p. 265]. Now the motifs of spiritual death from which life can be resurrected, of sacrificial and vicarious suffering, of sterility and barrenness and fertility, of appearance and reality, all converge to bring about her final illumination: "I was being unmade. I was no one" [p. 307]. At the final judgement of the voices, she hears the words, "You also are Psyche." Now she kisses Psyche's feet, acknowledging her to be a goddess. She concludes: "I ended my first book with the words no answer. I know now, Lord, why you utter no answer. You are yourself the answer. Before your face questions die away. What other answer would suffice? Only words, words; to be led out to battle against other words" [p. 308].

By now it should be apparent that the novel is really about love. The fourth alteration Lewis achieves is to take some hints from Apuleius but to go beyond him in focusing our attention ultimately on the subject of love—both its proper forms and the ethical ambiguities which jeopardize its proper expression. The author of *The Screwtape Letters* saw beyond the mere jealousy of Apuleuis's sisters and located the motif of that love which, when unsanctified, becomes tyrannical and possessive, which rots and stinks and turns into hatred. In fact, the best commentary on the novel is Lewis's *The Four Loves*; all four of his categories—*Storge*, Friendship, Eros, *Agape*—weave in and out of the novel so as to make these works complements of each other. Mr. Kilby is correct in pointing out that the ambiguities in Orual's love for Psyche were part of an entire lifetime of antagonism towards the gods.[6] Not until she gets squared away with them does she divest herself of her wish to control and possess; for that matter, not until she encounters the gods honestly does she achieve her own maturity. Lewis's modifications of Apuleius's tale discussed so far are tributary to his analysis and diagnosis of the totality of man's relationships—love of the gods leading to love of fellow human beings.

What can be said by way of summary? To put it simply, Lewis elicited in the story potentialities which Apuleius could not fathom. To be sure, some qualities of Lewis's own conception of the story are present in the original tale, and commentators have addressed themselves to the allegorical force of some of the episodes: the fragile quality of love, the need for trust, the toxin of jealousy. Significances of several kinds also attach to the lamp, the encounter of the mortal and the immortal, the soul's aspiration towards love (or reason), the motif of the quest, the vegetation rituals, the all-but-impossible tasks to be performed, the preference of monogamy over promiscuity. In all this, the original tale has filiations with romances of all kinds. But Lewis, surely regarding this as one of the good stories that God left to survive so as to act as a bridge between man and Himself, transformed a good tale into a profound one. Roy Battenhouse's observations about the qualities of myth are relevant at this point:

> Myths serve the artist as first principles by which both to explore and to explain. They enable a poet to make a beginning and to make toward an end. They determine his plot or fable. They define his logic. Without myth the effort at poetry cannot rise above indiscriminate sensibility, or blind reporting, or a hesitant groping amid winds of doctrine toward the ever elusive story of man.[7]

Thus, where Apuleius's tale is morally tentative and ambiguous, Lewis's involves commitment. Despite his disclaimer that Psyche is an instance of "the *anima naturaliter Christiana* making the best of the Pagan religion she is brought up in and thus being guided (but always 'under the cloud,' always in terms of her own imaginations or that of her people) towards the true God" [*Letters*, p. 274], she profoundly illuminates, at the highest reaches of the myth, the mission, scope, and sacrifice of Christ himself.

What Lewis has done is similar to what Christopher Fry has done in his *A Phoenix Too Frequent* with Petronius's cynical tale of the Ephesian Lady, and what Milton did in his *Samson Agonistes* with models provided him by the writers of Greek tragedy. Such achievements remind us of what especially a secular society prefers to ignore: that Christianity has resources of insight and wisdom not available to those who deny transcendence or the reality of Christian revelation.

Joe R. Christopher

Archetypal Patterns in *Till We Have Faces*

MANY readers consider *Till We Have Faces* C. S. Lewis's best piece of fiction. Obviously no single paper is able to "prove" this, but this study can offer some parallels, some analogies, which will serve to illuminate part of the richness of this book. These parallels are here called archetypes because the author believes them to be universal human patterns incarnated in Lewis's fiction; however, it should be added that he approaches this amorphous field of criticism as a litterateur, not as a Freudian or a Jungian. Therefore, the parallels tend to be from literature, biblical or other, rather than from psychiatrically interpreted myth. This (or any) archetypal approach has not been emphasized in previous discussions of the novel, and the result will, it is hoped, not be simply a literary study (if such a chemically pure substance exists) but one with religious and human implications.[1]

A passage from the book will suggest something of both form and matter, as well as introduce the content. It describes the preparations for the birth of a royal child (who turns out to be a girl, Istra):

> Of course no one in the house went to bed on the night of the birth, for that, they say, will make the child refuse to wake into the world. We all sat in the great hall between the Pillar Room and the Bedchamber, in a red glare of birth-torches. The flames swayed and guttered terribly, for all doors must be open; the shutting of a door might shut up the mother's womb. In the middle of the hall burned a great fire. Every hour the Priest of Ungit walked round it nine times and threw in the proper things. The King sat in his chair and never moved all night, not even his head. I was sitting next to the Fox. [p. 14]

194   TILL WE HAVE FACES

This paragraph, although technically written by Orual as an adult, captures part of a child's viewpoint in its unquestioning acceptance of the use of sympathetic magic. Indeed, several times in Lewis's book the reader not only understands more of the cultural background than do the characters but is left wondering about patterns on which no character comments. Is it an accident, for example, that Glome has its poor harvest after Tarin is gelded [pp. 25-26], or that the King dies at midwinter of a wounded thigh [pp. 184-85, 213-14]? As in "The Knight's Tale"—except that in Chaucer's poem the reader also sees the supernatural machinery—the characters in the first part of this novel fail to understand the full meaning of what happens to them.

In the discussion which follows, this novel of two parts, with twenty-one and four chapters respectively, shall be divided into six sections. The author claims nothing for his divisions except critical utility for his purposes. Since the final section corresponds with the whole of Lewis's second part, the division is primarily a means of isolating patterns in the first part.

The first division, the first chapter, introduces Orual, Redival, the Fox, the kingdom of Glome, and the goddess Ungit. The early fellowship of Orual and Redival is described in a subordinate clause, and the purchase of Lysias, the Fox—a Greek slave—is announced. This division is the exposition, or the background information, of the story.

The second section, chapters two through nine, telling the life of Istra (or, in Greek, Psyche), the third of the sisters, is more complex. The first and most obvious point to make about her life is that it is in the archetypal pattern of the hero, resembling at times (as would be expected) the life of Christ. Her birth is not a virgin birth, to be sure, but her mother dies in the labor and her father rejects her, for he wanted a boy, a male heir to the crown [pp. 19, 22]. So here, in a sense, is the parentless child, like Moses in the bulrushes. She grows up to be the most beautiful girl in the kingdom, so beautiful that the people begin to ask her blessings on children that they may become like her [pp. 27-28]. When the plague comes to Glome, the common mob cries for her to come out of the palace and touch the sick, for she nursed the Fox through his sickness and therefore is credited with having healing hands [pp. 30-32]. Finally, when the priest of Ungit demands a human sacrifice be made to end the drought, Psyche is chosen as the perfect victim, the unstained offering [pp. 49, 55]. If, unlike Christ, she is not crucified on Golgotha, yet she is chained to a Holy Tree on the Gray Mountain [pp. 48, 98, 107]; and if, unlike Christ, she is not resurrected from the dead and does not ascend to God the Father, yet she is taken from the Tree by one god and carried to a secret valley, divided from the world of men by a cold stream, where she is united with another god, her beloved [pp. 101, 110-15].[2]

Why does Lewis use this pattern? One may approach an answer through a quotation from Lewis's *Reflections on the Psalms*—a book published two years after *Till We Have Faces*. This quotation considers double meanings in biblical literature, basing itself in a discussion of Psalm Forty-five, which tells of a wedding:

> Few things once seemed to me more frigid and far-fetched than those interpretations, whether of this Psalm or of the *Song of Songs*, which identify the Bridegroom with Christ and the bride with the Church. Indeed, as we read the frank erotic poetry of the latter and contrast it with the edifying headlines in our Bibles, it is easy to be moved to a smile, even a cynically knowing smile, as if the pious interpreters were feigning an absurd innocence. I should still find it very hard to believe that anything like the "spiritual" sense was remotely intended by the original writers. But no one now (I fancy) who accepts that spiritual or second sense is denying, or saying anything against, the very plain sense which the writers did intend. The Psalm remains a rich, festive Epithalamium, the *Song* remains fine, sometimes exquisite, love poetry, and this is not in the least obliterated by the burden of the new meaning. (Man is still one of the primates; a poem is still black marks on white paper.)[3]

And, one may add to Lewis's position, Istra is still a princess in a barbaric kingdom at the literal level of his fiction, whatever else she may mean, however much she may fit an archetypal pattern.

Lewis continues with four applications of the erotic imagery he is considering—a long passage but quite valuable:

> And later I began to see that the new meaning [of Psalm 45 and *The Song of Songs*] is not arbitrary and springs from depths I had not suspected. First, the language of nearly all great mystics, not even in a common tradition, some of them Pagan, some Islamic, most Christian, confronts us with evidence that the image of marriage, of sexual union, is not only profoundly natural but almost inevitable as a means of expressing the desired union between God and man. The very word "union" has already entailed some such idea.

Before considering the other three applications by Lewis, perhaps one should pause over this mystical marriage. That erotic imagery is used in the sacrifice of Istra is made explicit by the Priest of Ungit, for, after he has said that the Accursed, the wickedest person in the kingdom, must be sacrificed to the Brute, which many say is a shadow, he describes the Great Offering this way:

"It is not done in the house of Ungit," said the Priest. "The victim must be given to the Brute. For the Brute is, in a mystery, Ungit herself or Ungit's son, the god of the Mountain; or both. The victim is led up the mountain to the Holy Tree, and bound to the Tree and left. Then the Brute comes. That is why you angered Ungit just now, King, when you spoke of offering a thief. In the Great Offering, the victim must be perfect. For, in holy language, a man so offered is said to be Ungit's husband, and a woman is said to be the bride of Ungit's son. And both are called the Brute's Supper. And when the Brute is Ungit it lies with the man, and when it is her son it lies with the woman. And either way there is a devouring . . . many different things are said . . . many sacred stories . . . many great mysteries. Some say the loving and the devouring are all the same thing. For in sacred language we say that a woman who lies with a man devours the man. That is why you are so wide of the mark, King, when you think a thief, or an old worn-out slave, or a coward taken in battle, would do for the Great Offering. The best in the land is not too good for this office." [pp. 48-49—ellipses included in the original]

Since Psyche speaks of the god of the mountain as her husband [p. 122], the application of Lewis's comments about the mystical marriage to her marriage is not difficult. In fact, it is basic to the myth which Lewis has retold in his book, to the myth which Apuleius first told in *The Golden Ass*. In the Roman writer's fiction, Psyche (which is Greek for *soul*) is loved by Cupid, son of Venus; in the British writer's fiction, Istra (which is Glomish for *psyche*) is loved by the god of the Gray Mountain, son of Ungit. Thus the human soul (Psyche, Istra) is joined to divine love (Cupid, the god of the mountain); and thus the mystical marriage is consummated, for *eros* is, by analogy, *agape*.

To return to Lewis's applications of the erotic imagery in the Bible:

Secondly, the god as bridegroom, his "holy marriage" with the goddess, is a recurrent theme and a recurrent ritual in many forms of Paganism —Paganism not at what we should call its purest or most enlightened, but perhaps at its most religious, at its most serious and convinced. And if, as I believe, Christ, in transcending and thus abrogating, also fulfils, both Paganism and Judaism, then we may expect that He fulfils this side of it too. This, as well as all else, is to be "summed up" in Him.

For Lewis, therefore, Istra's life resembles Christ's because the life of Christ is the center of reality, and all other happenings take their meaning and pattern from it—that her life (within the fiction) took place before His does not matter, since His truth is eternal,

outside the limits of time. This certainly answers the question of
why Lewis used the pattern. But, one may ask, what of the reader—
how is he to evaluate the archetype of the hero and the mystical
marriage? If he, like Lewis, is a Christian, and if he, like Lewis,
Dante, and others, believes in the salvation of the good pagan,
then he may find in Istra the fictional representation of a virtuous
pagan, whose life suggests that of Christ simply because Christ's
life is the archetypal way of salvation. This reader will say, "Lewis
has here presented the Way, the Truth, the Life—or, at least, the
truth about the way pagan life is, at its best." For the reader who
is not a Christian but who is sympathetic to the romance form—who,
for example, enjoys the Homeric parallels in Joyce's *Ulysses* as
much as the Dublin grime—there will be little problem: he will
suspend his disbelief and read on, reminding himself that Jung
said archetypes occur in literature as they do in dreams. And one
can only assume that the reader who is not sympathetic to the prose
romance genre—whether Christian or non-Christian—will not get
beyond the cover blurbs.

This, however, is not an application of Lewis's comments on the
pagan use of erotic imagery to *Till We Have Faces*. Lewis clarifies
his view of pagan usage a few sentences later than the passage
already quoted: "For the Pagans, the god is the bridegroom of the
mother-goddess, the earth, but his union with her also makes fer-
tile the whole tribe and its livestock." In light of the comments
by the priest of Ungit, it is presumably acceptable to substitute
Istra for the mother-goddess, since she is at least the perfect sacrifice. Therefore, on the pagan level this union between a god and a
sacrifice creates fertility for the tribe: more specifically, Psyche is
sacrificed in order to bring rain to the land of Glome. And, after
the offering, the rain *does* come [pp. 82, 84, 110].

The last two of Lewis's applications may be quoted together:

> Thirdly, the idea appears, in a slightly different form, within Judaism.
> For the mystics God is the Bridegroom of the individual soul. For the
> Pagans, the god is the bridegroom of the mother-goddess, the earth,
> but his union with her also makes fertile the whole tribe and its live-
> stock, so that in a sense he is their bridegroom too. The Judaic con-
> ception is in some ways closer to the Pagan than to that of the mystics,
> for in it the Bride of God is the whole nation, Israel. This is worked out
> in one of the most moving and graphic chapters of the whole Old
> Testament (*Ezekiel* 16). Finally, this is transferred in the Apocalypse
> from the old Israel to the new, and the Bride becomes the Church,
> "the whole blessed company of faithful people." It is this which has,
> like the unworthy bride in Ezekiel, been rescued, washed, clothed,
> and married by God—a marriage like King Cophetua's.

It is difficult to see in *Till We Have Faces* any union of people to God, the Hebraic view, but a case may be made for the Christian view, the union of the church with God. This does not become clear until the end of the book, but what Lewis is describing is not simply an individual's—Psyche's—marriage to God. The god of the Gray Mountain prophesies to Orual that she too will be Psyche [p. 174]. At the end of the book, when Orual has been made spiritually and physically beautiful by the preparation brought from the Dead-lands, then Orual sees her reflection in a garden pool: her appear-ance is identical with that of Psyche, that of the beautiful soul [pp. 307-08]. The waiting together of Istra and Orual for their god to come, at the end of the last vision, does not suggest the in-dividual union with God which is the mystical goal, but a community union, a fellowship of faith, a spiritual harem (in an extreme image), or, in short, the one, holy, catholic Church.

Lewis concludes his comments on Psalm 45 and *The Song of Songs* this way:

> Thus the allegory which at first seemed so arbitrary—the ingenuity of some prudish commentator who was determined to force flat edifica-tions upon the most unpromising texts—turned out, when you seriously tugged at it, to have roots in the whole history of religion, to be loaded with poetry, to yield insights. To reject it because it does not im-mediately appeal to our own age is to be provincial, to have the self-complacent blindness of the stay-at-home.

As has been suggested, at least three of Lewis's four erotic inter-pretations also can be applied to the marriage of the god and Psyche in *Till We Have Faces*. The point is not that these interpretations *have* to be made, but that the archetypal situation allows, and to some degree encourages, them.

The third section, chapters ten through fifteen, detailing the conflict between Orual and Psyche in the valley of the god, may be considered archetypally as another *Paradise Lost* (not, like Lewis's versions in *Perelandra* and *The Magician's Nephew*, a Paradise Re-tained).[4] Psyche, commanded by her beloved not to look upon him, is approached as Adam was approached by Eve, Eve implicitly demanding him to eat the fruit because of their sexual love, Orual explicitly demanding Psyche to disobey her husband's commands because of their friendship and family love [pp. 159-64]. As Lewis observed in *The Four Loves*, affection, friendship, and eros may all be perverted:[5] here, Orual distorts affection and friendship in her relationship with Psyche, as she elsewhere distorts eros with her counsellor Bardia [e.g., p. 224]. But of course at the time Orual does not understand that she is distorting these loves: she feels, for example, that she is concerned for Psyche, not jealous of her; that she must rescue Psyche from some animalistic god (if Bardia is right about why the god prohibits Psyche from seeing him— pp. 135-36) or from some wandering vagabond (if the Fox is correct when he says Psyche must be mad, having been rescued from the tree by a criminal and believing him a god—pp. 141-44). Only when she reads her complaint against the gods does Orual realize that she accepted these answers because subconsciously she did hate Psyche for being chosen by the god; subconsciously she was jealous of her [cf. pp. 81-82, 200-01]. Eve is not so clear in her self-understanding in *Paradise Lost*, nor are most men in their blindness to their own sins. But perhaps on the Day of Judgement, the day when they have to read their autobiographies aloud to the assembled multitudes, they will be.

The next section, chapters sixteen through twenty, tells of Orual's life as queen—more specifically, as the veiled queen. Two important points should be made here. First, the reader will feel a difference of tone in this part. Partially, this comes from the disappearance of archetypes—no *Imitation of Christ*, no *Paradise Lost*. This is the period in which Orual has no religious visions, when she works without hope; indeed, when she works so that she may forget what she has done to Psyche and may forget the god which appeared to her then. The tone in the first four chapters of this section shifts to that of a Sabatini sword-play romance. Lewis wants to show Orual taking over the queenship, so he provides his reader with a fleeing prince and the queen's fight for him as his champion [pp. 190-93, 218-19]: this is familiar material, and if the sexes were reversed one would expect it to end in marriage. Northrop Frye, in his "Theory of Modes," would say that the tone drops from the level of romance to that of high mimesis. Also, romance, with its closeness to myth (and hence, in Frye's terms, to archetype), gives way to politics, to work—bargaining with Arnom over "the Crumbles" [pp. 187-89], planning an honorable way around war with Argan [pp. 194-99], and (in the final chapter of this section, which summarizes the rest of the queen's reign after the duel) achieving these objectives:

> I had all the laws revised and cut in stone in the center of the city. I narrowed and deepened the Shennit till barges could come up to our gates. I made a bridge where the old ford had been. I made cisterns so that we should not go thirsty whenever there was a dry year. I became wise about stock and bought [brought?] in good bulls and rams and bettered our breeds. I did and I did and I did—and what does it matter

what I did? I cared for all these things only as a man cares for a hunt or a game, which fills the mind and seems of some moment while it lasts, but then the beast's killed or the king's mated, and now who cares? [pp. 235-36]

A minor point can be made about this shift in tone: the politics in the palace and temple are hinted at in the death of the old Priest and King Trom. Arnom says about the Priest: "If I have any skill, he'll not last five days" [p. 187]. The statement is ambiguous—Arnom is the most skilled doctor in the realm—but sinister. Two hints appear concerning the king:

Arnom and the Fox went to the Bedchamber and fell into talk about the King's condition (those two seemed to understand each other well). [p. 205]

They both had medical vocabularies?

The Fox was sitting by the bedside—why, or with what thoughts, I don't know. It was not possible he should love his old master. [p. 213]

Orual underestimates the Fox's power of love? These hints establish part of the tone of this section also; not all of the politics and work are openly displayed.

The second main point to be made about this section concerns the meaning of the queen's veil. Here the reader may be reminded if not of an archetype—it is hardly that—then of a parallel, in Nathaniel Hawthorne's story of "The Minister's Black Veil." Both veils are, in different ways, ambiguous. Orual had first worn hers when going to the Holy Tree, for she did not want to be recognized [pp. 93, 154]; later she began to wear it constantly [cf. pp. 180-81]. Now, as she becomes queen, she finds its psychological value [pp. 228-29]. Lewis probably means this to suggest that the queenship becomes a mask for Orual, an outward personality behind which the grieving, the unhappiness, the bitterness, can go on. Orual thinks of her queenship—not precisely of her veil—as the emergence of a second personality. As she used the image of damming rivers when she was trying to forget the loss of Psyche [pp. 184, 189], so she thinks she is burying not only Psyche but herself when she covers the well [pp. 234-35]. The opposite of this veil image appears at the end of the book when Orual is stripped of all her clothes just before she delivers her complaint against the gods and thus realizes her true character [p. 289]. One remembers that Lewis's original title for this book was *Bareface*.[6]

Orual comments at one point that the veil "is a sort of treaty made with my ugliness" [pp. 180-81]. Since her ugliness is one of the main poisons of her life, causing her conscious resentment of Redival and subconscious resentment of Psyche, this veiled efface-ment is a means of suppressing her problem while she must work in the world. She finds the veil useful, in dealing with ambassadors, for example [p. 229], but this is not unusual: sometimes a private adjustment rebounds to one's social credit—the man who stops drinking too much may find more, not fewer, invitations to parties arriving.

This identification of the veil and the Queen (not Orual) does not exhaust the meaning of the symbol: it also stands for the flesh. Orual recounts guesses about the face beneath the veil:

> Some said (nearly all the younger women said) that it was frightful beyond endurance; a pig's, bear's, cat's or elephant's face. The best story was that I had no face at all; if you stripped off my veil you'd find emptiness. But another sort (there were more of the men among these) said that I wore a veil because I was of a beauty so dazzling that if I let it be seen all men in the world would run mad; or else that Ungit was jealous of my beauty and had promised to blast me if I went bareface. [pp. 228-29]

The guess about the beauty and Ungit's jealousy is one of the ways in which the god's prophecy that Orual shall be Psyche is fulfilled. But these guesses are also guesses about Orual's soul (the veil, the flesh): is it bestial? or nothingness? or divinely beautiful? In the final vision, after Psyche has brought the casket of beauty from the Deadlands, it turns out that Orual's visionary self *is* divinely beautiful. But first she had to descend into the earth and see that she was as ugly as Ungit.

So much for the years of work: Orual works when she sees no meaning; indeed, works in order to suppress personal meaning—perhaps thereby being meritorious (to move back by analogy from the fictional world to the real world), for, as Screwtape observed, it pleases the Enemy—that is, God—for a human to do his duty in a world which seems to him meaningless.

The fifth section, chapter twenty-one, sums up the Job-like cry of Orual. In their making of Psyche's story into a myth, the gods have lied about her: they have said that she saw the god's castle and that she was jealous of her sister [pp. 243-44]. She denies both these charges and others in this autobiography, which she has written to answer the gods. She concludes, after her charge of un-fairness, with this paragraph:

I say, therefore, that there is no creature (toad, scorpion, or serpent)
so noxious to man as the gods. Let them answer my charge if they can.
If may well be that, instead of answering, they'll strike me mad or leprous
or turn me into beast, bird, or tree. But will not all the world then know
(and the gods will know it knows) that this is because they have no
answer? [pp. 249-50]

So also Job cries to his four accusers about God:

> If indeed you magnify yourselves against me,
>   and make my humiliation an argument against me,
> know then that God has put me in the wrong,
>   and closed his net about me.
> Behold, I cry out, "Violence!" but I am not answered;
>   I call aloud, but there is no justice.
>   [Job 19:5-7, RSV]
> Why are not times of judgment kept by the Almighty,
>   and why do those who know him never see his days?
>   [Job 24:1, RSV]

Orual is a Job, and for both a reversal occurs. God finally speaks
to Job out of the whirlwind, not answering his charges directly;
but the vision of God itself is a satisfactory answer for Job, who
says:

> I had heard of thee by the hearing of the ear,
>   but now my eye sees thee:
> therefore I despise myself, and repent in dust and ashes.
>   [Job 42:5-6, RSV]

Likewise, Orual writes near the end of the second part of her
autobiography:

> I ended my first book with the words *no answer*. I know now, Lord,
> why you utter no answer. You are yourself the answer. Before your face
> questions die away. What other answer would suffice? [p. 308]

The final section of the six in this analysis covers the most
complex division of *Till We Have Faces*, and thus receives the
greatest space in this essay. But the way back is sometimes the
best way forward: two autobiographical aspects of the novel (autobiographical on Lewis's part, not Orual's) here serve as an introduction, the first of these coming from the second section, from
chapter seven. This first autobiographical element is *Sehnsucht*, or
Romantic Longing. No attempt will be made here of anything like
a full description; it has been discussed, earlier in this volume,

in the essays by Scott Oury and Eliane Tixier.[7] But a simple identification is useful to show Lewis using his own experiences in the
fiction. In his autobiography, he includes this brief passage in his
description of his Belfast childhood:

> Every day there were what we [his brother and he] called "the Green
> Hills"; that is, the low line of the Castlereagh Hills which we saw from
> the nursery windows. They were not very far off but they were, to
> children, quite unattainable. They taught me longing—*Sehnsucht*; made
> me for good or ill, and before I was six years old, a votary of the Blue
> Flower. [*Surprised by Joy*, p. 7]

In *Till We Have Faces* it is Psyche who feels the longing for the
mountain:

> It was when I was happiest that I longed most. It was on happy days
> when we were up there on the hills, the three of us [Psyche, Orual, and
> the Fox], with the wind and the sunshine . . . where you couldn't see
> Glome or the palace. Do you remember? The colour and the smell, and
> looking across at the Grey Mountain in the distance? And because it
> was so beautiful, it set me longing, always longing. Somewhere else
> there must be more of it. Everything seemed to be saying, Psyche come!
> But I couldn't (not yet) come and I didn't know where I was to come to.
> It almost hurt me. I felt like a bird in a cage when the other birds of its
> kind are flying home. [p. 74—ellipsis in the original]

This is not what is usually called an archetypal passage, but it
certainly reflects more than Lewis's individuality, as his allusion to
the German Romantics and their blue cornflower makes clear.
Indeed, it may be considered a particular Romantic archetype.

Another way in which *Till We Have Faces* is autobiographical lies
in its basic plot: in the psychological reversal which Orual undergoes in this last section of the novel. Lewis pictures the reversal
in his own life in his early, allegorical *Pilgrim's Regress*: the main
character, John, drawn by a vision of a far island with mountains
on it, journeys westward through much of the book, only to find
near the end that he has circled the earth, and there, across a sea,
lies his "island"—the hills which were just across a brook (the River
of Death) from him in his boyhood. Only—and this is the reversal
—there is no boat, and John must retrace his steps. In *The Pilgrim's
Regress*, as in Bunyan's *The Pilgrim's Progress*, the journey is the
symbol for living through time. In *Till We Have Faces* Orual's
autobiographical form permits the psychological reversal without
the symbol. And, of course, it is not surprising that this fictional
autobiography was published close to the same time—the year after—

as Lewis's own autobiography, *Surprised by Joy*, appeared, with
its telling of his return to Christianity, to the faith of his childhood.[8] Apart from *A Grief Observed*, they are his two most intro-
verted writings, and a critic may guess that the autobiography
prepared the way for the fiction, which Northrop Frye would
classify as a confession-romance. It is as difficult to speak of this
reversal as an archetype, as it was of Romantic Longing; but the
experience of a return to faith is hardly rare in the twentieth century. The lives of T. S. Eliot and W. H. Auden both illustrate it.[9]
The pattern is thus well known, if not archetypal.

Therefore, despite the thesis which Lewis argues in *The Personal
Heresy*, about the invalidity of reading literary works in order to
make contact with the author, his own works reflect his experiences,
his life. This shall be further demonstrated in the second of the three
points to be made about the last four chapters of *Till We Have Faces*.
For clarity in this densely packed material, chapter divisions shall
be ignored and three interwoven strands picked out: first, Orual's
realization of the truth about her own motivations; second, the
burdens she bears for Psyche (and that which Psyche bears for her);
and third, the archetypal pattern of the final vision.

Although Orual's realization of the truth about her motivations
affects her attitudes towards the gods, she has already been considered as Job; hence, her understanding of her relationships with
other persons can be isolated. The first of these people is her older
sister, Redival. As she writes her autobiography, Orual remembers
the fun she and Redival had as children, before the Fox was purchased [p. 254]. Then Tarin reappears and comments on how lonely
Redival was when he met her.

> I am sure still [writes Orual] that Redival was false and a fool. . . .
> But one thing was certain: I had never thought at all how it might be
> with her when I turned first to the Fox and then to Psyche. For it
> had been somehow settled in my mind from the very beginning that I
> was the pitiable and ill-used one. She had her gold curls, hadn't she?
> [p. 256]

The second person about whom she re-thinks her relationship is
Bardia, after he dies. This episode is more complex than the first
because it involves Orual's realization of her Ungit-like aspects. It
begins straightforwardly enough with a disagreement between
Orual and Ansit, Bardia's wife, after his death; this is a reinterpretation of character through an understanding of a different point of
view, something like that offered by Tarin about Redival. But Ansit
adds to the specific statement of the Queen's overworking her
husband the generality that she has so used all around her:

Perhaps you who spring from the gods love like the gods. Like the Shadowbrute. They say the loving and the devouring are all one, don't they? . . . Faugh! You're full fed. Gorged with other men's lives, women's too: Bardia's, mine, the Fox's, your sister's—both your sisters'. [pp. 264-65]

Although this part of the episode ends Orual's love for Bardia, her reinterpretation of her character in terms of Ansit's words develops further.

Orual next attends a religious ceremony in the house of Ungit, and she thinks how the seed of men, the lives of the girls who are the sacred prostitutes, and the silver are all drained into the temple and nothing is given back. (The satisfaction of the peasant woman who prays to Ungit on pp. 271-72, while Orual is there, indicates that Orual is not seeing the whole truth.) Thereafter she dreams that her father takes her into a subterranean chamber (because Ungit is an earth goddess and because the unconscious mind of psychoanalytic studies is popularly pictured as *beneath* the conscious mind and popularly called the *sub*conscious); in this buried chamber her face is shown in a mirror: and this face is the face of Ungit [p. 276]. With her realization of the truth of Ansit's words—that she is Ungit (or the Shadowbrute), that she as Queen has drained the country as she believes the house of Ungit has—Orual tries to reform herself, to practice Platonic philosophy, to be calm and dispassionate and wise, but she finds herself unable [pp. 281-83].

Orual then writes:

I had only one comfort left me. However I might have devoured Bardia, I had at least loved Psyche truly. There, if nowhere else, I had the right of it and the gods were in the wrong. And as a prisoner in a dungeon or a sick man on his bed makes much of any little shred of pleasure he still has, so I made much of this. [p. 285]

The reinterpretation of her relationship to Psyche is, of course, the third and final step in her understanding of her own motivations. This comes abruptly in the vision in which she reads her complaint against the gods (the first part of the book, transformed in the vision to a small, shabby scroll), whereupon she learns her true motives:

I know what you'll say. You will say the real gods are not at all like Ungit, and that I was shown a real god and the house of a real god and ought to know it. Hypocrites! I do know it. As if that would heal my wounds! I could have endured it if you were things like Ungit and the Shadowbrute. You know well that I never really began to hate you until Psyche began talking of her palace and her lover and her husband.

In other words, the myth which the gods told about her, which began her writing of her defense, was true. Orual continues:

> Why did you lie to me? You said a brute would devour her. Well, why didn't it? I'd have wept for her and buried what was left and built her a tomb and . . . and. . . . But to steal her love from me! Can it be that you really don't understand? Do you think we mortals will find you gods easier to bear if you're beautiful? I tell you that if that's true we'll find you a thousand times worse. For then (I know what beauty does) you'll lure and entice. [p. 290—ellipses included in the original]

This depiction of natural love gone wrong (and only the first dozen sentences in Orual's speech have been quoted) resembles a similar portrait Lewis drew eleven years before: Pan, a Ghost in *The Great Divorce*, wants back her son, Michael, to love him. But this psychological understanding, while penetrating (how many men want to possess, to control, their "loved" ones?), is unrelated to the archetypal patterns; the identification of Orual and Ungit, on the other hand, strikes a deeper note—it is surely archetypal to resemble an earth goddess.

The second strand running throughout these last four chapters is the concept of what Charles Williams called the Way of Exchange. Because this is the most esoteric of the concepts in the book, some explanation of its background is useful before the discussion of how it functions in the novel. At the time of the Crucifixion, Scripture reports the jibe of the chief priests: "He saved others; himself he cannot save" [Mark 15:31; Matthew 27:42]. One's reaction *is* to call that a jibe, but Charles Williams called it a definition: nobody, not even Christ, could save himself—he could (and one can) save others and, in turn, only be saved by someone else. It is a definition of the Way of Salvation. But its application need not be only in terms of salvation: it also applies to the burdens of the world. Williams discusses this in various works (in his *Descent into Hell* he calls it in a chapter title "The Doctrine of Substituted Love"); here is a brief passage from his essay entitled "The Way of Exchange":

> Compacts can be made for the taking over of the suffering of troubles, and worries, and distresses, as simply and as effectually as an assent is given to the carrying of a parcel. A man can cease to worry about *x* because his friend has agreed to be worried by *x*. . . . No doubt the first man may still have to deal directly with *x*; the point is that his friend may well relieve him of the extra burden.[10]

That Williams, in this same essay, turns to the writings of the Desert Fathers for an illustration suggests that the concept is not commonly held in Christian thought; but Williams was serious about the idea—and about its application.

In his discussion of Williams's Arthurian poems, Lewis comments on the doctrine of Exchange or Substitution:

> We can and should "bear one another's burdens" in a sense much more nearly literal than is usually dreamed of. Any two souls can ("under the Omnipotence") make an agreement to do so: the one can offer to take another's shame or anxiety or grief and the burden will actually be transferred. This Williams most seriously maintained, and I have reason to believe that he spoke from experimental knowledge.[11]

That phrase "experimental knowledge" has nice connotations to the modern world, suggesting as it does some sort of scientific knowledge gained from scientific experiments; but of course what Lewis means here is not that at all—he means personal experience. Presumably Williams was able to bear others' burdens. And, eventually, Lewis too was able to do it. Nevill Coghill, in his reminiscence about his friend, writes:

> It was Charles Williams who expounded to [Lewis] the doctrine of co-inherence and the idea that one had power to accept into one's own body the pain of someone else, through Christian love. This was a power which Lewis found himself later to possess, and which, he told me, he had been allowed to use to ease the suffering of his wife, a cancer victim, of whom the doctors had despaired. . . . Once, shortly after his marriage, when he brought his wife to lunch with me, he said to me, looking at her across the grassy quadrangle, "I never expected to have, in my sixties, the happiness that passed me by in my twenties." It was then that he told me of having been allowed to accept her pain.
>
> "You mean" (I said) "that her pain left her, and that you felt it for her in your body?"
>
> "Yes," he said, "in my legs. It was crippling. But it relieved hers."[12]

A suggestion exists in Lewis's letters that the exchange may have gone beyond just the bearing of his wife's pain:

> Did I tell you that I also have a bone disease? It is neither mortal nor curable; a prematurely senile loss of calcium. I was very crippled and had much pain all summer, but am in a good spell now. I was losing calcium just about as fast as Joy [his wife, who had a temporary remission of her cancer] was gaining it, a bargain (if it was one) for wh. I am very thankful. [*Letters*, p. 280]

This Doctrine of Exchange was said above to be not widely held in Christianity, but that refers only to one Christian bearing such burdens for another Christian. In the archetypal sense that Christ bears the sins of the world, and that He bears the burdens of the individual Christians, it is an essential part of the Christian faith. In what follows, both Orual and Psyche may be said to partake of this Christ archetype.

The application of this Doctrine to *Till We Have Faces* explains much of the significance of these last four chapters and also under-lies the prophecy of the god to Orual earlier in the book: "You also shall be Psyche" [p. 174]. It explains basically the significance of Orual's dreams or visions of sorting grain, of trying to gather the golden wool, and of crossing the desert to the mountains to collect a cup of water. When she first dreams of gathering the wool, she notices that, after the rams have knocked her down, someone else gathers the golden fleece from the brambles [pp. 283-84]. Later, in her last vision, when she watches the pictures of Psyche's life after being driven from the valley, Orual sees the same point made about the desert crossing:

> In the next picture I saw both Psyche and myself, but I was only a shadow. We toiled together over those burning sands, she with her empty bowl, I with the book full of my poison. She did not see me. And though her face was pale with the heat and her lips cracked with thirst, she was no more pitiable than when I have seen her, often, pale with heat and thirsty, come back with the Fox and me from a summer day's ramble on the old hills. She was merry and in good heart. I believe, from the way her lips moved, she was singing. [p. 300]

The conversation between the Fox and Orual which immediately follows in the vision makes this point clear:

> [Orual asks,] "But are these pictures true?"
> "All here's true."
> "But how could she—did she really—do such things and go to such places—and not . . . ? Grandfather, she was all but unscathed. She was almost happy."
> "Another bore nearly all the anguish."
> "I? Is it possible?"
> "That was one of the true things I used to say to you. Don't you re-member? We're all limbs and parts of one Whole. Hence, of each other. Men, and gods, flow in and out and mingle."
> "Oh, I give thanks. I bless the gods. Then it was really I—"
> "Who bore the anguish. But she achieved the tasks. Would you rather have had justice?"
> "Would you mock me, Grandfather? Justice? Oh, I've been a queen and I know the people's cry for justice must be heard. But not my cry. A Batta's muttering, a Redival's whining: 'Why can't I?' 'Why should she?' 'It's not fair.' And over and over. Faugh!" [pp. 300-01—ellipsis included in the original]

Thus Orual, partially cleansed (one assumes) by her confession of her possessive desire for Psyche, is able to no longer want justice (the basis for her complaint against the gods, that they were not just) but to give love: to delight in her service of Psyche.

But the Way of Exchange is twofold in this book. Orual has borne the anguish of Psyche's tasks for Psyche, but the fourth task, the descent into Hades—here called "the Deadlands"—to get the casket of beauty from the Queen of that realm for Orual, is done by Psyche alone. In the myth, Venus sends her; in this story the equivalent figure would be Ungit, but Orual has already realized that she is Ungit—"the swollen spider, squat at [the] center [of Glome], gorged with men's stolen lives" [p. 276]—and thus the reader is prepared for Psyche's first words upon her return:

> But Maia, dear Maia [the childhood nickname of Orual], you must stand up. I have not given you the casket. You know I went a long journey to fetch the beauty that will make Ungit beautiful. [pp. 305-06]

However, the trip down to the Deadlands, told in one of the pictures which Orual and the Fox observe, is not just a painful task but a symbolic journey: the people of Glome, the Fox, and Orual with her wounded arm (her means of blackmailing Psyche earlier into looking at her husband) all attempt to stop her [pp. 302-04]. The reader of Lewis will be reminded of the shadowy figures who attempt to dissuade John from diving into the baptismal pool in *The Pilgrim's Regress*. For both John and Psyche, those they have known try to dissuade them from their religious duties; for Psyche, her past life is the burden she must bear alone.

Although Psyche so bears it, she does not bear it for herself. As indicated, she brings back the casket of beauty for Orual. And, after Orual receives the gift, comes the descent of the god—of Psyche's husband—to judge Orual:

> He was coming. The most dreadful, the most beautiful, the only dread and beauty there is, was coming. The pillars on the far side of the pool flushed with his approach. I cast down my eyes.
> Two figures, reflections, their feet to Psyche's feet and mine, stood head downward in the water. But whose were they? Two Psyches, the one clothed, the other naked? Yes, both Psyches, both beautiful (if that mattered now) beyond all imagining, yet not exactly the same.
> "You also are Psyche," came a great voice. [pp. 307-08]

Since *psyche* means *soul*, Lewis thus indicates that Orual's soul has at last been purified, beautified—that Orual too (in Christian terms) has been saved. Her ugliness that she hid from the world behind a veil (as most people hide their ugliness from the world by a veil) has been transformed into beauty. And the means of her salvation, her transformation, her baptism (as suggested by the pool and the coming of the Spirit), is Psyche's bearing of a burden for her, bringing the deathly (and deathless) beauty out of death for her, just as Orual's bearing of Psyche's burdens in her first three tasks allowed Psyche to re-achieve her divine marriage. The Exchange is complete.

The third strand in these last four chapters is an interweaving of Dantean imagery which reinforces the Christian meaning of Orual's final vision. When Orual is haled into the underworld court to read her complaint against the gods, she thinks, "In my foolishness I had not thought before how many dead there must be" [p. 289]. This echoes Dante's thought on seeing the Futile in the Vestibule of Hell:

> . . . i' non avrei mai creduto,
> Che morte tanta n' avesse disfatta.
> [*Inferno*, III.56-57]

[I had not thought death had undone so many.—T. S. Eliot's paraphrase in *The Waste Land*, I.63]

After her reading of her scroll before the black-veiled judge (perhaps suggested by the brilliantly veiled Nature of Spenser's "Mutabilitie Cantos"), Orual is led by the Fox—as Dante by Virgil—from the Underworld to a garden:

> He was leading me somewhere and the light was strengthening as we went. It was a greenish, summery light. In the end it was sunshine falling through vine leaves. We were in a cool chamber, walls on three sides of us, but on the fourth side only pillars and arches with a vine growing over them on the outside. Beyond and between the light pillars and the soft leaves I saw level grass and shining water. [p. 297]

Here, taking the place of the allegorical pageants in the Garden of Eden for Dante, are the moving pictures which the Fox and Orual watch [pp. 297-304]. Then, with the coming of Psyche carrying the gift of beauty for Orual, analogous to the coming of Beatrice to Dante, the Fox disappears from the story, but unlike Virgil (another limited, humanistic guide) without comment [p. 305]. After the sisters' reconciliation, comes not a Beatific Vision—as that with which Dante's poem closes—but the hint of one:

> "You also are Psyche," came a great voice. I looked up then, and it's strange that I dared. But I saw no god, no pillared court. I was in the palace gardens, my foolish book in my hand. The vision to the eye had,

I think, faded one moment before the oracle to the ear. For the words were still sounding. [p. 308]

A critic may hesitate to call these Dantean parallels an archetypal pattern, for they are so close to Dante's poem that they seem rather to belong to the realm of literary borrowings. Yet Dante's *Divine Comedy* has been a major statement of the Christian way, of the Christian understanding of the world; and Dante's symbolic journey through the world has been held to be at least as universal as *The Pilgrim's Progress*. Thus, as the experience of *Sehnsucht* can be considered a Romantic archetype, so also this Dantean conclusion may be held a Christian archetype.

Are Christian and Romantic archetypes really the "universal human patterns" announced at the beginning of this essay? One can only answer by analogy. The Oedipus story, held by Freud to be universal in its psychological meaning, could be called by the same principle merely a Greek (rather than a Christian or Romantic) archetype. The proof of the pudding is in the eating. Therefore, if there are more than just one or two eccentric Romantics who feel the call of *Sehnsucht*, the pattern is a widespread human one. If it turns out after death that the Christians are right and that there is then an opportunity finally to understand one's self fully (to see face to face what was here seen in a mirror obscurely) and—if one wishes—to be reunited with loved ones and united with the Source of all Love, then the Christian archetype will be universal indeed. Often a literary study ends up making the work seem interesting as an artifact but unrelated to the reader's life. In this case the patterns which have been traced are, to a greater or lesser degree, like many people's experiences. Or rather, many people's experiences are like the patterns which are seen more clearly in this fiction because, being a fantasy, it is more like the dreams which Jung analyzed. Even such esoteric notions as Williams's Way of Exchange are no doubt practiced by a few individuals, perhaps by many across the centuries. Lewis's book is thus a romance—or *A Myth Retold*—which is also a reflection of its readers' (current or potential) experiences.

It is partially for this reason that *Till We Have Faces* seems to this critic to be Lewis's greatest achievement as a fiction writer. It captures in mythic form his own experience of a return to faith while, through the use of a feminine protagonist with her own problems, it avoids being simply a disguised autobiography.[13] Indeed, it surpasses the prose romancers who were Lewis's masters—George MacDonald and William Morris—in its depth of psychological understanding of Orual and others, although another paper would be necessary to properly illustrate this. And this characterization is not alien to the reader. He too has many times been jealous of a sibling; he too has hidden his own motivations from himself; he too has buried himself in work to avoid confronting more ultimate problems. *Till We Have Faces* is rich with analogues (if they are not more) to the Bible and, in the latter part, to the Dantean journey; even if these are not caught as allusions by an unwary reader, they may have a lasting influence (aesthetic or religious) on him. As indicated above, the novel is equally rich with the archetypal patterns of life, the great patterns in which the common reader may also find himself participating: among others more mundane, the self-sacrifice because of love, the bearing of another's burdens, the purgation of worldly desire, and the divine marriage or beatific vision.

Orual writes, "When the time comes to you at which you will be forced at last to utter the speech which has lain at the center of your soul for years . . . you'll not talk about joy of words" [p. 294]. She is speaking of her complaint against the gods. Lewis first thought of writing the story of Cupid and Psyche during his under-graduate days, and it stayed with him, "thickening and hardening with the years," until the proper form came to him in 1955.[14] It too was "the speech which ha[d] lain at the center of [his] soul for years," but it was no complaint: it was, rather, a vision. And this reader at least can testify that in Lewis's words embodying this vision he finds a deep and deeply moving joy.

Notes

INTRODUCTION

1. *A Preface to Paradise Lost* (London: Oxford University Press, 1942), p. 3.

2. A thorough and convenient listing is *C. S. Lewis: An Annotated Checklist of Writings about him and his Works*, compiled by Joe R. Christopher and Joan K. Ostling, The Serif Series: Bibliographies and Checklists, No. 30, ed. William White (Kent, Ohio: The Kent State University Press, 1974).

3. *The Allegory of Love* (Oxford: Clarendon Press, 1936), p. 2.

4. "Sometimes Fairy Stories May Say Best What's To Be Said," in *Of Other Worlds: Essays and Stories*, ed. Walter Hooper (London: Geoffrey Bles, 1966), p. 35.

5. "Sir Walter Scott" (1956), in *They Asked for a Paper: Papers and Addresses* (London: Geoffrey Bles, 1962), p. 98.

6. *The Personal Heresy: A Controversy* (London: Oxford University Press, 1939), p. 103.

7. *An Experiment in Criticism* (Cambridge: At the University Press, 1961), p. 132; see also p. 83 and *A Preface to Paradise Lost*, pp. 2-3.

8. *Studies in Medieval and Renaissance Literature*, collected by Walter Hooper (Cambridge: At the University Press, 1966).

9. [16 April 1952]. Regarding Lewis's unpublished letters, see the Preface, p. ix.

THE THING ITSELF:
C. S. LEWIS AND THE VALUE OF SOMETHING OTHER

1. *An Experiment in Criticism* (Cambridge: At the University Press, 1961), p. 140. For editions of Lewis's works cited in brackets but not footnoted, see the list of "Frequently Used Texts," pp. vii-viii.

2. John Wain, "Pleasure, Controversy, Scholarship," *Spectator*, 193 (1 October 1954), 404, as quoted by Dabney A. Hart, "C. S. Lewis's Defense of Poesie" (Unpublished Ph.D. dissertation, University of Wisconsin, 1959), p. 392.

3. Owen Barfield, in an address entitled "C. S. Lewis," given at Wheaton College (Illinois), 16 October 1964.

4. Chad Walsh, "The Elusively Solid C. S. Lewis," *Good Work*, 30 (Winter

1967), 17-24, reprinted in *Shadows of the Imagination: The Fantasies of C. S. Lewis, J. R. R. Tolkien, and Charles Williams* (Carbondale: Southern Illinois University Press, 1969), pp. 1-2.

5. Hart, "C. S. Lewis's Defense of Poesie," p. 391.

6. *A Preface to Paradise Lost* (London: Oxford University Press, 1942), p. 53.

7. *The Abolition of Man* (New York: Macmillan, 1947), p. 11.

8. From an unpublished letter to Gracia Fay Bouwman, 19 July 1960.

9. *Surprised by Joy*, pp. 17-18. Subsequent references to the process of his conversion will be drawn from *Surprised by Joy* unless otherwise noted; page numbers will appear in brackets following the reference. Though it may immediately seem as if "desire" and "Joy" fall into the category of one's own makeup, or qualities one adds to the object, it will become apparent that Lewis found them to have the qualities of otherness, i.e., of "the object itself."

10. "The Weight of Glory: Preached originally as a sermon in the Church of St. Mary the Virgin, Oxford, on June 8, 1941," in *"The Weight of Glory" and Other Addresses* (New York: Macmillan, 1949), pp. 4-5.

11. *The Four Loves* (London: Geoffrey Bles, 1960), p. 21.

12. *Reflections on the Psalms* (New York: Harcourt, Brace and World, 1958), p. 2.

13. N. W. Clerk, pseud., *A Grief Observed* (London: Faber and Faber, 1961), p. 16.

14. Hart, "C. S. Lewis's Defense of Poesie," p. 4.

15. "Dante's Similes" (1940), in *Studies in Medieval and Renaissance Literature*, collected by Walter Hooper (Cambridge: At the University Press, 1966), pp. 76-77.

16. "Myth Became Fact" (1944), in *God in the Dock: Essays on Theology and Ethics*, ed. Walter Hooper (Grand Rapids: Eerdmans, 1970), p. 66.

17. "C. S. Lewis Discusses Science Fiction with Kingsley Amis," *Science Fiction Horizons*, 1 (Spring 1964), 6

18. "The Way" is closely analogous to the essential feature of myth, as Lewis describes it: "A particular pattern of events"—*George MacDonald: An Anthology* (1946; rpt. Garden City, New Jersey: Doubleday, 1962), p. 19. That phrase might as easily describe the shape of a person's life.

19. W. H. Auden, "Red Lizards and White Stallions," *Saturday Review of Literature*, 29 (17 April 1946), 22.

TRIADIC PATTERNS IN LEWIS'S LIFE AND THOUGHT

1. Owen Barfield, "On C. S. Lewis and *The Great Divorce*," *Mythprint*, 13 (January 1976), 2.

2. Barfield, "On C. S. Lewis and *The Great Divorce*," p. 2.

3. Barfield, "On C. S. Lewis and *The Great Divorce*," p. 7.

4. A description of the action of the Word of God becoming flesh in the historical Jesus of Nazareth and then rising from the dead—cf. *The Problem of Pain*, p. 84.

5. Lewis writes about the dangers of the "modern" heresy in *The Abolition of Man* (London: Oxford University Press, 1943), the prose counterpart of *That Hideous Strength*. He takes the popularizers of the evolutionary myth to task in "The Funeral of a Great Myth" (n.d.) and "The Poison of Subjectivism" (1943), which are collected in *Christian Reflections*, ed. Walter Hooper (London: Geoffrey Bles, 1967). His inaugural address at Cambridge, *De Descriptione Temporum* (1955; reprinted in *Selected Literary Essays*, ed. Walter Hooper [Cambridge: At the University Press, 1969]), falls upon the same theme. The Arthurian elements in *That Hideous Strength* come more from Charles Williams than from Malory, as we

see in *Arthurian Torso: Containing the Posthumous Fragment of The Figure of Arthur by Charles Williams and a Commentary on the Arthurian Poems of Charles Williams by C. S. Lewis* (New York: Oxford University Press, 1948).

6. Co-inherence is a term used by Charles Williams. For a full treatment of Williams's terminology, see Mary Shideler, *The Theology of Romantic Love: A Study of the Writings of Charles Williams* (Grand Rapids: Eerdmans, 1962), and the critical introduction by Anne Ridler in Charles Williams, *The Image of the City and Other Essays*, ed. Anne Ridler (London: Oxford University Press, 1958). Shidler tells us that the origin of the term for Williams comes from the Genesis story. In creating the disparity between male and female God introduced the principle of the variation and interdependence of creatures. The interaction that takes place he calls co-inherence; the source of its existence and continuation is God; exchange is its basic principle of activity; and joy and love are its fruits. Basically it means that we live *from* others if not also *for* others. Self-sufficiency is the opposite of all co-inherent exchange.

7. Owen Barfield, *What Coleridge Thought* (Middletown, Conn.: Wesleyan University Press, 1971), pp. 30-31.

8. Barfield writes: "Polarity is, according to Coleridge, a 'law'; it is a law which reigns through all Nature; the duality of the 'opposite forces' is the *manifestation* of a prior unity; and that unity is a 'power.' . . . Polarity is dynamic, not abstract. It is not 'a mere balance or compromise,' but 'a living and generative interpenetration.' Where logical opposites are contradictory, polar opposites are generative of each other—and together generative of new product. Polar opposites exist by virtue of each other *as well as* at the expense of each other; 'each is that which it is called, relatively, by predominance of the one character or quality, not by the absolute exclusion of the other.' Moreover each quality or character is present *in* the other. We can and must distinguish but there is no possibility of *dividing* them. . . . The apprehension of polarity is itself *the basic act of imagination*" [*What Coleridge Thought*, pp. 35-36; original italics].

9. Northrop Frye, *Anatomy of Criticism: Four Essays* (Princeton: Princeton University Press 1957), p. 122.

10. The quotes from Hopper concerning the anagoge-in-depth are cited from Stanley Romaine Hopper, " 'Le Cri de Merlin!' or Interpretation and the Metalogical," in *Anagogic Qualities of Literature*, ed. Joseph P. Strelka (University Park: Pennsylvania State University Press, 1971), pp. 26-27 [original italics]. Hopper's concluding quotation is from Pascal.

11. Frye, *Anatomy of Criticism*, p. 125.

12. In his essay "Myth Became Fact" (1944)—*God in the Dock: Essays on Theology and Ethics*, ed. Walter Hooper (Grand Rapids: Eerdmans, 1970), pp. 63-67— Lewis explains how the cosmic Christ is "heaven," just as on earth Jesus was the kingdom in his person. "Now as myth transcends thought, Incarnation transcends myth. The heart of Christianity is a myth which is also a fact. The old myth of the Dying God, *without ceasing to be myth*, comes down from the heaven of legend and imagination to the earth of history. . . . By becoming fact it does not cease to be myth: that is the miracle. . . . If God chooses to be mythopoeic—and is not the sky itself a myth—shall we refuse to be *mythopathic*? For this is the marriage of heaven and earth: Perfect Myth and Perfect Fact" [pp. 66-67; original italics]. Lewis further explains the relation of myth to reality on p. 66, where he says, "what flows into you from myth is not truth but reality (truth is always *about* something, but reality is that *about which* truth is), and, therefore, every myth becomes the father of innumerable truths on the abstract level" [original italics].

13. Barfield, *What Coleridge Thought*, p. 145 [original italics].

14. Barfield, *What Coleridge Thought*, p. 148.

15. J. R. R. Tolkien, "On Fairy-Stories," in *Essays Presented to Charles Williams*, ed. C. S. Lewis (1947; rpt. Grand Rapids: Eerdmans, 1966), p. 81.

16. N. W. Clerk, pseud., *A Grief Observed* (London: Faber and Faber, 1961), p. 49.

The Creative Act: Lewis on God and Art

1. Unpublished letter to a Mr. Lennox, 25 May 1959.

2. See Clyde S. Kilby, *The Christian World of C. S. Lewis* (Grand Rapids: Eerdmans, 1964), p. 100; and William Luther White, *The Image of Man in C. S. Lewis* (Nashville, Tenn.: Abingdon Press, 1969), p. 122.

3. For a man with a reputation for having shunned women for many years, Lewis creates heroines of amazing depth and psychological validity.

4. The Lady's freedom is similar to that illustrated in the picture of Christ which Lewis creates in an unpublished (and undated) letter to Owen Barfield in which Lewis says, "In Gethsemane it is essential freedom that is asked to be bound, unwearied control to throw up the sponge. Life itself to die. . ." [No. 50 in Barfield's letters in the Marion E. Wade Collection, Wheaton College]. The Lady could understand all that was involved in submission as only one could who was in contact with Maleldil-Christ.

5. If, of course, one makes the intended connection of Maleldil with Christ, then one can consider that He once had human form on earth.

The Cosmic Trilogy of C. S. Lewis

1. *Mere Christianity*, p. 19. This volume contains three series of radio talks, published originally as *Broadcast Talks* (in the United States, *The Case for Christianity*), *Christian Behaviour*, and *Beyond Personality*.

2. *The Problem of Pain*, p. 129—epigraph to chapter ix.

3. Cf. *Mere Christianity*, p. 36: "Christianity agrees with Dualism that this universe is at war. But it does not think this is a war between independent powers. It thinks it is a civil war, a rebellion, and that we are living in a part of the universe occupied by the rebel."

4. *The Christian Doctrine*, Book I, chapter ii [Bishop Sumner's translation].

5. "God is totally present at every point of space and time, and *locally* present in none" [*Miracles*, p. 87].

6. For the description, see *That Hideous Strength*, p. 52.

7. *Perelandra* (1943; rpt. New York: Macmillan, 1965), pp. 55-60.

A Preface to Perelandra

1. *The Allegory of Love* (London: Oxford University Press, 1936), p. 271.

2. *A Preface to Paradise Lost* (New York: Oxford University Press, 1942), p. 96 —further references to this book, hereafter cited as *"Preface,"* will be given in the text. In *The Great Divorce* the same theme is stressed through the "plain man" who "only wanted his rights." The answer is "oh, no. It's not so bad as that. . . . You'll get something far better." The plain man is still unhappy because he only wants what he deserves: "I'm a decent man and if I had my rights. . . ." The answer is that it is not quite true: "You weren't a decent man. . . . We none of us were. . . . Lord bless you, it doesn't matter" [pp. 33-35]. It was Lewis's firm

belief that only by acknowledging our faults and giving up any claim to "rights" can we enter into the Joy. This is what Satan refused to do.

3. C. S. Lewis, *Spenser's Images of Life*, ed. Alastair Fowler (Cambridge: At the University Press, 1967), p. 65.

4. All citations of Milton are from *The Student's Milton*, ed. Frank Allen Patterson (New York: Appleton-Century-Crofts, 1961).

5. Victor Hamm, "Mr. Lewis in Perelandra," *Thought*, 20 (1945), 279.

6. See *Out of the Silent Planet*, pp. 135-40, for a masterful, Swiftian, deflation of the rhetoric of Scientism. Lewis wrote to Green that Olaf Stapledon's *Last and First Men* and J. B. S. Haldane's *Possible Worlds* "have the desperately immoral outlook which I try to pillory in Weston" (Roger Lancelyn Green and Walter Hooper, *C. S. Lewis, A Biography* [New York: Harcourt Brace Jovanovich, 1974], p. 163). Lest Weston be misunderstood as the representative of science per se rather than the cult of Scientism, Lewis deliberately included, in *That Hideous Strength*, the noble figure of William Hingest. (See also *Letters*, pp. 166-67, for an account of "Westonism.")

7. *The Great Divorce* was, as the title suggests, written to combat this equation which Blake had made between God and the devil: "The Jehovah of the Bible being no other than he who dwells in flaming fire"—"The Marriage of Heaven and Hell," plates 5-6, *The Complete Writings of William Blake, with Variant Readings*, ed. Geoffrey Keynes (London: Oxford University Press, 1966), p. 150.

8. Dabney Hart, "C. S. Lewis's Defense of Poesie" (Unpublished Ph.D. dissertation, University of Wisconsin, 1959), p. 235.

9. According to Roland Frye in his *God, Man and Satan* (Princeton: Princeton University Press, 1960), in the reformed tradition hell is not geographically located, but is a permanent state of mind existing "whenever the Satanic idol is accepted, this is, wherever the wholeness of God is rejected in favor of a lesser good or a positive evil. And the lesser good becomes a positive evil whenever it assumes its own supremacy" [p. 39]. This becomes relevant to Adam's predicament as well, choosing conjugal love over love for God. Theology itself may be such a lesser good. In *The Great Divorce* one man refuses heaven because he has to read a paper on Friday: "We have a little Theological Society down there" [p. 45]—an obvious reference to *Paradise Lost*, Book II, where the devils debate predestination and free will. Neither Lewis nor Milton sees theology per se as inappropriate to the damned; salvation lies in the will, not knowledge.

10. Lewis is not alone in his objections to Milton's anthropomorphism. His censure of Milton's God is shared, for example, by Marjorie Hope Nicholson, *John Milton: A Reader's Guide to His Poetry* (New York: Farrar, Straus, and Giroux, 1963), pp. 225-27; John Peter, *A Critique of Paradise Lost* (New York: Columbia University Press, 1960), pp. 15-16; and William Empson, *Milton's God* (London: Chatto and Windus, 1961), pp. 119-20.

11. Lewis is probably indebted to Milton for the "gem" of *Perelandra*, the Great Dance. In *A Preface to Paradise Lost* Lewis said *Paradise Lost* is "not the writing of a man who embraces the Hierarchical principle with reluctance, but rather of a man enchanted by it. . . . This is perhaps the central paradox of his vision. Discipline, while the world is yet unfallen, exists for the sake of what seems its very opposite—for freedom, almost for extravagance. The pattern deep hidden in the dance, hidden so deep that shallow spectators cannot see it, alone gives beauty to the wild, free gestures that fill it" [pp. 80-81]. Though the dance of the heavens was a Renaissance commonplace (see Davies's "Orchestra," for example), there does seem verbal parallel between Lewis's interpretation of Milton and his own fictional representation.

12. Peter Kreeft, *C. S. Lewis: A Critical Essay* (Grand Rapids: Eerdmans, 1969), p. 40. Most critics believe that Lewis has excelled in his portrayal of his good characters. Walter Hooper, for example, claims that "in *Perelandra* Lewis reverses Milton's failure: Ransom is far better drawn than Weston"—*The Bulletin of the New York C. S. Lewis Society*, 2, No. 2 (1970), 7.

13. William Norwood, "The Neo-Medieval Novels of C. S. Lewis" (Unpublished Ph.D. dissertation, University of Texas, 1965), pp. 89-92. The theme of temptation is central to virtually all of Lewis's fiction. See, for example, Charles A. Huttar, "C. S. Lewis's Narnia and the 'Grand Design,'" in the following section of this book. On the concept of the Fall in Lewis see R. J. Reilly, *Romantic Religion: A Study of Barfield, Lewis, Williams, and Tolkien* (Athens: University of Georgia Press, 1971), pp. 128ff, for a provocative, but wrong, analysis. Reilly has read into Lewis's works the anthroposophic ideas of his friend Owen Barfield. Though Barfield did influence Lewis, Lewis specifically rejected any theology which made a collective Mankind replace the individual.

14. *The Screwtape Letters with Screwtape Proposes a Toast* (New York: Macmillan, 1961), p. ix.

15. Cf. Northrop Frye, *Return of Eden* (Toronto: University of Toronto Press, 1965), p. 79, who declares that when Adam chooses to fall with Eve the reader sympathizes. Right or not, this is what the reader would have done too, "and that, of course, is exactly Milton's point." See also Stanley E. Fish, *Surprised by Sin: The Reader in Paradise Lost* (London: Macmillan, 1967), p. 269, who agrees with Lewis that Adam should have chastened Eve and then interceded for her.

16. Hamm, "Mr. Lewis in Perelandra," p. 282.

17. Millicent Bell, "The Fallacy of the Fall in *Paradise Lost*," *PMLA*, 67 (1953), 870-71; cf. Wayne Shumaker's response, *PMLA*, 70 (1955), 1186-87.

18. Norwood, "Neo-Medieval Novels," p. 89. On the idea of the "magic fruit" see, for example, *De Doctrina*, Book I, chapter x, where Milton declares that the forbidden fruit is "in its own nature indifferent"; it served merely as "a test of fidelity" [*The Student's Milton*, p. 986]. There was no magic involved; the tree took its name from the event rather than vice versa.

19. Clyde S. Kilby, *The Christian World of C. S. Lewis* (Grand Rapids: Eerdmans, 1964), p. 99.

20. John M. Phelan, "Men and Morals in Space," *America*, 9 October 1965, reprinted in *The Bulletin of the New York C. S. Lewis Society*, 6, No. 5 (1975), 7.

21. In "Religion: Reality or Substitute?" (1941), Lewis uses the scene of Eve looking in the pool as an illustration for the difference between first and second things. This scene "I used to think the most grotesque, but now think one of the most profound, in *Paradise Lost*. I mean the part where Eve, a few minutes after her creation, sees herself in a pool of water, and falls in love with her own reflection. Then God makes her look up, and she sees Adam. But the interesting point is that the first sight of Adam is a disappointment; he is a much less immediately attractive object than herself. Being divinely guided, Eve gets over this difficult *pons asinorum* and lives to learn that being in love with Adam is more inexhaustible, more fruitful, and even better fun, than being in love with herself. But if she had been a sinner, like ourselves, she would not have made the transition so easily"—*Christian Reflections*, ed. Walter Hooper (London: Geoffrey Bles, 1967), pp. 39-40.

22. Charles Marriot, Review of *Perelandra*, *Commonweal*, 40 (May 1944), 90.

That Hideous Strength: A Double Story

1. "The Inner Ring: The Memorial Oration at King's College, the University of London, 1944," in *"The Weight of Glory" and Other Addresses* (New York: Macmillan, 1949), p. 61.

2. "A Reply to Professor Haldane," in *Of Other Worlds: Essays and Stories*, ed. Walter Hooper (New York: Harcourt, Brace and World, 1966), p. 80.

Narnia: The Author, the Critics, and the Tale

1. "It All Began With a Picture . . . ," in *Of Other Worlds: Essays and Stories*, ed. Walter Hooper (London: Geoffrey Bles, 1966), p. 42.

2. Chad Walsh, *C. S. Lewis: Apostle to the Skeptics* (New York: Macmillan, 1949), p. 10.

3. "On Three Ways of Writing for Children," in *Of Other Worlds*, p. 31.

4. *The Four Loves* (London: Geoffrey Bles, 1960), p. 73.

5. Quoted in Kathryn Lindskoog, *The Lion of Judah in Never-Never Land* (Grand Rapids: Eerdmans, 1973), p. 16.

6. "Sometimes Fairy Stories May Say Best What's to be Said," in *Of Other Worlds*, p. 37.

7. *The Allegory of Love* (Oxford: Clarendon Press, 1936), p. 45.

8. "Transposition" (1949), in *They Asked for a Paper* (London: Geoffrey Bles, 1962), p. 178.

C. S. Lewis's Narnia and the "Grand Design"

1. See Israel Baroway, "The Bible as Poetry in the English Renaissance: An Introduction," *Journal of English and Germanic Philology*, 32 (1933), 447-80, and other articles by Baroway on related subjects in *JEGP*, 33 (1934), 23-45; *Modern Language Notes*, 49 (1934), 145-49; and *ELH* [*Journal of English Literary History*], 2 (1935), 66-91; 8 (1941), 119-42; and 17 (1950), 115-35.

2. Stanley Wiersma, *Christopher Fry: A Critical Essay* (Grand Rapids: Eerdmans, 1970), pp. 19-20.

3. See Austin Farrer, *A Rebirth of Images: The Making of St. John's Apocalypse* (London: Dacre Press, 1949), reissued in a completely revised version as *The Revelation of St. John the Divine: Commentary on the English Text* (Oxford: Clarendon Press, 1964).

4. See Lewis's essay on "Historicism" (1950), in *Christian Reflections*, ed. Walter Hooper (London: Geoffrey Bles, 1967), pp. 100-13.

5. See C. A. Patrides, *The Grand Design of God: The Literary Form of the Christian View of History* (London: Routledge and Kegan Paul, 1972), p. 119. Patrides's footnotes provide a full bibliographical guide not only to the history of this idea but also to modern studies of the Judeo-Christian concept of history.

6. "It All Began With a Picture. . . ," in *Of Other Worlds: Essays and Stories*, ed. Walter Hooper (New York: Harcourt, Brace and World, 1966), p. 42.

7. Chad Walsh, *C. S. Lewis: Apostle to the Skeptics* (New York: Macmillan, 1949), p. 10.

8. Walter Hooper, "Past Watchful Dragons: The Fairy Tales of C. S. Lewis," in *Imagination and the Spirit: Essays in Literature and the Christian Faith presented to Clyde S. Kilby*, ed. Charles A. Huttar (Grand Rapids: Eerdmans, 1971), pp. 301-09.

9. Hooper, "Past Watchful Dragons," pp. 310-11.

10. Hooper, "Past Watchful Dragons," pp. 297-301.

11. *A Preface to Paradise Lost*, (London: Oxford University Press, 1942), pp. 15-16.

12. Parallel difficulties exist in attempting to project *recent* observation (i.e., within the history of man) on a time scale of billions of years. Discoveries in radio astronomy have led German scientist H. von Ditfurth to at least entertain the antiuniformitarian hypothesis "that *other laws* governed the universe when it was young"—*Children of the Universe: The Tale of Our Existence* (New York: Atheneum, 1974), p. 41 [original italics].

13. For the general idea of this paragraph, see "Religion and Rocketry" (1955), in *The World's Last Night and Other Essays* (New York: Harcourt, Brace and World, 1960), pp. 83-92.

14. In *A Preface to Paradise Lost*, pp. 65-69, 113, 118, Lewis cites Augustine as a locus classicus for this idea.

15. On Hierarchy see *A Preface to Paradise Lost*, ch. xi; on the Tao, *The Abolition of Man* (London: Oxford University Press, 1943).

16. Cf. the classic statement of this doctrine in the Athanasian Creed: "He is God and man, . . . not two but one Christ. He is one, however, not by the transformation of his divinity into flesh, but by the taking up [*adsumptione*] of his humanity into God"—J. N. D. Kelly, *The Athanasian Creed* (New York: Harper & Row, 1964), p. 21. The doctrine of Christ's Ascension also points to the permanence of the divine-human union.

17. Man's "dominion" over the rest of creation can only be understood in conjunction with his participation in and responsibility to the created world. For a typical statement see D. Bonhoeffer, *Creation and Fall* (New York: Macmillan, 1959), pp. 39-40. The author of the Epistle to the Hebrews (2:5-9) sees man's "dominion" as not yet fulfilled, except prototypically in Christ, the God-Man.

18. Hooper, "Past Watchful Dragons," pp. 310-11.

19. See *Comus*, 1. 758; *Paradise Lost*, II.226: IX.549ff., 670ff.

20. For a full discussion of these and other parallels, see Hooper, "Past Watchful Dragons," pp. 325-32.

21. Cf. Mark 15:34. See C. A. Huttar, "Samson's Identity Crisis and Milton's," *Imagination and the Spirit*, p. 157.

22. *The Discarded Image* (Cambridge: At the University Press, 1964), p. 58.

IMAGINATION BAPTIZED, OR, "HOLINESS" IN THE CHRONICLES
OF NARNIA

1. Chad Walsh, Preface to *Imagination and the Spirit: Essays in Literature and the Christian Faith presented to Clyde S. Kilby*, ed. Charles A. Huttar (Grand Rapids: Eerdmans, 1971), p. vii.

2. "It All Began With a Picture . . . ," in *Of Other Worlds, Essays and Stories*, ed. Walter Hooper (London: Geoffrey Bles, 1966), p. 42.

3. *George MacDonald, An Anthology* (London: Geoffrey Bles, 1946), p. 21.

4. William Morris, in *Selected Literary Essays*, ed. Walter Hooper (Cambridge: At the University Press, 1969), p. 219.

5. Unpublished letter to Arthur Greeves, 4 February 1933. Further references to Lewis's unpublished letters to Greeves will be included within brackets in the text.

6. "The Weight of Glory" (1941), in *"The Weight of Glory" and Other Addresses* (New York: Macmillan, 1949), p. 5.

7. See *The Weight of Glory*, p. 4 and *Surprised by Joy*, p. 167.

8. I think one can use here Lewis's very words although they were specifically applied to Morris, for this was exactly what he meant by Holiness when he used

it to characterize *Phantastes*. Note also this comment on Morris: "For the first (and last?) time [in *Love is Enough*] the light of *holiness* shines through Morris's romanticism"—from a letter to Arthur Greeves, 30 June 1930, quoted in Roger Lancelyn Green and Walter Hooper, *C. S. Lewis, A Biography* (London: Collins, 1974), p. 107.

9. "All my deepest, and certainly all my earliest, experiences seem to be of sheer quality. The terrible and the lovely are older and solider than terrible and lovely things"—*Letters to Malcolm*, p. 86. One could say that this is also how he first discovered Holiness: as a quality, perhaps even before he knew the term or met holy people.

10. *Phantastes, A Faerie Romance* (1858; rpt. London: Ballantine, 1971), p. 76.

11. Bede Griffiths, *The Golden String* (London: The Chiswick Press, 1954), p. 11.

12. Griffiths, *The Golden String*, p. 33. This work, Griffiths's autobiography, was published a year before *Surprised by Joy* and tells a similar story. Indeed, Lewis's and Griffiths's conversions took place during the same period. In *Surprised by Joy*, which he dedicated to Griffiths, Lewis wrote: "My chief companion on this stage of the road was Griffiths, with whom I kept up a copious correspondence" [p. 234]. In an unpublished letter to Griffiths in 1934 he also acknowledged, "We both, in places, travelled the same road to Christianity."

13. "On C. S. Lewis and the Narnian Chronicles," An Interview with Walter Hooper. Propos recueillis par Eliane Aymard, in "Caliban V," *Annales de la Faculté des Lettres et Sciences Humaines de Toulouse*, Nouvelle Série, Tome IV, Fascicule 1, janvier 1968, p. 137.

14. The use of paradox in such matters is not surprising, as the theologian Henri de Lubac pointed out: "Plus la vie s'élève, s'enrichit, s'intériorise, plus le paradoxe gagne du terrain. . . . La vie mystique est son triomphe"—*Paradoxes, suivi de Nouveaux Paradoxes* (Paris: Seuil, 1959), p. 72.

15. Unpublished letter to Arthur Greeves, 12 September 1933: "God will be guiding me—as quickly as He can to where I shall get what I really wanted all the time. It will not be very like what I now think I want: but it will be more like it than some suppose. In any case it will be the real thing, not a consolation prize or substitute. If I had it I should not need to fight against sensuality as something impure: rather I should spontaneously turn away from it as something dull, cold, abstract and artificial."

16. *The Allegory of Love, A Study in Medieval Tradition* (London: Oxford University Press, 1936), p. 45.

EPISTEMOLOGICAL RELEASE IN THE SILVER CHAIR

1. This idea owes its origin to Michael M. Murrin, who teaches modern fantasy at the University of Chicago: he pointed out that the juxtaposition of worlds has an epistemological function in *The Silver Chair*.

2. "Hamlet: The Prince or The Poem?", in *Selected Literary Essays*, ed. Walter Hooper (Cambridge: At the University Press, 1969), p. 99.

3. *The Faerie Queene*, I.i.18-19. All quotations of *The Faerie Queene* are from the Variorum *Works*, ed. E. Greenlaw, et al. (Baltimore: The Johns Hopkins Press, 1932-57).

4. The enchanted chair also appears in Milton's *Mask at Ludlow*; indeed, Milton's Lady—magically immobilized and fiercely articulate—may be another model for Lewis's immobile but desperately lucid prince. If so, the relationship supports the argument that knowledge is thematically important in *The Silver Chair*, since the Lady's issue with Comus is similar to Guyon's issue with Mammon. Only Spenser's chair, however, is specifically called silver.

5. The association of a silver chair with Proserpina is the clue to this mysterious artifact's origin in the Eleusinian mysteries, as John Upton first noted in the eighteenth century. See his note on *FQ*, II.vii.63 [Variorum *Works*, II, 268-69]. For a more recent investigation, see Frank Kermode, "The Cave of Mammon," in *Elizabethan Poetry*, ed. J. R. Brown and B. Harris (London: Edward Arnold, 1960), pp. 151-73. Kermode's erudition is intelligently qualified by Bartlett Giamatti in *The Earthly Paradise and the Renaissance Epic* (Princeton: Princeton University Press, 1966), pp. 233-34.

6. Whether the reader's release was epistemological or imaginative (or whether the second can be the former) was an important question for Lewis, if we can judge from his "Great War" with Owen Barfield on the subject. See *The Bulletin of the New York C. S. Lewis Society*, 6, No. 10 (1975), 3-18. Like Plato, Lewis maintained that the imagination does not have a cognitive function but that it can give, in Bacon's words, "some shadowe of satisfaction to the minde of Man in those points wherein the Nature of things doth denie it." How important that shadow was for Lewis, however, can be judged from the volume of his own imaginative work.

7. J. R. R. Tolkien, "On Fairy-Stories," in *Essays Presented to Charles Williams*, ed. C. S. Lewis (1947; rpt. Grand Rapids: Eerdmans, 1966), pp. 75-81. Lewis, "On Three Ways of Writing for Children," in *Of Other Worlds*, ed. Walter Hooper (New York: Harcourt, Brace and World, 1966), pp. 29-30.

8. Tolkien, "On Fairy-Stories," pp. 60 and 76.

TILL WE HAVE FACES: AN INTERPRETATION

1. From an unpublished letter to Arthur Greeves, dated about October 1916.
2. See Nevill Coghill, "The Approach to English," in *Light on C. S. Lewis*, ed. Jocelyn Gibb (London: Geoffrey Bles, 1965), p. 63.
3. *Poems*, ed. Walter Hooper (London: Geoffrey Bles, 1964), p. 102.

FROM MT. OLYMPUS TO GLOME: C. S. LEWIS'S DISLOCATION OF APULEIUS'S "CUPID AND PSYCHE" IN TILL WE HAVE FACES

1. *Till We Have Faces* (London: Geoffrey Bles, 1956), p. 1.
2. See Lewis's "Note," p. 313 of the Eerdmans edition of *Till We Have Faces*. All succeeding references to the novel are from this edition.
3. *The Works of Francis Bacon*, ed. J. Spedding, R. L. Ellis, and D. D. Heath (New York: Hurd and Houghton, 1872), XIII, 122-25. Bacon saw in Venus the older generation of love, a general sympathy, a widely diffused cosmic affection, whereas Cupid represented to him the newer generation of love, that is, love between individuals. He finds equivalents for Cupid's blindness (God's providential power, the source of law and order and beauty, but not always imperceptible to man); his arrows (distance, without which nothing could move); his infant state (he is primary, uncomplicated, like an atom); and his nakedness (this is consistent with his primary quality, for compounds are clothed and masked).
4. Walter Pater, *Marius the Epicurean* (New York: The Book League of America, 1929), p. 43. Pater's version appears on pp. 43-64.
5. From Lewis's introduction to *George MacDonald: An Anthology* (New York: Macmillan, 1947), p. 21.
6. Clyde S. Kilby, *The Christian World of C. S. Lewis* (Grand Rapids: Eerdmans, 1964), p. 52.

7. Roy Battenhouse, "The Relation of Theology to Literary Criticism," in *Religion and Modern Literature*: *Essays in Theory and Criticism*, ed. G. B. Tennyson and Edward E. Ericson, Jr. (Grand Rapids: Eerdmans, 1975), p. 87.

ARCHETYPAL PATTERNS IN TILL WE HAVE FACES

1. Perhaps the best popular guide to archetypal criticism (which it combines with myth criticism) is found in Chapter 4 of *A Handbook of Critical Approaches to Literature*, by Wilfred L. Guerin, Earle G. Labor, Lee Morgan, and John R. Willingham (New York: Harper and Row, 1966). The source of most literary archetype-hunting (as contrasted to the Jungian hunts) is the Third Essay in Northrop Frye's *Anatomy of Criticism* (Princeton: Princeton University Press, 1957). A Jungian approach to the basic story (not Lewis's retelling) is Erich Neumann's *Amor and Psyche: The Psychic Development of the Feminine: A Commentary on the Tale by Apuleius*, trans. Ralph Manheim, Bollingen Series LIV (New York: Pantheon Books, 1956); it contains a discussion, particularly in the "Postscript" [pp. 153-61], of other criticism.

2. A briefer comparison of Orual and Christ can be found in Nathan Comfort Starr's *C. S. Lewis's "Till We Have Faces": An Introduction and Commentary*, The Seabury Reading Program: Religious Dimensions in Literature, No. RDL5, ed. Lee A. Belford (New York: The Seabury Press, 1968), pp. 18-19. Starr's chapbook approaches Lewis's book by means of a letter which Lewis wrote to Clyde S. Kilby [*Letters*, pp. 273-74.] Ten other essays or related materials on *Till We Have Faces* are listed in Joe R. Christopher and Joan K. Ostling, *C. S. Lewis: An Annotated Checklist of Writings about him and his Works*, The Serif Series: Bibliographies and Checklists, No. 30, ed. William White (Kent, Ohio: The Kent State University Press, 1974), pp. 117-19.

3. *Reflections on the Psalms* (New York: Harcourt, Brace and World, 1958), pp. 128-29. Subsequent quotations in the text extend through p. 130.

4. The phrase "Paradise Retained" for *Perelandra* was first used by Victor M. Hamm, in "Mr. Lewis in Perelandra," *Thought*, 20 (1945), 271-90.

5. *The Four Loves* (London: Geoffrey Bles, 1960), pp. 50-68 (on the perversions of Affection), 91-103 (on the perversions of Friendship), and 127-32 (on the perversion—specifically the idolatry—of Eros).

6. Roger Lancelyn Green and Walter Hooper, *C. S. Lewis: A Biography* (New York: Harcourt, Brace, Jovanovich, 1974), p. 261.

7. The fullest study of this topic is by Corbin Scott Carnell, *Bright Shadow of Reality: C. S. Lewis and the Feeling Intellect* (Grand Rapids: Eerdmans, 1974); see p. 116 in particular. Carnell offers a brief Jungian reading of the novel on pp. 115-16.

8. Cf. Fr. Zogby's fuller discussion of this point earlier in this volume. According to the Green and Hooper biography, *Surprised by Joy* was begun by March 1948 and the manuscript was complete in 1955 [p. 257]; *Till We Have Faces* was written in 1955, being in typescript for the publisher in February 1956 [p. 261].

9. An interesting biographical point is that Auden gave partial credit to Lewis for his return to Christianity. In his poem "A Thanksgiving" (collected posthumously in *Thank You, Fog: Last Poems*—New York: Random House, 1974), he writes that "Wild *Kierkegaard*, [Charles] *Williams*, and *Lewis* / guide[d] me back to belief" [ll. 17-18].

10. In *The Image of the City and Other Essays*, ed. Anne Ridler (London: Oxford

University Press, 1958), pp. 151-52. Perhaps the fullest discussion of what Williams thought about Exchange is in Mary McDermott Shideler, *The Theology of Romantic Love: A Study in the Writings of Charles Williams* (New York: Harper and Brothers, 1962), Chapter 8, "The Way of Exchange."

11. Charles Williams and C. S. Lewis, *Arthurian Torso* (London: Oxford University Press, 1948), p. 123.

12. "The Approach to English," in *Light on C. S. Lewis*, ed. Jocelyn Gibb (London: Geoffrey Bles, 1965), p. 63. Shideler discusses the bearing of pain on pp. 155-56 of her book. An amusing example of something of the same sort, but done without conscious acceptance of the burden, is described by W. H. Lewis, C. S. Lewis's brother, in his Diary, Vol. XXI, p. 36, now in the Marion E. Wade Collection, Wheaton College, Wheaton, Illinois: "*Saturday 4th. April* [1950]. Tolkien rang up this morning and asked me to meet him at the Bird and Baby ['the Eagle and Child,' a pub], he being in these parts to be fitted with a set of false teeth. He had a remarkable story, told him by his dentist, Mr. Pegler, which I can account for only by supposing Charles's theory of Substitution to be fact and not fantasy. A girl child, after a night of great pain, was brought to Pegler, who found on investigation that it wd. be necessary to cut into the inflamed flesh round a bad tooth without administering an anest[h]etic. The child was warned that the treatment wd. be extremely painful: but unavoidable, and she must be very brave. As Pegler cut into the diseased tissue, a pain of such severity shot through his own jaw that he dropped his lancet and stamped up and down his surgery. When the agony had worn off a little, he returned to his patient—sitting in the chair with a slash in her jaw—and asked her if she was in much pain? The child laughed and replied that she had felt nothing at all!" (The author wishes to thank the Research Committee of Tarleton State University for a grant which allowed him to study at the Wade Collection in the summer of 1975.)

13. Green and Hooper suggest [p. 263] that much of Orual's character is based on Joy Davidman, to whom the novel is dedicated. Chad Walsh, in his Afterword to a recent edition of *A Grief Observed* (New York: Bantam Books, 1976), adds a few details to the parallel [pp. 143-44].

14. The quotation comes from Lewis's statement on the dust jacket of *Till We Have Faces* (New York: Harcourt, Brace and Company, 1957).

Index

Abstraction, 141, 142
Adonis, 142
Aesop, *Fables*, 159
Aesthetics, and religion, 136
Alexander, Samuel, *Space, Time, and Deity*, 5
Allegory, 25, 52, 130, 191, 198; Lewis's definition of, 110; cf. symbolism, 116
Anthropocentric view of universe, 128, 129
Anthroposophism, 218(n13)
Apocalypse, 116, 132-35
Appearance, and reality, 146, 166, 190
Apuleius, *Metamorphoses*: and *Till We Have Faces*, 33, 178, 182-91 passim, 196
Aquinas, St. Thomas, 22, 52
Archetype: defined, 193; theory of, 223(n1)
Aristotle, 164; quoted, 53
Arnold, Matthew, 9
Art: process of, xiii; poetry as, xv; receiving vs. using, xvii, 9; universe as, 40; control in, 41-47; Creation as, 46; as path to God, 141-42
Arthur, 26, 99, 214(n5)
Artist: as subcreator, 29, 31; God as, 41, 121; similar to God, 42, 47
Athanasian Creed: echoed, 39; quoted, 117-18, 220(n16)
Atmosphere, 11-13, 164, 186
Atomism, challenged by Lewis, 23

Atonement, 131
Auden, W. H., 19, 204, 223(n9)
Augustine, St., 52, 220(n14); quoted, 81, 101
Autobiographical form, of *Till We Have Faces*, 203

Bacchus, 142
Bacon, Sir Francis, 183, 222(n3); quoted, 222(n6)
Balder, 142
Baptism, 22, 28, 55, 210; of the imagination, 136, 140, 184, 185
Barfield, Owen, 2, 10, 20, 25, 32, 33, 37, 109, 215(n7), 216(n4), 218(n13), 222(n6); quoted, 21, 23, 24, 215(n8)
Baroway, Israel, 219(n1)
Battenhouse, Roy, quoted, 191
Baynes, Pauline, 161
Beauty, 138, 155-57, 173, 179, 209
Bell, Millicent, 85
Bible, 119-20, 121, 122, 174, 212; Cited: Ephesians, 65; Ezekiel, 197; Genesis, 85, 123-27 passim, 129, 130, 215(n6); Hebrews, 157, 220(n17); Isaiah, 112; Job, 124, 201, 202; John, 117, 124; I Kings, 112; Luke, 114; Mark, 112, 114, 117, 206, 220(n21); Matthew, 114, 132, 133, 206; II Peter, 133; Psalms, 124, 195, 198; Song of Songs, 195, 198; Revelation, 132, 133, 144, 181
Blake, William, 75; quoted, 217(n7)

Contributors and Editor

J. R. CHRISTOPHER is an Associate Professor of English at Tarleton State University, Stephenville, Texas. He is author of several articles on Lewis and co-compiler of *C. S. Lewis: An Annotated Checklist*.

JOHN D. Cox, Assistant Professor of English at the University of Victoria, Victoria, British Columbia, has published articles on modern Fantasy and Renaissance drama. He is presently completing a book about the soldier as lover on the Elizabethan and Stuart stage.

MARGARET PATTERSON HANNAY, author of several articles on Lewis and a doctoral dissertation on Lewis's literary criticism, is a Lecturer in the English Department at the State University of New York, Albany.

FATHER WALTER HOOPER was personal secretary to Lewis and is one of the executors of the C. S. Lewis estate. He has edited a number of collections of Lewis's essays and is co-author of *C. S. Lewis: A Biography*.

CHARLES A. HUTTAR, Professor of English at Hope College, Holland, Michigan, has written a number of essays on Milton, Shakespeare, other Renaissance writers, and the Oxford Christians. He is Book Review Editor of the *Christian Scholar's Review* and editor of *Imagination and the Spirit: Essays in Literature and the Christian Faith presented to Clyde S. Kilby*.

CLYDE S. KILBY, Professor of English at Wheaton College, Wheaton, Illinois, is author of *The Christian World of C. S. Lewis* and of many articles and reviews on Lewis, and is curator of the Marion E. Wade Collection at Wheaton College.

JANICE WITHERSPOON NEULEIB is an Assistant Professor of English at Illinois State University, Bloomington-Normal. She wrote a dissertation on the concept of evil in Lewis and has published several articles on his works.

Scott Oury teaches English at Triton College, River Grove, Illinois. He wrote an M. A. thesis on the importance of "the object itself" in Lewis's life and thought.

Richard L. Purtill is a Professor of Philosophy at Western Washington State College, Bellingham, Washington. He is author of *Lord of the Elves and Eldils: Fantasy and Philosophy in C. S. Lewis and J. R. R. Tolkien*, as well as five other books and numerous scholarly articles.

Peter J. Schakel is an Associate Professor of English at Hope College, Holland, Michigan. He organized and served as chairperson of a Seminar on Lewis for the Modern Language Association conventions in 1975 and 1976.

Wayne Shumaker, Professor of English at the University of California at Berkeley, is author of several critical books, including *Elements of Critical Theory, Unpremeditated Verse: Feeling and Perception in Paradise Lost*, and *The Occult Sciences in the Renaissance*.

Eliane Tixier is an Assistant Professor of English at the University of Toulouse-Le Mirail, Toulouse, France, and is working on a doctoral dissertation on "The Religious Thought of C. S. Lewis."

Steve J. Van Der Weele is Professor of English at Calvin College, Grand Rapids, Michigan.

Chad Walsh, author of *C. S. Lewis: Apostle to the Skeptics* and numerous articles and reviews on Lewis, was for many years Professor of English at Beloit College, Beloit, Wisconsin. He has now retired, is a Visiting Professor at Juniata College, Huntingdon, Pennsylvania, and is writing a book-length critical study of Lewis.

Edward G. Zogby, S. J., is Assistant Professor of Religious Studies and Chairman of the Department at Le Moyne College, Syracuse, New York. He recently completed at Syracuse University a dissertation entitled "C. S. Lewis: Christopoesis and the Recovery of the Panegyric Imagination."